International Interiors 4

International Interiors 4

Lucy Bullivant

Co-ordinating Researcher: Jennifer Hudson

Laurence King

Published 1993 by
Laurence King Publishing

A catalogue record for this book is
available from the British Library.

ISBN 1 85669 036 9

Designed by Esterson Lackersteen,
London, with Adam Hay.

Printed in Singapore

Researchers
Annett Francis (USA)
Jennifer Hudson (UK)
Noriko Takiguchi (Japan)
Philippa Thomas (UK)

Frontispiece: The 'dragon waterfall'
in Now & Zen, London, designed by
Rick Mather Architects (page 132).
Photograph: Peter Cook.

Acknowledgements
The author would like to thank
Jennifer Hudson for her
conscientious and good-humoured
assistance with the research and
co-ordination of documentation
throughout this project; Annett
Francis in New York and Noriko
Takiguchi in Tokyo for their
invaluable help in co-ordinating
research material from the USA and
Japan respectively; Philippa Thomas
for excellent research support during
the early stages of work; and the
many architects, designers and their
staff globally who contributed
information and visual material for
their enthusiastic co-operation.
Numerous photographers and
agencies helped by lending visual
material, and the following credits
are given for photographs appearing
in this volume (page numbers are
given in brackets):

Matthew Antrobus (68; 69 bottom)
Architekturfoto Engelhardt & Sellin (90-3)
Bin Asakawa/ZOOM (156-7)
Olivo Barbieri (174; 175 bottom)
Gabriele Basilico (152-3)
Peter Blundell Jones (58 centre; 225 top)
Luc Boegly/Archipress (124-6; 182 bottom; 183 top)
Richard Bryant/ARCAID (42-3; 45; 82-5; 133; 210-11; 213)
Lluís Casals (166-7; 182 top)
Robert César/Archipress (94-5; 142-3)
Martin Charles (24-5; 146; 225 bottom, left and right; 230-1; 233)
Mario Ciampi (118-121)
Jeremy Cockayne/ARCAID (106-9)
Peter Cook (16-19; 48-55; 100; 102-3; 132; 148
bottom right; 151; 154-5; 168-71; 194; 202-3)
Stéphane Couturier/Archipress (26-9; 186-9)
Richard Davies (195; 197)
Sophy de Martino (44)
Klaus Frahm (160-3)
© Scott Frances/Esto (20-3)
Ferran Freixa (184-5; 226-9)
Mitsumasa Fujitsuka (238-9)
Chris Gascoigne/ARCAID (147; 148 top and bottom left; 149; 150)
Dennis Gilbert (69 top; 70-1; 86-9; 101; 198-201)
© Jeff Goldberg/Esto (206 top; 207-8; 209 right)
© John and Kate Gollings Pty Ltd (46-7)
Alain Goustard/Archipress (244-5)
Yoshiharu Hata (134-5)
Paul Hester (218-19)
Hiroyuki Hirai (32-5)
Isao Imbe (96-7)
Lourdes Jansana (220-3)
Ken Kirkwood (196)
Kenji Kobayashi (242-3)
Waltraud Krase (178-181)
Michael Mack (114-17)
Duccio Malagamba/ARCAID (183 bottom; 190-3; 234-7)
Peter Mauss/Esto (136 left; 137; 139)
Michael Moran (12-15)
Grant Mudford (56-7; 64-5; 72-3)
Nacása & Partners (141)
Paul Ott (58 top and bottom)
Raimon Ramis (175 top; 176 bottom)
Jo Reid and John Peck (66-7)
Sharon Risedorph (158-9)
Paolo Rosselli (122-3)
Jordi Sarra (128-131)
Daria Scagliola/Stijn Brakkee (36-9)
Peter Schütte/Joop van Reeken Studio (40; 41 top)
Peter Seidel (212)
© Shinkenchiku-sha (74-7; 214-17; 240-1)
Hisao Suzuki (110-13; 176 top; 177; 204-5)
Tom Vack (136 right; 138)
Fridtjof Versnel/Jeroen van Putten (41 bottom)
Paul Warchol (60-3; 78-9; 81; 105; 206 bottom; 209 left)
Andrea Zani (30-1)
Gerald Zugmann (164-5).

Special thanks are also due to Mark Dytham
and Julia Schulz-Dornburg for their advice and
assistance with specific projects; to William Owen
for moral support; and to Lynne Bryant of ARCAID,
London, and Françoise Morin at Archipress, Paris,
for their recommendations.

Contents

Introduction   6

1 Workspaces, Offices & Studios   10

2 Restaurants, Cafés, Bars, Clubs & Hotels   98

3 Stores, Showrooms & Retail Centres   144

4 Cultural & Public Amenity Buildings   172

Biographies   246

Credits   250

Addresses of Architects, Designers & Suppliers   254

Index of Architects, Designers & Projects   256

Introduction

This is a pivotal time for architects and designers in the developed world: buffeted by events which simultaneously accentuate the need to survive and the need to reflect changing patterns of culture, they continue to work in a climate of withering market forces. The day-to-day experience for many has become one of squeezed budgets in the public and private sectors, delayed projects and the forced lay-off of skilled labour; at the same time there is furious pitching for work, and tempting, high-prestige competition themes, often with no guarantee that the winner will build. Thought and labour are wasted in the face of necessity: in cities everywhere, growing numbers of people without even a basic shelter curl up at the doors of 'signature' buildings.

What scope can the recession-blighted design professions have to alter these fundamental imbalances? A growing environmental lobby is starting to make its impact on new building design, but still falls victim to hard economics and short-term thinking. Commentators have pointed out how even the most prestigious architect can exert little influence amid this maelstrom.

In recent years, critics, users and designers have all begun to question the over-aestheticized but fragmented nature of the contemporary architecture and interior design scene, as well as the comparative lack of attention given to the design of basic public amenities. The emphasis on marketing-led design has been attacked for its elevation of superficial stylistic elements, at the expense of what people want from the work or leisure spaces they occupy. The primary social function of public spaces has been obscured by the need to generate funds or project an image, and correspondingly a confusion has arisen between design for sale and design for use. As the twenty-first century approaches, the potential for a more thoughtful synthesis of aesthetics and function in even the smallest, most economical space remains unfulfilled in many sectors of public life.

The coining of slogans will not provide a solution to these problems. Reviewing new interiors selected for its Annual Design Review, the July/August 1992 issue of *ID* magazine concluded: 'Gimmicks are out, honesty's in'. This sentiment has been widely expressed in the design world of late. It implies that honesty in design is not just an appropriate response to the disillusion of the early 1990s, but is now a fashionable position to adopt. But what does 'honesty' really mean? From a pragmatic point of view, it signifies an increasing necessity in the face of tight design budgets to use materials with greater economy and responsibility; to assert a plainer, less image-conscious and more durable aesthetic in order to give the interior and its function a clearer, rational and humane form, employing user-friendly materials and energy systems. From a cynical point of view, it is another way of persuading consumers to part with their money.

If 'honesty' is to avoid becoming a gimmick itself, it has to be understood as a greater responsiveness to users' needs on an emotional as well as a practical level, otherwise the result is the bland illusion of utility – a mere function fetish. A designer is not just a technician concerned only with practicality, but applies his or her knowledge to create a dialogue between a space and its transient or permanent occupants. If an interior is to work on a number of levels, its designer must marry the mechanics of operation – which might be eating, buying, working or waiting – with a profound appreciation of the psychological and emotional dimensions of human existence.

In this volume, interior design is broadly defined, being seen not, as it so often has been in the past, as a specific discipline divorced from wider, architectural concerns, but as a central part of architectural practice (which encompasses issues of urban planning). The projects selected represent conceptual clarity and thoroughness, in many cases a calmer, less overtly expressive approach to design language, but above all, a well-developed sense of ingenuity and imagination regarding physical space in a range of building types. They display the architects' and designers' often passionate concern with visual and tactile qualities, most importantly when aesthetic appeal has sprung directly from a thoughtful analysis of the complex social role of an interior environment. Such a response means creating a workspace which is humane as well as efficient for all its users and, in the case of the transformation of an existing historical structure, ensuring that it meets these requirements whilst retaining elements of its original character.

Increasing numbers of clients – whether they are private companies, charitable organizations or organs of the state – have come to regard design as a powerful marketing tool, and this has manifested itself in both good and bad ways. In the field of fashion retailing it has been widely perceived as a high-profile, expressive discipline which creates exciting, money-making environments, sometimes on a minute scale, displaying great ingenuity, an astute grasp of geometry, a well-developed sense of theatrics and a distinctive image to lure the customer. Luxury consumption is a cyclical business, fuelled by a steady succession of novelties, and until recession started to strike, the 'turn-me-round', high fashion end of retailing was a giddy dance of the styles.

Now, however, the fashion industry is being forced to consider a widespread rejection of newly designed products in favour of second-hand clothes, 'grunge' anti-fashion or simply timeless classics bought from traditional retail establishments. New, innovative retail interiors – whether in New York, Paris or Tokyo – are now on the whole very small-scale. By contrast, more enlightened middle- and mass-market retailing operations are focusing on strategy in place of high style: better customer service, with advances in layout, circulation, lighting, back-up facilities and access taking on paramount importance.

If clients a few years ago flocked to exploit design skills – many possessing only a limited view of how design could contribute to corporate culture, other than by presenting an enhanced public image to increase profit – reduced budgets have now forced them to consider their needs much more carefully. Now the ability to create a lot from a little with ingenuity, economy and a clear vision is a priority for client and designer alike.

One particular feature of this volume is that the selection is weighted towards both corporate and government workspaces, and cultural and public amenity buildings – museums and galleries, educational and sports buildings, transport termini and tourist facilities. This is not just because the global recession has begun to limit severely the potential for innovative developments in the retail/leisure sphere, but because of the wealth of good, larger-scale projects with a longer lead time, initiated, in many cases through competitions, during the mid-1980s but not completed until the early 1990s. The two areas are linked by the fact that the government offices featured also provide public amenities. In all cases, the projects included show responses to considerable programmatic and technical challenges.

The demand for new office and industrial buildings may be falling in Western Europe, as a result of cautious economic strategies, but other trends, like the increasing internationalization of most sectors of economic activity, and the application of new technology, are acting as agents of dramatic change in the workspace. New perceptions of need and technological advances, and the prospect of the electronically networked 'virtual' office, demand that design keeps pace and maintains some correspondingly human and contextual qualities. The proliferation of new cultural buildings in the developed world underlines an increased awareness of their potential role as symbols of renewal and change within urban and rural communities. For such buildings to be more than just symbols demands a sensitivity to site, users, artefacts and the commercial agenda of the client, with all their frequently conflicting needs.

The selection also includes some of the most accomplished recent examples of innovative, design-led projects for sectors of the service industries – like the Paramount Hotel, New York, Jigsaw and Now & Zen, London and Bar Maddalena, Prato, Italy – as well as offices for clients in this area – including Warner Brothers, New York, Tour sans Fins, Paris, Lynne Franks PR, London, Matsumoto Corporation, Japan, D.E. Shaw, New York and Chiat/Day, London and Los Angeles. It also identifies another, growing phenomenon with which at least two of these projects are connected: the creative rehabilitation or conversion of buildings from another era. The thoughtful recycling of existing stock is not only an economic solution to changing needs, but one which affords a considerable design challenge; the transformation of an existing, redundant environment into a useful resource, rather than a faithful recreation of the past.

To bring out a building's original strengths – however ramshackle its condition – or to redefine the structure of its fabric to accommodate new or increasingly hybrid functions – is a task which entails a large-scale engagement with architectural aesthetics. In the inner city, in particular, the politics of conversion are inevitably entangled with conservation issues. When the original building is a famous architectural landmark in a high-density urban area, like the Guggenheim Museum, its alteration becomes a long-drawn-out affair, with everyone expressing views about the merits of the conversion and the desirability of adapting a historic design to give it a more contemporary, technologically refined guise.

On a practical level, the experience of working with such a host of restrictions – everything from existing elements which have to be retained, client requirements which demand drastic modifications or the accommodation of new acoustic and service elements within confined spaces – is both demanding and inspiring. In the process of conversion the life of the building is not only resuscitated but is redirected, and the question of what form its new identity should take to match its changed role arises.

The most talked about workspaces of the last few years – many of them American-designed, both in the United States and in Europe – have been speculative projects conceived purely as slick commodities. Thought for the end user is not a priority, and the image of work they represent is an outdated, hierarchical one. By contrast, ambitious new schemes like The Ark in Hammersmith, London, draw on advanced Scandinavian thinking to create a much more user-friendly and informal environment for corporate culture, with an air-cooling system, and circulation space which enriches the building, rather than being squeezed by the demand to maximize space for letting. In energy terms alone, projects of this kind are still a rarity in Britain – the energy-conscious scheme for speculative workspaces at 20-22 Stukeley Street is an exception to the rule. Of the many positive ecological aspects slowly being introduced in the design of some buildings, reducing the physical demands made by air-conditioning and heating systems is becoming a priority, although the technology for individual control of the internal environment is still very expensive. The new office building for JCJ Haans in Tilburg, The Netherlands, uses solar energy, and its compact housing of services gives it a greater spaciousness and clarity.

Working environments need to express their functions in ways that allow them to be equally enjoyed by staff and visitors. The offices for D.E. Shaw in New York represent the computer-driven nature of the business in a serene symbolic form, whilst accommodating a wide range of electrical equipment. Like New Line Cinema East or the Warner Brothers' New York headquarters, the project occupies one of the city's many standard format high-rise blocks. These unprepossessing sites with their confined, rectilinear dimensions can be given a focused, user-friendly ambience which also promotes the company's image. In Europe, expressive, small-scale office interiors are often shoehorned into unexceptional existing spaces, as Chiat/Day and Lynne Franks PR, London and the Julia Binfield studio in Milan demonstrate. As the government buildings included here show, old, formidable and inflexible structures still used when they have become almost intolerable operationally, can benefit greatly from extensions or new structures with an imaginative attention to detail, colour, texture, circulation and more informal patterns of work – aspects which need not necessarily be confined to creative sectors of industry, like advertising. Both the private and public spaces of the new Second Chamber for the Dutch Parliament in The Hague, Reykjavik City Hall and the Plenary Chamber of the German Federal Parliament in Bonn – all projects predictably long in the making – make attempts to give essentially formal buildings a more open and informal character, in keeping with what we can at least hope are genuinely improved patterns of political debate and consultation.

Apart from economics (and therein lies the problem), there is no reason why a more utilitarian application of such aesthetics should not work with larger-scale industrial buildings, like the B Braun complex at Melsungen in Germany. Very few industrial buildings are designed by architects, however, and so often the user-friendliness of a busy environment like a works canteen is neglected in favour of an infrequently used management conference room. Clients like BASF-France, who commissioned high-quality furniture and fittings to be enjoyed by staff throughout their new offices in Paris, are all too rare in a field where companies often cling to interior design reflecting outmoded, vertical management structures.

Along with the movement to create buildings for work which reflect horizontal and informal management, there has been a discernible shift towards lightness and transparency in all types of public building structures as a response to their underlying solidity and complexity of function, or geographical context. Stansted Airport terminal building in Essex, England, for example, is a low, light shed structure with concrete side slabs and a PVC canopy roof free of services – which are banished to an undercroft – extensive glazing and clear, logical routes from arrival to take-off points. The equally low-volume Yatsushiro Municipal Museum has a light, steel-frame roof with exhibition space concealed underground, and at S-Lattice in Tokyo the lattice structure and dual-use features reduce interior detail. Transparency implies a desire to celebrate advanced technological structures and materials, and to provide as much programmatic clarity as possible. There is a degree of irony in creating a framed window on the world at a time when land use is becoming so constrained, but the move towards transparency also stems from a wish to enjoy the psychological and physiological benefits of natural light. This priority in design tactics features in practically all the projects in the book, with the exception of a few of the smaller club or bar spaces which have a more autonomous spatial character, divorced from the exterior environment.

The desire for maximum flexibility in modern interiors often produces bland, characterless results. Smaller details within architectural interiors – the best being entirely ungratuitous – can exert a strong influence on the way in which the building works, at the same time lending the interiors a distinctive character which gives the user scope to 'read' the design, rather than 'swallow' it in one sight. These are elements, compact details or devices which, to paraphrase architect Karen Bausman, work best at the scale at which we operate and, whilst they perform a functional task, also convey subtle messages about our activities, aspirations and desire for personal control. An interior might incorporate simple but innovative ideas, for instance, the advanced atrium windows and flexible light fittings at 20-22 Stukeley Street; the electronic weather monitor at the Paramount Hotel; the artistic screens at Warner Brothers; subtly oversized door-frames – bringing to mind the work of that master of expressive detail Carlo Scarpa – at New Line Cinema's New York offices; playful video columns in the Circulo de Lectores publishing centre in Madrid; or the mobile, cylindrical walls and the perforated control cupboards at the Knoll showroom in Frankfurt. All these details show that there is scope for our relationship with the high and low technology of modern interior spaces to become more interactive.

This volume focuses on innovation and responsive imagination in interior design, showing personal choices which form only the tip of a huge iceberg in terms of recent architectural projects completed globally between the end of 1990 and December 1992. No more than 20 per cent of all the new buildings in the world are designed by an architect, so theoretically – particularly in the wake of political and economic changes in Eastern Europe, China and the Far East – there is great scope for the wider application of architectural skills. The increasingly internationalized nature of interior design activity has threatened to make cultural context seemingly irrelevant and to cast the subject as a novelty-seeking consumer. However, there are many compelling examples within all sectors of industry – including culture – where success has resulted from the soundness of the overall concept and the way it is developed; superficial appearance is only part of the equation, particularly if users can vote with their feet (something which unfortunately they are not often able to do). An imaginative, thoughtful embrace of context and subject, and a critical responsiveness to change are the important qualities that the designer of public interiors needs to demonstrate. This is not only a more 'honest' approach, but one which will help sustain us as individuals.

Workspaces, Offices & Studios

Anderson/Schwartz Architects 12
Isaac Mizrahi & Company
New York, USA

Ron Arad Associates 16
One Off Ltd
London, UK

Bausman-Gill Associates 20
Warner Bros. Records
New York, USA

Behnisch & Partners 24
Plenary Complex of the German
Federal Parliament
Bonn, Germany

Berbesson Racine et Associés 26
Agence Berbesson Racine et Associés
Asniéres, France

Olivier Brenac and Xavier Gonzalez 28
Tour sans Fins
Arche de la Défense, Paris, France

Luisa Calvi, Marco Merlini, 30
Carlos Moya
Julia Binfield
Milan, Italy

David Chipperfield Architects 32
Matsumoto Corporation
Okayama, Japan

Jo Coenen & Co. 36
J.C.J. Haans
Tilburg, The Netherlands

Pi de Bruijn, de Architekten Cie 40
The Second Chamber of Parliament
The Hague, The Netherlands

Stefano de Martino, Rem Koolhaas, 42
DEGW London Ltd
Chiat/Day Advertising Inc.
London, UK

Denton Corker Marshall 46
The Australian Embassy
Tokyo, Japan

Ralph Erskine, in collaboration with 48
Lennart Bergström and
Rock Townsend
The Ark
London, UK

Spencer Fung Architects 52
Designers' Guild
London, UK

Frank O. Gehry & Associates, Inc. 56
Chiat/Day/Mojo
Venice, California, USA

Volker Giencke 58
Odörfer
Klagenfurt, Austria

Steven Holl Architects 60
D.E. Shaw & Company
New York, USA

Franklin D. Israel Design Associates 64
Limelight Productions
Los Angeles, California, USA

Jestico + Whiles 66
20-22 Stukeley Street
London, UK

Ben Kelly Design 68
Lynne Franks PR
London, UK

Eric Owen Moss 72
Scott Mednick Associates
Culver City, California, USA

Kazuyo Sejima Architect & Associates 74
Saishunkan Seiyaku
Women's Dormitory
Kumamoto City, Kumamoto Prefecture,
Japan

Smith-Miller + Hawkinson Architects 78
New Line Cinema East and West
New York and Los Angeles, USA

James Stirling, Michael Wilford and 82
Associates, in association with
Walter Nägeli
B Braun Melsungen AG
Melsungen, Germany

Studio Granda 86
Reykjavik City Hall
Reykjavik, Iceland

STUDIOS Architecture 90
Knoll International
Frankfurt am Main, Germany

Jean-Michel Wilmotte 94
BASF-France
Levallois-Perret, Paris, France

WORKSHOP 96
S-Lattice
Sendagaya, Tokyo, Japan

Anderson/Schwartz Architects
Isaac Mizrahi & Company
New York, USA

'Calm and serene in its bare bones simplicity' is how Ross Anderson describes the new headquarters/showroom in New York City for the young fashion designer Isaac Mizrahi; but, he adds, 'it is also able to dress for the occasion', a fitting versatility for a space that has to show off products as well as keep the show running. Offices for twenty, a design studio, showrooms, fitting rooms and a runway and seating area for 250 people are accommodated into 12,000 square feet on two floors of a SoHo loft building. Seasonal fashion shows take place here amidst the existing ductwork and piping of the industrial building, but the ancillary offices and services needed by this busy designer have been given equal care and attention.

The fifth floor houses the showroom and show area, with large, north-facing industrial skylights providing indirect natural light. The interior space here was designed to meet Mizrahi's request for a neutral backdrop for the clothing, with partitions, fittings and furniture (mostly in wood and steel) evolving from 'a concise palette of materials'. The resourcefulness of the architects' response has produced a lively environment which is versatile enough to accommodate visits from fashion editors and private clients, as well as hectic work schedules.

A sizeable, pink-tinged plywood and poplar slotted wall with openings at regular intervals dominates the layout, enclosing open-plan sales offices, storage and a sound booth, and separating visitors from private offices and conference rooms at the back. It serves as a dramatic backdrop for the fashion shows taking place on a high-gloss floor, a rectangular pool of shiny white epoxy reflecting both the architecture and the fashion parade. Bench seats are installed for shows, and models slip out from the slotted wall and on to the runway. Although this area is not vast, its character was enhanced by the removal of dropped soffits above, creating 13-foot-high ceilings throughout the space.

The front showroom areas for men and women are part of this area; they are roomy

Left: Fashion shows take place along the shiny white floor between the showroom and a slotted plywood and poplar wall. The space is big enough for bench seats to be installed.

Right: The folding, wing-like wall which defines the main design studio.

and easily adjustable, with racks, tables, table-like display cases and video. Anderson Schwartz's furniture is straight from the schoolhouse, a modern interpretation of Shaker function and simplicity, providing nothing more than is needed and, like the space itself, doing so in an elegantly understated and resourceful manner. The table, which functions equally well as a desk or for dining, is strict in its simplicity and is made from maple veneer and steel. Its wax finish enhances the graining of the maple. The chair, with its rigorous proportions and legible construction, is made of the same materials. Together they are as much a statement regarding Mizrahi's own clean forms, if not his occasional flamboyancy, as the intentionally spare aesthetics of the workspace.

The fourth-floor space is identical in plan, its central partitioned area also enclosing offices, which are again quite narrow but are helped by low partitioning and horizontal slots giving tiny views out. The design studio is defined by a folding, wing-like wall on legs made of a row of fin-shaped pieces of strandboard within a poplar frame. This huge construction serves as display space on the outer side, and is connected to a thick wall of workstations.

On the other side of the reception, the fitting room's maple veneered walls trimmed in raw steel are placed diagonally. The boxy, enclosed space is simply furnished, with sisal carpeting. The architects have crafted an elaborate entrance: a pivoting, tapered panel of wood, rice paper and stainless steel, anchored to a concrete disk. Like the space as a whole, it is elegant and eminently usable.

1 Entrance
2 Fitting room
3 Design assistants' studios
4 Design studio
5 Reception/runway area
6 Open offices
7 Executive offices
8 Conference room
9 Showroom

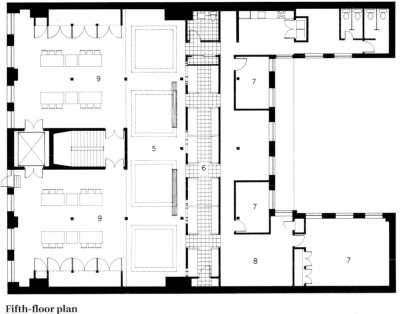

Fifth-floor plan

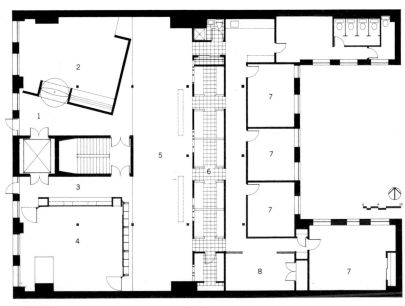

Fourth-floor plan

Ron Arad Associates
One Off Ltd
London, UK

When One Off Ltd moved from the company's small Covent Garden base to derelict courtyard premises off Chalk Farm Road, the change of location meant that the thriving furniture workshop, studios and showroom could finally exist alongside owner Ron Arad's architecture and design office in spaces big enough to accommodate the seemingly endless flow of new ideas.

Rather than waiting until the conversion was complete, the company immediately began working in the dilapidated sheds, designing and converting the new studios and workshops from within the building site whilst carrying on their other projects. The result, say the designers Ron Arad and Alison Brooks, is 'a physical metaphor for the studio's creative process where there is a continuity between the workbench and the drawing board. Both workshop and office are in the same volume of space, literally under the same winged roof, separated only by a layer of transparent, flexible PVC.'

Designing their own space gave the team, which included One Off staff, a great opportunity to experiment. The designers introduced a landscaped floor, an expanded metal and fabric roof, soft, rotating windows, and columns and a bridge whose sculptural appearance belies their functional role. All these elements are contained within the 150-square-metre first-floor showroom/office space. In contrast to this upper area, the rest of the building complex was left almost unchanged. The façade has been brightened up with blue paint, but the stairs and double front door retain a worn appearance which makes the intervention within more striking.

The floor of the showroom is one of the interior's most extraordinary features. After starting off quite tamely, it begins to sweep upwards, becoming a three-dimensional 'hill' of veneered wood which then quickly descends. The idea of introducing a wall between the showroom at the front and the design office area at the rear was rejected in favour of this sensuous floor shape. It creates a storage space below, reached by a hatch at the side of the studio.

Ron Arad's mezzanine office at the far end of the steel bridge. A cut-out shape in its welded and sculpted steel-plate wall takes its cue from the figure-of-eight window columns opposite. The two-part wooden chair, 'Schizzo' (on the bridge), was designed for Vitra.

The rusty metal trellis around the first-floor showroom entrance of the old building provides a suitably enigmatic introduction to its interior spaces.

The route across the wooden-strip floor of the first part of the showroom opens out under the curved, single membrane of the roof. Light streams into the double-height space through the rotating window arabesques which echo the organic forms of Arad's designs: the blue 'Spring' chaise, red leather 'Offspring' chair and 'Chair on a Pedestal', all pieces produced in 1991 for Moroso, plus the squat metal form of the 'Rolling Volume' chair.

At the back of the room there is a narrow mezzanine of steel where Arad has his office (reached by steps welded on to the rusted steel wall). A curved bridge made of 10 millimetre thick steel plate welded into a hollow box section, stretches from the 'hill' to this mezzanine. Its sinuous form acts as a distributor of hot and cold air issuing from an air handling unit located underneath.

Working on the roof with the engineer Neil Thomas of Atelier One, the designers were searching for something translucent, lightweight (so that it did not place too great a load on the structure of crumbling bricks below) and relatively quick to build. Their solution was a prefabricated tensioned membrane restrained by the curvature and compressive forces of an expanded metal shell, an economical idea rarely applied (another example is the Herron Associates' PVC roof for Imagination's London headquarters in Store Street), which was approved by the district surveyor and should last for fifteen years. Internally, its metal curves resemble a row of fish bones.

The roof is supported by a row of two-metre-high columns – actually triangulated connections but well disguised by their swirling calligraphic shapes. They also act as a radial track for flexible, rotating windows based on a 1-metre radiused flange. The windows are made of 8 millimetre thick industrial Perspex, stiffened at the edges with a sprung-steel frame, and can be opened into any position and fixed in place according to the shape of the column. The arabesque forms of the windows are echoed by a huge curling shape like a Greek epsilon which is cut into the upright holding up the mezzanine.

One Off is a project which sprang from pure need, with sketches of what might be done to occupy a crumbling building, and gradually became a more ambitious and elaborate undertaking, finished only minutes before the opening party. For Arad, 'designing furniture is the same as designing architecture', and the interior provides the perfect backdrop for his witty, sculptural forms.

18

Bausman-Gill Associates
Warner Bros. Records
New York, USA

Bausman-Gill's projects frequently involve imaginative three-dimensional collages. These play both a functional and aesthetic role as partitions and framing devices within interior spaces, helping to 'capture space at the scale we inhabit'. Not just art for art's sake, these assemblages are carefully ordered representations of sequences and structures the user can easily assimilate. The architects' habit of joining the construction crews to help build part of every project they design has taught them about translating their artistic concerns into three dimensions. Their approach works effectively at a variety of scales, and an interior project such as Warner Bros., led by partner Karen Bausman with colleagues Alison Berger and Adi Shamir, is innovative and yet pragmatically ordered, without any loss of attention to detail and craftsmanship.

The New York headquarters of Warner Bros. Records are located high up within the Rockefeller Center on two floors with a total of 22,000 square feet. Apart from a reception area, private offices and semi-public workspaces, there is a series of medium-sized listening and video rooms. After meetings with the clients it was decided that the plan should reflect a clear, hierarchical arrangement of offices to accommodate the different ranks of staff. The inclusion of informal meeting rooms for visitors, an art department, conference rooms and listening rooms necessitated a versatile treatment of the plan's inner and outer core.

Ranging workstations at more expansive points on the plan, the architects placed the service elements within the dense inner core. This central storage area is clad in wood panelling stained a deep purple, to which are attached CD racks, files, file racks and workstations, all within easy reach of the offices, facing the main corridor. As with Bausman-Gill's earlier job for Elektra Entertainment further down the same high-rise building, which also involved designing an efficient and aesthetically pleasing method of filing the client's product, it made sense to expose the storage as a design element rather than hiding it.

It was also vital to find a way of integrating the two floors into a whole. Bausman explains that this was done by creating a horizontal cut through the floors, and dropping into it a vertical backdrop which transmits light from the perimeter wall it mimics. The staircase's undulating metal handrail stands out boldly against a backdrop of wire cloth panels. The vertical channels of the structure are echoed by the framework of the workstations and display racks.

Two translucent screen walls located at right angles to the dense building core provide a fixed point of reference for the project. One, located behind the ornamental stair, allows daylight deep into the interiors. The second wall is a suspended metal, glass and wood screen depicting Thomas Edison's first sound studio. This emblematic image representing the history of sound recording is entitled 'Edison's Apparition' and back lit to project the image fully. Developed from maquettes exploring the interplay of silhouette and shadow, it acts as a terminus for the axis created by the vertical wall of diffused light.

Most of the materials used were chosen for their natural character and durability: Pakistani slate, terrazzo, wood cabinets and panelling, sisal matting for floors and metal fittings housing CDs, files and workstations. But the architects have not left nature unadorned: rich-hued gold and aubergine have been rubbed and painted on to wall surfaces. These subtle painterly effects give the interiors a sense of depth, and a warm, sumptuous atmosphere.

The video viewing room also has a translucent screen. The plaster recesses behind the video cabinet are finished with metallic dust to reflect the light.

'Edison's Apparition', the assemblage/collage by Karen Bausman and Alison Berger, which is displayed on a vertical screen at one end of the public corridor, loosely dividing public circulation and private office space.

The architects placed the service elements within the inner core of the office, behind aubergine-stained wood panelling walls which feature at strategic points throughout the offices. Carefully planned storage units are attached to the walls.

Right: Elegant wooden CD racks within the central core of the office.

Far right: An aubergine stain gives depth to the grained wood panels which are framed by brass channels and detailed with custom-designed hardware.

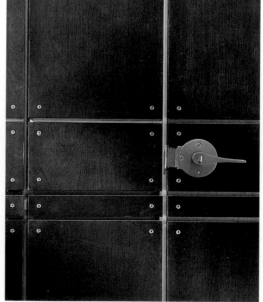

Behnisch & Partners
Plenary Complex of the German Federal Parliament
Bonn, Germany

The new restaurant for MPs on the building's upper floor, west of the Chamber, features murals by Nicola de Maria.

Right: The circular, open form of the Plenary Chamber, facing an updated version of the Eagle Wall. The Chamber is flanked by double-height walls in front of the viewing balconies.

The building of the new Plenary Chamber Complex in Bonn was 'a long, lively complex business', as Günter Behnisch tactfully puts it, involving consultation with a huge number of people, an evolution in perceived needs and a prolonged construction period.

It had become clear by the end of the 1960s that new buildings needed to be provided for the *Bundestag* and the *Bundesrat*, the two chambers of the Federal German Parliament, whose functions had outgrown the old *Bundeshaus*. A site on the banks of the Rhine was mooted, but later rejected in favour of improving the existing buildings in the Rhine Valley, whilst at the same time developing a new 'Federal District' surrounding the complex. All the different buildings of the Constitution would be sited here, with a space reserved for the public in the middle.

The old complex was a 'pot-pourri' of elements, and upon closer inspection the architects discovered that the existing Plenary Chamber had obviously been put up in a hurry, and could not be redesigned in a way that would have made the desired new seating arrangement possible. So, despite sentimental ties, the decision was made to demolish it and build a new chamber.

The existing buildings vary in quality, the best being an old college *Akademie*, a notable example of 1930s modernism, and the MPs'

high-rise 'Langer Eugen'. The new Plenary Chamber, a total cube, adopts the clarity and asceticism of the first, but combined with a greater diversity, one which Behnisch regards as 'more diaphanous, less material, with materials, constructions and formal orders of our age'. It was essential to avoid creating a setting that was cut off from natural light and the riverside landscape, so the architects have given its outer shell a lightness of character, and forged clear links with natural elements: the 'bird's nest' staircase in the Speaker's area emulates a tree; some of the internal routes have a garden path-like quality; and the area beneath the skylight in the Chamber resembles an outdoor setting beneath trees.

The brief asked for seating corresponding to the present day Constitution and encouraging discussion rather than speeches, so that the deputies could make shorter contributions from their seats. In the old building they were positioned opposite the raised seats occupied by the Government, Speaker and *Bundesrat,* but here they sit in a circle, around a shallow, dish-shaped floor rising towards the periphery. Seats have been added for guests of honour and the press, arranged at right angles around three sides of the Chamber, facing the centre of the circle. A new 'Eagle Wall' has also been added.

Above: The structure of the building is open, with a variety of circulation routes connecting floor levels.

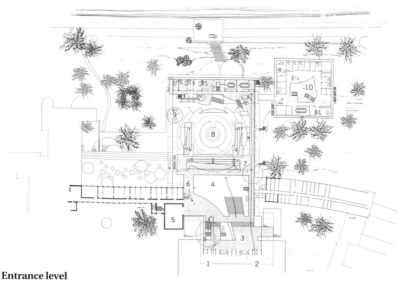

1 Visitors' entrance
2 Entrance for members and staff
3 Foyer
4 Void over lobby
5 Cloakroom
6 Visitors' approach to chamber
7 Route to *Bundestag* president's area
8 Chamber
9 Quiet retreat
10 Void over hall in president's annexe

Entrance level

The building's main foyer is a sociable space where several routes meet and intersect. The entrance lobby reached from here was originally going to be open to the public, and thus part of the Parliament plaza. However, safety regulations have become increasingly stringent over the years, and unfortunately, where people should have been able to stroll casually through the glass partitions, there are now bulletproof glass security checkpoints, destroying the unity of the plaza and the lobby. Several architectural features based on the unity of these two elements are now hard to understand; for Behnisch, 'such contradictions are part of the story of the new building and how it evolved'.

There are two entrances to the lobby from the plaza; the right-hand one is for MPs, and from here the foyer is reached, with the Chamber and Speaker's Rooms closely linked. The left-hand entrance is for visitors, who can either go down to the lecture rooms or up to the viewing gallery. The Chamber is surrounded by side lobbies and foyers with a number of views of both the outside and the interior. The entrance opposite the Rhine is clearly defined, with a broad staircase and a fine view of the surrounding landscape. The offices of the Speaker and her staff are on galleries above the foyer facing the river, with views into the Chamber, and further afield to the Siebengebirge mountains. The restaurant has a winter garden and café terrace.

The inclusion of numerous works of art has enriched the Chamber, adding depth to the architecture, even if it cannot make up for less successful programmatic changes introduced over the years in response to evolving requirements. A Sam Francis painting occupies a space between the Eagle Wall and the riverside landscape; swirling ceiling works by Nicola de Maria enliven the restaurant; outside, next to the river, is a steel sculpture by Mark di Suvero, and further works by Joseph Beuys, Rebecca Horn and Hermann Gloeckner will follow, adding their individual contribution, for, as Behnisch put it, as artists, being 'almost completely detached from any weight of materials or practical functions, they can fly higher'.

Berbesson Racine et Associés
Agence Berbesson Racine et Associés
Asnières, France

The streamlined boat logo on architects Philippe Berbesson and Marie Racine's letterhead is not there simply to indicate their ability to navigate clients through the problems of building projects; they recently chose to relocate their offices and now occupy a 40-metre boat moored at the landscaped site of Port Van Gogh on the River Seine at Asnières, 6 kilometres north-west of the centre of Paris. Looking for a large, bright and independent space with its own personality, the architects decided that 'Sycomore', an old pinnace used to ship coal, could, with some conversion, become their corporate home.

The rules of boat building are obviously quite different to those governing an immobile building structure, and the conversion took five months, at a cost of 3,500,000 francs. The boat now provides 260 square metres of workspace, accommodating up to sixteen people. This unconventional environment functions effectively as a relaxed and informal office, and its owners can also travel along the river whenever they want a change of scenery.

The bottom of the hull and the engine room were left untouched, and the architects concentrated on the upper deck and the steerage areas, creating openings at the lower levels and external longitudinal alleyways. Their principal aim was to create an open space with easy vertical circulation and communication between the two levels. In order to keep movement and views between spaces clear, it was also important to avoid introducing enclosed corridors.

The views from one end of the boat to the other are superb. The boat's long volume demanded a symmetrical layout, with circulation through the middle or on both sides, and the main stair is centrally located in the strong axis running from the front. On either side of the staircase there are oak lecterns for books and documentation. In the rear studio individual workspaces are arranged along a long, transverse drawing table, with reading desks and book shelves opposite. This area is kept as open as possible, and all other elements – another studio, meeting room, offices, kitchen, dining room, modelling studio, toilets and equipment rooms – are compactly incorporated at the lower level. Only here, where there are a few private rooms, are there any doors, some of which are sliding, so that in general long perspective views along the boat are not impeded.

With its nautical theme, the interior departs from the traditional image of a workspace. The principal materials are wood and steel: all the furniture is custom-designed in oak with steel bases; oak doors have brass portholes; the stairs are of painted steel, and floors and internal bays are also varnished oak. Berbesson and Racine have not allowed the office function to extend to interior details, which are mostly elements commonly used in boats, such as the stainless steel cables and guys supporting the stair rail, cup door pulls and ventilating cowls. Natural light, enhanced by the reflectiveness of the water, penetrates the long, narrow volume and is supported by internal and external fixtures, including hanging lights designed by the architects which give all the polished brass fixtures a lively glint.

Port Van Gogh is at once 'the country, the city and the sea', says Marie Racine, and this resourceful conversion gives her access to the benefits of all three. Visiting clients never fail to be impressed, and the redefined boat fulfils their requirements for a peaceful, comfortable and yet unusual environment.

'Sycomore' provides a tranquil, waterborne working base at Port Van Gogh on the Seine.

Longitudinal section of the converted pinnace

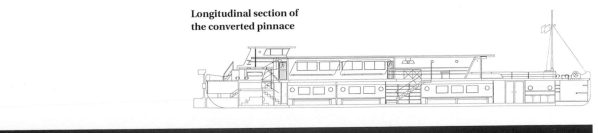

Below: The main upper studio, seen from the bow. On one side, a six-metre-long desk faces the water, with a series of individual working desks, all designed by the architects and complemented by Charles Eames office chairs. Incandescent and natural light are mixed to make the most of the interior perspectives and the high degree of water reflection.

Above: The glowing interiors at the stern of the converted boat, overhung by bracket lights, reveal their relaxed, domestic character through an open glazed window.

Right: The upper studio, seen from the stern. The long volume dictated a symmetrically planned layout.

Olivier Brenac and Xavier Gonzalez
Tour sans Fins

Arche de la Défense, Paris, France

Below and right: Fine venetian blinds in the director's office, hung in front of glass walls, provide a semi-transparent veil of colour between spaces. Rows of clear glass bands are suspended from the ceiling directly below recessed spots. Opaque, sand-blasted glass squares positioned just at the point where the light hits, create strong white shapes which are reflected in the glass walls. The furniture is an eclectic mix of pieces by Le Corbusier, Charles Eames, Andrée Putman, Jean Nouvel and Jean-Michel Wilmotte, and the carpet is by Eileen Gray.

The concept behind the design of the offices for Tour sans Fins – the developers of the building of the same name which Jean Nouvel is designing next to the Arch at La Défense – is movement from darkness to light. This simple idea, inspired by the plans for the remarkable 'endless tower' itself, has been ingeniously realized within the tiny dimensions of the space. The offices, which are located on the 33rd floor of the Arch, have dramatic views of the site of the new building.

The 250-square-metre space in the edge of the Arch includes private offices for senior and secretarial staff, as well as a meeting room, reception and information/exhibition area. Small but beautifully organized, architects Olivier Brenac and Xavier Gonzalez intended it to express imaginatively the client's innovative vision and cultural inclinations.

The floor plan is a triangular one, divided into individual spaces by huge glass walls lined with fine, saffron venetian blinds. These allow the privacy in this open environment to be altered by degrees.

The theme of dark evolving into light is dramatically embodied in the wall following the long diagonal of the triangular plan. It starts in the dark corner of the meeting room and runs through the information area towards the light coming from the windows of the president's office at the end. The wall is a collage of Japanese paper tinted with pastels, created by Gatimalau, a group of artists. Visible from every area of the office, it simultaneously creates a sense of transparency and depth which is reminiscent of impressionist painting techniques.

Colour reinforces the theme of transition from dark solidity to translucence. The earthy tones of copper, sienna and clay in the meeting room are followed in the adjoining information area by a palette of antique red, orange, saffron and gold, interrupted by a patch of ink blue. Finally, in the president's office, colour gradually disappears, leaving only white, reflecting the light from the windows.

The process of applying this leitmotif within the space was not without difficulties because the presence of mechanical ducts meant that the height of the suspended ceiling varied from 2.20 – 50 metres. This problem was resolved by introducing glass bands to soften the transition from one ceiling height to another. In the large waiting area where the ceiling is lower, two bands are set flush with the ceiling; once they have passed into the president's office, they become floating objects, suspended from steel rods, which catch the light from spots above and hanging pendant lights.

Glass bands are also incorporated at intervals across the space turned on their edge, running parallel to – and 100 millimetres away from – the top of the glass partition. This allows a gap for a light fitting between the two glass panes, which can illuminate space on both sides. A *trompe-l'oeil* effect, using the sense of shifting planes, is created by squares sandblasted on to the band, which appear to float in space, sometimes horizontally and sometimes vertically, in a subtle interplay between real and reflected imagery.

The triangular-shaped office floor is divided by clear glass partitions. The long wall facing the central reception/information space is a collage of Japanese paper, topped by a strip of silkscreened sky and clouds to make up for the lack of windows on this side of the building, and to underline the panoramic views to be had on its opposite side.

Luisa Calvi, Marco Merlini, Carlos Moya
Julia Binfield
Milan, Italy

Making a creative work base which functions as a coherent unit out of old industrial building stock requires ingenuity, particularly if the budget is slim and the proportions are tiny. Architects Luisa Calvi, Marco Merlini and Carlos Moya used all their wits to turn an old workshop into a self-contained studio, 112 square metres in size, for Julia Binfield, a firm of young graphic designers and illustrators.

The studio occupies one floor with a meeting room, archive, bathroom and kitchen adjoining the main workspace. Its floor level was 70 centimetres higher than the other main connecting entry zone; however, the architects have skilfully maintained the site's spatial discontinuity, whilst creating a coherent environment. They moved the site's original entrance, replaced all the windows and removed original internal divisions, introducing breeze-block cavity walls to insulate the space which are left unplastered.

The trio imaginatively viewed the project as 'a submarine with an observation deck'. This theme is emphasized by the dramatic contrast in the quality of light between the principal space of the studio, with natural top lighting and windows along the street side, and the subsidiary spaces which are illuminated solely by artificial light. Whilst the studio is a combination of neutral and natural tones, colour makes a dramatic appearance in the kitchen the clients badly wanted (lime green walls, blue ceiling) and entrance hallway (red, with Isami Noguchi's 'Akari' paper light a dramatic white blob on the floor). Two moveable stair units in powder-coated steel (with galvanized sheet steel treads), and porthole doors accentuate the industrial and sub-nautical inspirations.

The small, lower-level meeting room is not divorced from the main studio but visible through a large, clear glass window, a bold link which plays on the disjunction in levels. Furnishings here are limited to Arne Jacobsen chairs and tables, conveying a sense of efficiency, but no greater luxury than the studio with its plain, pine-board floors and Ernesto Rogers office chairs. Some furniture and storage units were designed specifically for the space, but they can easily be adapted for other clients. Solid constructions that were built to last, they include plywood bookshelves, welded stainless steel worktables and moveable stair units.

The studio has a spatial unity which the architects intended to be 'oriented towards the urban context'. Their sensitivity towards the client's long cycles of work, relaxation and revival has helped to create a humane and flexible working environment.

Right: The main studio, with its pine-board floors and custom-made bookshelves in poplar plywood, seen from the window of the conference room. In the foreground is one of the 'Costanza' suspension lamps by Paolo Rizzato.

The conference room, with its glazed wall and sliding door, framed in stretched metal sheet, has Leccablocco walls and a large window facing the main studio. The furniture is by Arne Jacobsen, the illustrations by client Julia Binfield.

Mobile, custom-made stair units provide access from the stone-tiled entrance lobby to the kitchen. A folding screen conceals the box/storage room. Access to the conference room is via a glazed sliding partition.

David Chipperfield Architects
Matsumoto Corporation
Okayama, Japan

The new Matsumoto Corporation headquarters were built to celebrate the seventy-fifth anniversary of the construction company, based on Okayama in the south-west of Japan. The company had decided to use the event to overhaul their corporate identity, and engaged David Chipperfield Architects to undertake the design of a new building on the existing site – one which represents the architect's largest built work in Japan to date. It is located in an area of historical interest, close to the centre of the city, where the height of any new building is controlled by regulations. The design overcomes this restriction, however, lending the company headquarters a refined and distinct character which could be read as a shrewd statement in concrete, steel and timber about the optimum use of space.

To reduce the weight of the building, the structure is a steel frame with sandblasted stainless steel cladding. The orientation of the site was also a critical factor: because of tight shadow regulations, the mass of the building has been pulled back to the southern boundary, which runs at ninety degrees to the street. This main block compactly houses all the principal office functions. Its south-facing orientation inspired the creation of a large sun louvre façade with light-diffusing screens which give an open, banded effect. Behind this façade there is a double-height atrium punctuated by tall, steel-clad columns, running the length of a white frame structure holding two floors of open-plan offices (the upper floor housing reception/presentation rooms).

Although there is an elevator at the rear of the office, the two floors are connected by a long, prominent staircase in the atrium to encourage circulation by stair. Two service/stair cores are situated at either rear end of the working area. A third floor contains more self-contained executive offices, including the president's offices at one end, close to a balcony facing west to the hills. This level also incorporates a south-facing courtyard roof terrace with a plain timber board floor.

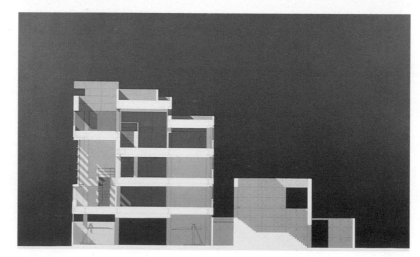

Left: Matsumoto's landmark building, close to Okayama city centre, from the south side, showing its two glazed, south-facing office floors.

Centre: The concrete-framed upper terrace of the open courtyard, overlooked by the office building to the right, and the reception, café and seminar room (in the background, centre), laid out on different levels like a row of pavilions. The main staircase leading into the building is situated at the far end of the glazed walkway which continues the axis between the two blocks. A wooden screen shields the lower courtyard area to the left.

Right: The wood-floored courtyard and adjoining passage underneath the glazed walkway at ground-floor level. (The café, below the reception, is to the right.)

Left: Cross-section of the headquarters building from south to north, showing the interior composition of the office block on the south side of the site.

The main block overlooks a terraced garden area on the northern strip of the building. The reception, café and seminar room are located here in the form of a row of pavilions on different levels bordered by a perimeter garden. The working sections of the offices are situated away from the south-facing façade down towards these spacious areas, which are much more open, but screened from the undistinguished urban mass behind. As with many of Chipperfield's buildings, there is no firm line of demarcation between interior and exterior. The interiors overlooking or opening on to the courtyard form a bond with it, while the open areas of the building become part of the inside, embraced within the overall structure.

The front entrance is on the east side of the site. A long main approach staircase links the two blocks of the building. The taller office block has a large framed aperture providing access to the ground-floor car park. On the right, the lower front of the seminar room is another strong geometric frame with a wide glazed portion admitting light to its double space and to the partially open entrance lobby behind.

The stair brings visitors in from the busy street to a first-floor entry point on the right. Straight ahead, a long, open walkway continues the strong axis running between the two blocks, while the entrance opens out into a courtyard area with café tables and chairs, and beyond that stairs to a raised terrace. These open areas are protected to the north by a high side wall containing a wooden screen which offers views out from the courtyard.

The light structure and basic materials used meant that the contract budget of £6,000,000 was not strained to its limits. Chipperfield's pragmatic, flexible approach does not rely on sophisticated techniques, but is based on a rationale which 'deals with what can be made apparent', making the most of the tactile qualities of plain materials in simply defined spaces. A building should 'not attempt to mystify', he maintains. 'The basic elements have their own mystery.'

Jo Coenen & Co.
J.C.J. Haans
Tilburg, The Netherlands

Architect Jo Coenen wanted his new office building for the importers J.C.J. Haans to make a major contribution to the improvement of the work place. It was to be a 'sparkling landmark', but also a calm, uncluttered internal environment. The result is a glass pavilion – a transparent cube of almost filigree lightness – set at the end of a long steel footbridge and surrounded by water. The project was built to accommodate fifty employees and includes five storeys of offices. The central entrance hall is on the third floor, with two floors of showrooms below. On the ground floor there is a café. Above the reception there are open-plan offices fronted by two projecting balconies.

The glass façade is not tinted, and this guarantees the building's transparency from both sides. Coenen explains that this decision was not a straightforward one: its technical realization demanded an innovative approach to both air-conditioning and façade engineering. Highly reflective, light-deflecting prisms are incorporated into the double glazing in such a way that the view outside is not hindered, and rays of sunlight can be most efficiently used for energy, irrespective of their seasonal angle. Winter sun, with its low angles, is directed right into the centre of the building, and radiated heat absorbed and stored by solid floor components. In the summer, louvres deflect the much steeper angles of the sun's rays, preventing the glass cube from becoming a hothouse.

The air-conditioning system is not obtrusive or extensive. Steel supports which form part of the primary structure also serve as conduits for air to ventilate rooms; this double function means that both bulky conduits and suspended ceilings were unnecessary. Putting air vents in the supports made it necessary to install sprinklers there too, and this, together with the use of a central installation shaft and in-floor conduits for electricity distribution, leaves the rooms free of obtrusive technical equipment. Air-cooling systems are neatly housed in custom-designed fitted cupboards in beech veneer; their perforated sliding doors also have useful sound-absorbing qualities.

For Coenen, this method of dealing with the building's services is vital, for then 'the architectural qualities of the design can be applied, without interference, to create the optimum of offices. The harmony in the rooms is never undermined or disturbed.' Furthermore, he points out, the lack of concealing cladding in the building's workspaces and communal areas gives more visual emphasis to its materials and neatly designed functional details, such as window profiles and stair rails.

The design of the furniture and fittings helps to give workspaces flexibility and a positive character. On each floor it is possible to create small areas of private space by means of curved, mobile partitions. These are attractive forms with steel structures, finished with perforated steel plates and beech veneer; decorative grooves cut into the wood emphasize their mobility. Beech is used extensively for the furniture and floors throughout, suggesting an internal warmth which contrasts with the openness and transparency of the building's structure.

Left: The five-storey glass pavilion, surrounded by lake, is reached via a steel footbridge running along a 60-metre wall.

Right: Curved wooden partitions can be moved easily on their wheels, allowing areas to be sectioned off when privacy is desired. Wooden floors and furniture help to create a warm atmosphere. The yellow wall is made of prefabricated concrete with coloured window frames.

Left: The canteen, overlooked by the curved balcony of the first office floor, is kept separate from the cube of working areas at the heart of the building, but shares their sense of openness.

Right: The layered balconies of the office floors receive plenty of light from the curtain-walled façade, which is supported by a system of structural steel rods. Grid gangways behind the curtain façade facilitate maintenance work, such as window cleaning.

Left: Custom-designed furniture includes fitted cupboards in veneered Multiplex and beech, and Norman Foster's 'Nomos' tables.

Pi de Bruijn, de Architekten Cie
The Second Chamber of Parliament

The Hague, The Netherlands

Proposals for a new building for the Second Chamber of Parliament in The Hague were first raised as long ago as 1863. However, it was not until the early 1970s that lack of space for MPs and the pressure of increasing numbers of public visitors made a separate extension essential. The brief of a competition held in 1977 asked for an open, accessible building linking people and Parliament, which reflected 'new methods of working and meeting' and also fitted in with existing government buildings in the Binnenhof complex and the centre of The Hague. After the entries received failed to reach the required standard, the Housing Minister invited tenders. After many discussions, Pi de Bruijn of de Architekten Cie was chosen as architect on the basis of his scheme which showed an 'overall image of strength and simplicity, contrast with the environment and strong architectural vision'.

The new building, which was completed in 1992, is created around three squares, the Binnenhof, Plein and Hofcingelplein. It develops a new axis, the width of the Binnenhof and the central fourteenth-century Ridderzaal, and makes other

government buildings on the site, new and old, seem complementary. A cast concrete structure, it is made up of meeting rooms, halls and offices linked to a central glass-covered hall, 24 metres high and 100 metres long, with bridges connecting refurbished offices to the new core. The hall is the most important spatial element of the project, and its three connected levels ensure the passages for visitors and users are physically separate but integrated in a single area. It has ground-floor information facilities for the press and public, and adjacent meeting rooms.

Structurally the new building is fairly traditional, but the architects' use of materials and application of details is very striking. To give a sense of continuity throughout, interiors and exteriors are clad with 'golden granite', a honey-coloured, speckled stone, which creates a dark, striped effect. The floors in the public area are tiled in strips of polished granite with a contrasting motif that de Bruijn sees as a 'beach pattern'. Recessed areas of glass link this central hall and two other Ministry buildings. The hall was planned as a passageway from the Hofcingelplein to the Plein, making it a

part of the public area. An architectural transparency has been achieved here, though security checks are required for access.

In order to emphasize the street-like character of the main hall, de Bruijn has kept colour to a minimum, with bright primaries reserved for a few small pavilions intended for meetings. However, each of the three blocks of meeting rooms is identified by soft shades of its primary colour (carmine red, corn yellow and ultramarine). Art features widely in the new buildings. The main hall shows Rudi van de Wint's visually complex and intensely coloured painting. The Government Art Supervisory Committee liked this 'almost theatrical foil for the clear lines of the architecture, reflecting the emotional element which often plays a role in the Chamber's decision-making processes'.

The new, saucer-shaped plenary hall, which takes its cue from the Greek or Roman amphitheatre, suits the Dutch system of coalition government and consultative politics, and its image is intimate rather than monumental. It allows the individual responsibilities of Cabinet and Parliament to be expressed, and its viewing gallery seats

Left: One of the committee rooms. Meetings are illuminated by wide-beam downlighters housed in floating ceiling panels. Aluminium louvres allow views of the street to be closed off.

Right: Perspective of the site of the Dutch Parliament. The Second Chamber is located next to the historic Binnenhof buildings in The Hague.

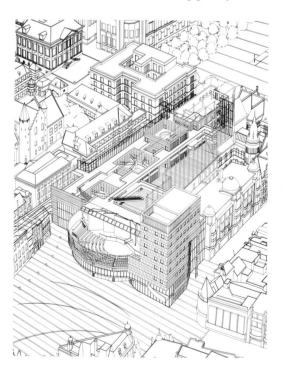

a maximum of three hundred members of the public (as opposed to sixty in the old chamber). The calm colours here reflect the Dutch landscape, with a green carpet, a blue, cupola-shaped ceiling, pearwood lecterns, natural-coloured worktops and, instead of benches, individual cobalt-blue leather and wood armchairs arranged in expanding rows.

'Formal autonomy' in the design was welcomed at the outset but, because of its long planning stage, the project evolved into a structure which binds a wide variety of new and old buildings into an integrated whole. With office space mainly confined to the older edifices or a nine-storey press tower, the new building is essentially composed of the main hall, meeting rooms, public areas and passageways. For the Minister of Housing and the Environment, the scheme has a timeless appeal and a metropolitan character, with colours and features exuding a positive image in place of the depressing greyness so often found in large government buildings. To the visitor, the interface between the public and Ministers achieved in the new Second Chamber reflects the consensual nature of Dutch government.

Above: The Central Hall, with its coloured meeting cubicles, acts as the main circulation route through the various parts of the building. Balconies provide access to the many committee rooms and street entrances at either end. Behind steel columns supporting the hall's glazed roof, the brickwork of the old buildings has been left uncleaned to heighten the contrast with the new elements.

Right: The new Chamber with furniture in leather and wood. A slit in the roof brings in direct light, and glare-free halide downlights are recessed into the ceiling. The spectators' gallery is dimly lit to accentuate the arena below. The walls behind the Speaker's chair are decorated with panels by Rudi van de Wint.

Stefano de Martino (design)
Stefano de Martino, Rem Koolhaas and DEGW London Ltd (project team)
Chiat/Day Advertising Inc.
London, UK

Next to one of the cast fibreglass panels slicing through the long room is a staircase to the mezzanine floor. Made of folded perforated steel, it has flat stringer on one side and hollow steel tube on the other.

Chiat/Day, an international advertising agency, have a high design profile which is underlined by their extraordinary head office in Los Angeles with its façade dominated by a huge pair of binoculars (see page 56). The location of Chiat/Day's London offices, in a tenth-floor penthouse at Berkshire House on High Holborn, did not permit such an ostentatious intervention into urban space but, committed to open, innovative working spaces, the agency wanted to create another mould-breaking design project. The interiors, which were initially refurbished by DEGW London as speculative office space, are a *tour de force* of imaginative open planning and detailing within a creative work environment.

Rem Koolhaas was originally approached to design the offices, but such were his other commitments that after early collaboration with the architect Stefano de Martino, the development of the project was completely handed over to de Martino, with Koolhaas' blessing. The converted space taken on by the architects encompassed two open floors and a mezzanine, with a double-height volume on the north side, overlooking the British Museum. It had a new vaulted roof, and a meeting-room area housed in a glass box structure jutting dramatically over the side of the building, which was intended to give occupants a sense of being suspended in mid-air.

At the outset, de Martino explains, the character of the space was one of 'bland linearity'. Its most exciting aspect was the rich range of urban views towards Bloomsbury, Covent Garden and Westminster. When seated, occupants can see a broad panorama from the south side, whilst from the north the view is confined to other tall buildings such as Centre Point, Senate House and the British Library's Reading Room. From a standing position, however, a 360-degree perspective of the whole cityscape rising towards Hampstead is visible. In his design, de Martino aimed to respond to the loftiness of the project's location.

Chiat/Day needed to accommodate about forty-five people working in groups of four or

Above: The conference room has a panoramic view over London. Its folding doors are made of clear polycarbonate roofing; the ceiling is perforated aluminium. The desk has perforated steel, copper and aluminium legs with a red linoleum and aluminium plate top. Placed around it are chairs by Charles Eames.

Right: The glass box structure of the meeting room gives the tenth-floor penthouse of the otherwise unexceptional Berkshire House a projecting façade.

A smaller meeting room is partitioned off by translucent walls. Its tables blend with the character of the space in a way that ready-made furniture could never do.

six, or in pairs (creative teams), and wanted to give each an open-plan environment but also some personal space. In addition, a range of meeting rooms of different scales was to cater for everything from one-on-one sessions to large presentations. The brief also had to incorporate services, including audio-visual and dark rooms, storage, a kitchen and showers.

Rather than redesigning the space provided, de Martino made a series of interventions which fulfil the brief and 'inhabit' the building, whilst leaving its existing fabric relatively untouched. To avoid separating the two floors into an upstairs and a downstairs zone, he included a series of translucent glass screens which link the space vertically. The screens slice through the void, connecting the floors and dividing the plan into different areas. There are no corridors blocking off areas of the interior; instead, the visitor follows an irregular sequence of enclosed spaces, each of which has its own identity.

The more intimate, small-scale areas above and below the mezzanine provide the working environment, while the double-height space is kept as a public area. With their subtle backlighting, the screens are perceived differently according to the viewing point; from the large public area, they appear as solids, but seen up close, within the dense grid of the workstations, they seem to become voids.

Three areas show best how de Martino uses screening to differentiate between parts of the project: the entrance screen between the lift lobby and the offices, holding together closed spaces like the production area, dark room and fire stairs, and extending the mezzanine into a wedge-shaped studio room; the central 'void' between two screens, with a variety of niche-like meeting rooms, a raised level on the tenth floor, a new stair and the second extension of the mezzanine into a half-suspended balcony; and lastly, the gable end, with the main conference room and associated facilities at the lower level, and the presentation room above.

The screens are made of translucent cast fibreglass panels with sandblasted steel frames, not mass-produced but batch-produced by the artist Terry Flowers. They look like delicate fragments of crumpled tissue paper, held firmly in place by the criss-cross steel bands. Other elements in the space have been given an individual treatment in keeping with the theme of openness and visual interest, and are also ingeniously economical. The folding doors to the main conference room, for instance, are made of translucent panels of plain polycarbonate roofing.

In a context like this, ready-made furniture would have been 'quite out of place' says de Martino. Apart from some Charles Eames chairs, he has custom-designed all the furniture, using a variety of woods and metals, including a reception desk in MDF and conference tables with aluminium and red linoleum tops and steel, copper and aluminium legs. In contrast to these cold and hard materials, the architect includes some soft elements in the reception area in the form of rock-shaped seats made of bright Lycra velour. In the smaller meeting rooms, tables with steel legs and amoeboid tops in fibreglass treated to look like copper introduce a playful note.

De Martino aimed to enrich the impoverished language of the office environment, created by the banal, 'component' mentality underlying much state-of-the-art office furniture. This, he believes, although technologically sophisticated, tends to exploit the user, making them feel like yet another component. The design of his light, expressive forms, with their rough and smooth textures emphasizes a dynamic and sensual combination of surface and mass.

Glass fibre and polyester resin was sandwiched between layers of crushed cellophane in order to create the luminous double-height screens connecting the main floor and the mezzanine vertically and horizontally – a good way to split space without reducing the amount of light. De Martino designed the majority of Chiat/Day's furniture, including the reception desk and a range of 'Blob' armchairs, made of Lycra velour over shaped foam on a wooden base.

1 Pit
2 Adjustable table
3 Meeting room
4 Kitchen
5 Ladies' toilets
6 Audio-visual room
7 Conference room

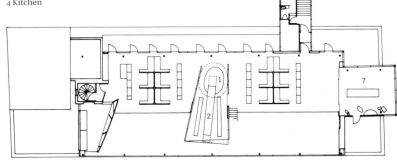

Mezzanine floor

Main level: tenth floor

Denton Corker Marshall
The Australian Embassy

Tokyo, Japan

The Australian Government began assessing the need for a new Embassy building in Tokyo during the mid-1980s. The site of the Ambassador's former residence, a Victorian mansion, was a vast plot about three kilometres south of the Imperial Palace, including a beautiful old garden. Its size and value encouraged the Government to consider selling the land, but in 1987 the decision was made to redevelop a third of it, and sell the lower end of the block, with a covenant protecting the group of huge old trees to the south. The new embassy was built along Mira Street to the north, in Minato-ku, and the finished building, designed with great assurance by Denton Corker Marshall, manages to convey the unerring confidence of officialdom as well as the imagination of the architects – a rare combination indeed.

It is a simple design, European in its formality, with a symmetrical layout. At the heart of the site is a central chancery building with an inner courtyard, flanked by two residential wings; on either side of a hill at the rear of the site there is a recreation building (to the west) and the Ambassador's residence (to the east). The building is approached from the north along Mita Avenue, a street with large houses in garden settings. A mesh blast screen over the front windows is functional but also has a lightness of touch. It is flanked by sculptural coats of arms, which are set in their own metal grid and which change like holograms as one approaches the building. In a playful twist of function, the same mesh shield becomes a sunscreen at the back of the building.

Traditionally, an embassy was a house for the Ambassador, so the architects tried to maintain this domestic image, but on a grand scale. The building had to present a confident and assertive image, so it has a dominant, centralized presence, but one which is not pompous or monolithic. 'Most embassies tend to be a few scattered buildings on a site; we used the residential wings to reinforce the size, to make it look bigger. The domestic feel comes with a change of scale and character', explains architect John Denton. Despite its scale, the project came together smoothly: 'It was built very quickly, cost $135 million, effectively built in 21 months, on time and at a fixed price.'

The four-storey chancery building is simple, formal and abstract, a composition of solid and void, light and shade. Enormous, stainless steel walls form its sides, cutting through the building, holding the edges of the entry courtyard and the foyer and framing the view into the garden. A series of frames fit between these walls, providing visual screening and, on the garden side, sunscreens. The two residential wings are broken down into smaller, more human dimensions: small punched windows, balconies and detailed aluminium panelling, contained within a series of grey cubes on black concrete bases, with white-framed glass sections above.

The architects used the project to experiment with materials and forms, and the design responds to the Japanese love of the qualitative nature of materials. The exterior of the building combines a black off-form concrete base, metal finishes, a white frame and glass. Inside, the finishes display a variety of layered textures in grey and white, with a few areas of contrasting colour (some of which are works of art): 'a reminder of the vivid Australian landscape', say the architects. Certain details show the application of a domestic theme, such as the larger-than-life stainless steel evocation of a traditional fireplace.

The Embassy is something of a hybrid: there are theatrical elements to the building, but it also has a particularly Western solidity which enjoys its privileged context, taking full advantage of the verdant surrounding landscape – which is particularly rare in Tokyo's dense urban fabric – with trees framing glimpses of its handsome detailing.

Left: The main façade and entrance to the building, showing the mesh blast screen over the front windows and the sculptural coats of arms.

Right: The architects' design responds to the Japanese love of high-quality materials. A stainless steel fireplace also shows their attempt to introduce a domestic ambience into the interior.

Far right: A meeting room with a restrained and handsome black and white décor.

A view from the landscaped garden of the warmly lit interior function-room spaces within the steel-frame-clad exterior.

Ralph Erskine, in collaboration with Lennart Bergström and Rock Townsend
The Ark

London, UK

The semi-elliptic, semi-triangular building that has taken shape on the edge of the site of a former car pound in Hammersmith, wedged between a motorway viaduct and the underground tracks, is a landmark development of speculative offices 'heralding a new approach to office design'.

The Ark was created by the Scandinavian construction company Åke Larson, well known in Britain for its innovative approach to design and building. Its concept was not an untested flight of fancy, but was modelled on similar environments constructed in Sweden by the company, whose role at The Ark combines that of client, project manager and potential tenant. Ralph Erskine has a close relationship with the developers, and his approach to their scheme was adventurous.

The building was conceived as one reflecting progressive corporate values – user-friendly, with natural light, an air-cooling system, natural materials and office space with character. It was designed for a working community 'where individual firms can have their own identity while enjoying contact with others in an unusual and stimulating environment'. The developers hope to find enough takers able to appreciate their enlightened corporate philosophy.

When Erskine began sketching the Ark, the interior environment was uppermost in his mind. He allowed the floors to rise up like stands in a football stadium, with the façade leaning out to give each floor the required width: ' the exterior was entirely dictated by the interior ... the result was an amusing and exciting exterior, but it was not actually something I was looking for'. The extensive, three-banded glazing (brown, clear, brown) reinforces his concept of an inner soul gazing out towards the world. The copper-faced spandrel panels of this angled cladding system will also, in time, develop a green patina, in line with the architect's organic concept of growth and change.

The interior incorporates 151,000 square feet of space to let on nine floors. This is arranged around a huge central space which Erskine wanted to give 'the organic complexity of a Venetian town centre' by means of a variety of cutaway features and differing ceiling heights. Two glass cupolas slope boldly down towards the lower, indoor and outdoor terraces on the sunny side of the building. A 10-metre tower, containing reception rooms, rises from the roof. At the centre of the interior, an inner 'building' rises from the ground floor linked by angled bridges and balconies to surrounding office levels. This gives intimacy and warmth to the space.

The understated main entrance reception has a polished granite floor and is reached via a large revolving door with a copper surround on the west side of the building. The ground-floor café/bar straight ahead is a relaxed environment fitted out with natural materials. There are leather-backed chairs and moulded, striped banquette seats, and wood is used extensively, with a curved ceiling and handrails in Oregon pine and walnut. The slatted floors are made from Belinga (a fully replenishable rain-forest hardwood from Nigeria).

Left: Panoramic views can be seen from the ninth-floor 'summit' meeting room, 69 metres above ground level, which features white cotton upholstered seating, a glass and steel table and a tall, conical floor lamp.

Right: View of the connecting bridges below the roof. Filtered fresh air is distributed within the building by ductwork, exhausted into the atrium and then to the outside via the ducts or the rooftop skylight.

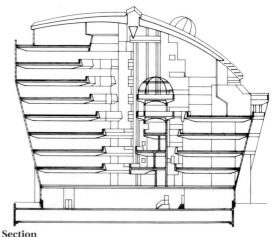

Section

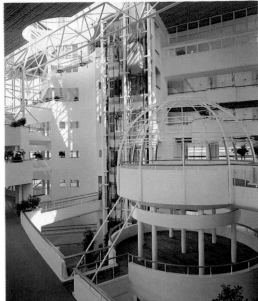

The open-plan, high-quality social area offers an attractive alternative meeting space. This communality and dissolution of barriers between work space and atrium slightly reduces the space allocation per person, but not at the expense of the standard of working conditions. An abundance of natural light makes individual areas, even in the smaller offices, seem larger.

Various types of office layout have been considered, and there is scope for cellular and landscape compositions which can be developed to the tenants' precise requirements. Offices along the façade are modelled on the 'combi-office' concept: partly open plan, with glazed fronts towards the middle of the floor giving views over the atrium, and conference areas, computer rooms and storage in a landscape area in the middle. Within these areas, more enclosed spaces can be built with alcoves, an idea previously used in Sweden.

The developers provide an extensive options catalogue of Scandinavian and classic modern furniture systems, flooring and colours, devised by the architects to blend in with the architecture of the building. This is particularly important as all the offices are visible from above. Occupants can choose from a selection of walls with glazed sections, and the atrium edge can be screened, though this was not the original intention. The suspended ceilings, made of Columbian pine, are indirectly lit and slope towards the façade, giving character to the rooms.

The building is sealed because of high noise and pollution levels in the area, but every room has individually controlled thermostats. Radiant panels in the ceiling provide cooling, using water, and this drastically reduces the space needed for plant rooms and eliminates extensive ducting. The air-cooling system, which is healthy and energy-saving as it does not recirculate stale air, is innovative in Britain. A slot running along the spine of the roof helps to bring in natural light, as well as assisting fire protection (part of it actually opens up).

The building's barrel shape incorporates nine storeys of offices facing the flyover, which reduce to five storeys, 'bowing to the smaller residential buildings on the south side'. One unexpected problem regarding increased acoustic levels as a result of the presence of the building's curved façade, is being actively addressed by the developers, for example, by planting trees at the perimeter of the site. On a more positive note, it is thought that the building might be helpfully deflecting some of the traffic noise emanating from the nearby flyover.

The way in which the interior of this innovative building – inspired by Erskine's vision of a miniature city – will function once it is full, will depend on the tenants' responsiveness to this progressive working environment.

Spencer Fung Architects
Designers' Guild
London, UK

Internal communication is not so easy for a company like the Designers' Guild, whose eighty-five staff spread out in departments on various sites around London. However, after some searching, this London firm of fabric designers and manufacturers finally found the spacious environment they needed for a single headquarters in the form of a three-storey Victorian coach-building works in North Kensington. Previously converted in 1980, the building offered lots of open space (a total area of 3,500 square metres) and an air of industry the firm was happy to adopt for its own busy enterprise. Here was a chance to create a semi-open layout closely geared to departmental requirements, encompassing a range of office and administration areas, design studios, meeting rooms and a café. The limited budget required a good basic design and a high degree of resourcefulness in finding materials and contractors, and the task of conversion had to be carried out on a tight schedule. With their thoughtful solution, Spencer Fung Architects managed to accommodate a wide range of company activities, without letting time or budget get the better of them.

The warehouse building offered good natural light conditions from large windows and central rooflights, and generously proportioned spaces on three floors positioned around a wide central stair core. Fung and his team have retained its open, bright atmosphere, designing individual ranges of free-standing partitions and storage units for each department. Fung does not attempt to play down the building's industrial origins, and the open reception, with its rows of heating pipes and the large chain pendant lighting fixtures running along the ceiling, provides a backdrop for the plain textiles hanging from painted steel display frames.

To turn the two floors into an open studio space, the architects adjusted the composition of the centre of the building, closing a floor void in the centre of the first floor, and partially closing a central stairwell on the second floor, to create a smaller, square floor void. The main steel

Right: The lower-floor reception doubles up as a display space for the client's textiles, with Fung's ceiling-mounted display frames and slatted display unit. The staircase to the upper floor was retained from the pre-converted building and remodelled by the architects. Leading away from the entrance space, and in the floor above, are a series of open workspaces designed for specific uses and defined by low partitions in white lacquered MDF.

Left: The staff café is contained within a distinctive, blue-painted box at the far left corner of the building, visible from the offices through a window slot. Old farmhouse furniture is combined with lemon-terrazzo-topped tables, a door in walnut with gun-metal steel door handles, modern chairs and uplighters to create a multi-faceted space.

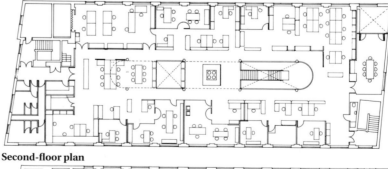

Second-floor plan

First-floor plan

Above and far right: Fung designed storage units for a range of specific uses within the different departments of the company, including this huge wall of niches holding fabric samples. On the balcony above there is a series of wooden lecterns for consulting fabric books, magazines and other documentation.

staircase was retained, but its handrails and balustrading were removed and new painted steelwork installed with rails and treads in walnut. The mullions of the large roof-light bring in natural light, and the skylights can also be opened up. Additional windows around the sides of the building assist ventilation, and concertina blinds will be introduced to soften the light.

The brief set was a very technical one: 'the client wanted an efficient layout in order to function efficiently', explained Fung. The challenge was to provide working areas geared to a variety of very specific departmental roles, whilst maintaining an open-plan layout to enable effective inter-group communication and access. This was achieved by introducing low-walled screening which provides both privacy and storage space. By designing individually tailored furniture and fittings, the architects could create a variety of spaces, each with their own focus and group identity.

The materials applied throughout the building are modest, basic and readily available: birch plywood, medium density fibreboard, walnut, painted and galvanized steel, linoleum and seagrass (sisal flooring). The design of the furniture and fittings is very much led by the wide range of functions required. However, Fung plays with a few of the finishes: the MDF, for instance, is treated with a semi-opaque white lacquer, giving it the milky, soft appearance of Marmarino plaster. By keeping the palette of materials predominantly natural, he ensured that the company's vibrant fabrics could be incorporated without making the whole environment look too busy. These are added only at strategic points such as the reception. In the same way, the sparing use of blue and lemon-yellow paint on key walls helps reinforce the functions of specific areas.

Storage facilities were an important aspect of the project and, apart from meeting-room furniture and chairs, the architects custom-designed all the furniture and fittings, creating storage units in a range of types and sizes, each individually conceived for a specific use. These include the design studio's navy and ochre boxes, made in robust cardboard and set in rack shelving, a huge wall of niches holding fabric samples, a series of wooden lecterns, cupboards housing a presentation screen, the metal display system in the reception – even filing trays.

The economy imposed upon the architects' choice of materials did not stop them from creating some more expressive small-scale pieces in the reception area. The main reception desk is a simple, sculptural form in a combination of walnut and birch, situated close to the entrance in front of an informal open meeting space. Against a vivid backdrop of fabrics, there is a range of café-style furniture. Alongside a group of small tables with round tops in lemon terrazzo is a Z-shaped counter in waxed steel with a co-ordinating blue top. This free-standing bar, overlooking offices opposite, divides the space from the central thoroughfare.

Furniture in the cellular offices and meeting rooms – including 'Piceno' tables and chairs in dyed white beechwood, designed by James Irvine for Cappellini – was sourced to blend with the natural tones of the setting, including sisal floors, and doors and presentation cabinets in walnut. The meeting rooms are set within a suite at one end of the building, made as open as possible – and suitable for receptions – by taking out existing cubicles. These are the only closed-off spaces, and the full-height glazing and aluminium partitions of the cellular offices maintain a high degree of transparency.

Even relatively small companies like the Designers' Guild find that it pays to offer good staff catering facilities with a relaxed, rather than a utilitarian atmosphere. As the staff café, an enclosed space in the far-left corner of the building, is rather small, a shift system operates. Its intimate and jaunty interior provides a contrast to the openness of the working areas. A blue wall punctuated by window slots signals its position, and the interior has a distinctly domestic character – one facet of an integrated environment which gathers previously dispersed elements.

Frank O. Gehry & Associates, Inc.
Chiat/Day/Mojo
Venice, California, USA

The iconic impact of Chiat/Day/Mojo's recently designed Main Street headquarters, with the giant pair of binoculars positioned enigmatically at its centre, owes its power to a meeting of minds between architect Frank Gehry, and artists and long-standing collaborators Claes Oldenburg and Coosje van Bruggen. The flawless symmetry of this unlikely urban object – its tapering cylindrical forms for Gehry conjuring up an image of the columns of Egyptian temples – is broken by the two very different elements which form part of the tripartite composition of the building; all three are intended to relate in scale and level of detail to the surrounding environment. While billboard artworks are two-a-penny within the urban landscape of this part of California, and sculpture is often precariously pinned on to less than inspiring façades, Gehry's project represents a more intimate and ambitious integration of the constantly evolving disciplines of sculpture and architecture.

The L-shaped site, originally owned by Gehry, was taken on by director Jay Chiat who urged his company's headquarters project forward, with Gehry as architect, until the discovery of hazardous waste during excavations delayed it for over two years. Its geographical location also slowed down further development. The building is four blocks from the Pacific Ocean, an area which Gehry explains has recently evolved from 'a funky beach town into a more urbane contemporary community'. The site is within the California Coastal Commission's jurisdiction, so the project had to go through an extensive review process. The building, says Gehry, reflects the dense but low-scale development the Commission aims to encourage within this area of Venice.

Low-scale it may be, but it is certainly not low-profile: the three-storey, 75,000-square-foot office space was designed specifically for the Chiat/Day/Mojo advertising agency (whose London headquarters are featured on pages 42 – 45). Their new building is sited on top of three levels of underground parking, reached by driving through the binoculars.

Directly behind the binoculars and above the drive-in entrance at first-floor level is the main conference room, dominated by Gehry's coiled snake lamp.

Sculptural binoculars on Main Street form the spectacular drive-in entrance to the headquarters, a tripartite composition with a sleek, curved white block nearest to the ocean and a copper-clad structure with tilting beams.

The binoculars, finished in a grey metallic stucco, are not there just for visual impact, but contain meeting rooms and work space. Each tall cylinder is topped by a skylight. The main conference room is located immediately over the entrance lobby, bridging the space on either side. Its tall, glazed frontage and amply proportioned side windows reveal the looming forms in front and bring natural light flooding into the space. A modestly sized table and chairs stand beneath a huge coiled light – all designed by Gehry.

The buildings flanking the binoculars have dramatically contrasting identities. One is fronted by a curved, white screen wall to provide shade from the western sun, and is smoothly shaped to link it with marine imagery. Its opposite 'partner' could not be more different: a copper-clad block of columns with tilting beams like legs holding up a downwards-sloping roof plane. Gehry combines the image of a densely grown forest with that of a structure apparently in the process of collapse.

A programme of artist-commissioned features was cancelled as an economy measure, and instead Gehry extended his design to include such elements as a huge, root-like reception desk. Oldenburg and van Bruggen created an enormous, pendulous light-bulb form within the tall, top-lit office spaces. These features do not overwhelm more practical functions of the offices: working spaces are sensibly planned out, and each employee has their own built-in workstation simply designed in plywood. The interior's tonal scheme is warm and welcoming, and enhanced by plenty of natural light. At the third level of the south façade, a very long skylight extends down through the building to the first floor, and other lightwells bring light down to the first and second floors.

The project, which came to fruition in August 1991, won a CC/AIA Honor Award the following year. While the construction was delayed, Chiat commissioned Gehry to convert a nearby warehouse into a temporary workspace for the company. His wonderfully improvisational interior design, which cost very little in comparison with the budget for the company headquarters ($15,000,000, excluding the fitting out of the interiors), produced a lively environment of sheet metal, fin-ply and cardboard. The company liked it so much that its creative department stayed there. The two projects – one an innovative landmark, the other a playful, *ad hoc* interior – have a compelling scenographic presence.

Volker Giencke
Odörfer
Klagenfurt, Austria

The Odörfer headquarters lie parallel to a busy ringroad near the southern edge of Klagenfurt, the capital of Carinthia and, according to the architect Volker Giencke, an area of 'sub-suburban density' which was once an agricultural landscape and is now blighted by a 'an uncoordinated series of selfish object-buildings' and 'conquered by the car'. It is, he adds, a scene representing 'the victory of architectural mediocrity ... with the exception of one building!'

The client wanted 'something new' at Odörfer to help affirm and reinvigorate its corporate identity. Used to low-budget projects, Giencke creates a solution which emphasizes 'economy of means, the experience of space and optical effects'. The passing motorist experiences the full visual impact of the building. Its great shimmering glass roof, with what Giencke calls a 'water-like reflectivity', rises 'unexpectedly out of the ground at 30 degrees to the horizontal'. Supported by a framework of stressed steel trusses, its glass panels overlap like roof tiles. Giencke regards its light construction as a kind of physical membrane between the exterior and interior of the building. The fact that it is almost north-facing also reduces the risk of solar penetration.

Odörfer specializes in sanitary and heating products, and the 5,000-square-metre floor area of its new building encompasses a showroom for sanitary equipment located 1.5 metres below the main entrance and sales area, a warehouse (4.5 metres above the entrance) and an office floor and caretaker's apartment above that on a bridge construction supported by steel girders. Giencke differentiated the building elements in line with these functions, and exhibition space, offices and storage areas are articulated by a range of dimensionally related structural systems; the result is a dramatic variation both in terms of the internal space and external treatment.

The exhibition area under the glass roof is built as a multi-levelled artificial landscape, bathed in light. In his approach to space Giencke acknowledges the influence of the German architect Hans Scharoun, who also introduced different levels to give his interiors a sense of activity and various vistas. Other immediately noticeable elements in the exhibition area include waterfalls and pools around the entrance which add visual interest and link the showroom with the yard.

The primary construction of the building is regular and disciplined; architectural pyrotechnics are reserved for areas where they were needed, such as the exhibition and entrance hall. However, Giencke has tried to introduce a 'knowing contrast' in his construction between light and heavy, and between regular and irregular elements; the concrete walls supporting the main trusses of the storage space are covered with glass which forms a transparent, reflective and continuous building façade. Also part of this lightweight construction are the fine stainless steel trusses supporting the glass roof.

The exhibition hall is equipped with a series of detailed elements: a 10-metre-long curved reception desk, running stair, basins, display cabinets, cubicles, light fittings and reflectors. All are functionally and economically designed in wood, glass, steel

grids and frames, with exotic plants evoking a greenhouse atmosphere. Coloured sail canvas is used to reduce the intensity of sunlight penetrating the transparent roof. The non-orthogonal elements of this area – the ground plane itself, partitions, staircases, sales counters and display stands – play against the structural order without breaking it, something Giencke feels is close in principle to Le Corbusier's 'plan libre'. The placing of elements to control movement and guide the visitor around the space is more organic.

A long heating duct runs from the entrance to the corner of the building's plant room, its dark aluminium cover plates creating a clear diagonal spine across the space, broken by the curved reception desk. Its visual impact is increased by a change of flooring material, with blue carpet to the right and a light, polished marble on the exhibition side.

The offices have a good, commanding position. A series of boxes running through the building between the storage and exhibition area at first-floor level, they are closely linked with the life of the exhibition space. They can also be reached via an outside staircase, giving access to an open corridor crossing the exhibition space below. The office windows on the south side open on to a sunlit rooftop gallery, a private world which also serves as the building's fire escape.

Odörfer was a relatively cheap building. As its budget did not allow for a very innovative construction, the architect has tried to use ordinary materials in an ingenious way, aiming for high-tech expression with a simple design. For Giencke, architecture is a process, and he characterizes his design method as 'late improvisation ... in response to the developing whole'.

Steven Holl Architects
D.E. Shaw & Company
New York, USA

Right: At night, fluorescent lighting fixtures concealed between the double-layered wall combine with the fluorescent paint to produce a soft, ethereal glow.

Space and light, rather than material and detail, are the determining elements of this office for a highly specialized financial trading firm occupying the top two floors of a 40-storey mid-town Manhattan skyscraper. Architect Steven Holl took his conceptual cue from his client's business which was set up in 1988 to monitor the shifts in prices for financial instruments, and is driven by 300 computers but few tangible processes. Working to a miniscule budget of around $50 per square foot, he devised a parallel design for a hauntingly beautiful interior that could not be further, aesthetically speaking, from the typical Wall Street office

D.E. Shaw's 65-person team includes computer scientists and mathematicians who prepare strategies for the traders. The company is geared up to execute transactions for almost twenty-three hours a day, so the challenge of housing this specialist group and $250,000 of computer equipment demanded a solution which was serene and spatially elegant, rather than bright and cosy. The brief set by the client was straightforward: they wanted a series of private offices and partially enclosed workstations, a conference room and small trading room. Holl interpreted these requirements with a suitably orderly plan, and then applied cutaway walls with hidden light sources.

Their effects are experienced most dramatically within the central reception area. This is a 31-foot, double-height cube, the high walls of which are carved and notched, creating irregularly shaped voids within the structure. Colour has been applied to the back and bottom surfaces of these 'fissures', and is projected into the space by both natural and artificial light. Only the projected colour is seen; the actual coloured surface remains invisible. Several openings have been left plain, and these allow natural light to enter. Holl points out that as the reflective effect weakens the intensity of the colour, a more vibrant result could have been achieved with fluorescent colour, perhaps less appropriate for an office but with the potential for considerable impact in

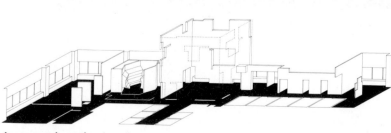

Axonometric section (1:250)

Above: In the reception area a layered stud and gypsum board wall faces the entrance, blocking out skyline vistas. Its inner layers are cut into geometric profiles backed with a coating of the fluorescent paint used for billboards.

Left: Offices lead off
from openings in the
cut-out wall of the main
reception area.

Left: The director's
office, with halogen
bulbs suspended on low-
voltage wires. Their
sandblasted, heat-
resistant glass cylinders
act as diffusers. The
conference table is made
of brushed aluminium
and sandblasted glass.
Its panels and openings
follow on a miniature
scale the wall gaps in the
reception area.

another type of interior.

It was the intangible, ephemeral nature of
trading that inspired Holl's economical
solution based on light and space. The
changing intensity of abstract light tableaux
can be seen as analogous to the energy
transmitted by satellite, and the enigmatic
spaces they reveal the endless possibilities
generated by technology. To give them their
curious glow, Holl uses yellow-green paint
originally developed for billboards; the effect
is continued at night with fluorescent fixtures
taking the place of daylight. Black vinyl tile
floors throughout provide a reflective base.

This imaginatively created artificial world
complements the intense, controlled and
abstract nature of the activities taking place
within it. However, it does not entirely
ignore the more chaotic urban landscape
surrounding the tower: the outside world is
visible from perimeter offices along the east
and west sides, where large windows (with
polarized glass to minimize glare on the
display monitors) provide skyline views.

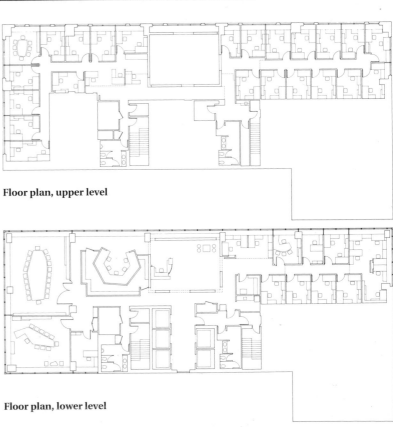

Floor plan, upper level

Floor plan, lower level

Franklin D. Israel Design Associates
Limelight Productions
Los Angeles, California, USA

Limelight's new production offices occupy a large, double-bay warehouse space in Hollywood. Like Frank Israel's earlier project there for Propaganda Films, it has rows of bow-string trusses arrayed along two matching bays. As with Propaganda, the remodelling of this compact site was carried out under tight budgetary constraints, but Israel is a versatile architect and he has created an unusual, varied environment which is both atmospheric and utilitarian.

Much of the design focused on providing a carefully articulated circulation route through the space, beginning outside at the building's western wall and continuing throughout the entire length of the interior. The entrance itself plays on Le Corbusier's cantilevered bris-soleil at Villa Stein. Inside, a canted wall becomes a long, low canopy defining the entrance area, with a back-lit shield of translucent fibreglass positioned at the east end of the axis. A free-standing wall moderates light entering from the skylights.

In a pattern which follows the trusswork above, Israel lined the perimeter of the space with individual offices surrounding a pool of workstations. These composite desk arrangements echo the layout of Frank Lloyd Wright's model workspaces in the Larkin Building and at Johnson Wax headquarters.

Conference rooms and public spaces are cleverly concentrated near the entrance so that the visitor perceives the complex to be far larger than it actually is. The grandeur of the long sweep of the entrance arcade, combined with the exploded scale of the central workstations, suggests a large multimedia empire, when in fact Limelight operates on a much more modest scale. As in Propaganda Films, the power of Israel's interiors derives from his strategy of enfolding smaller structures in a large shell and maintaining an intriguing ambiguity between public and private space.

Israel's work is always rigorously executed with a modest mix of ingredients. All the cabinetry was made from birch plywood, and the edges of all the laminated materials were exposed or stacked to 'celebrate their materiality'. Aluminium elements – fasteners, joints, wall bases, hardware and sheeting – were introduced as structural supports, and serve as the only embellishments in an otherwise utilitarian office interior. Glass and fibreglass provide a counterbalance to the predominantly opaque composition. A consistent logic was applied to Limelight's materials, details and colour scheme, and they work well together, creating a strong ambience.

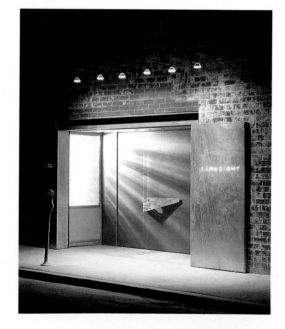

Above: Limelight's entrance, with its variant on a cantilevered bris-soleil, torqued and expanded out in forced perspective.

Right: In the extended entrance arcade a free-standing wall breaks rays entering through skylights. Visitors sit on banquette seating with Naugahyde vinyl covering.

In the reception area the canted wall becomes a low canopy. A back-lit shield 'totem' of translucent fibreglass counterbalances the opaqueness of other walls within the space.

Section

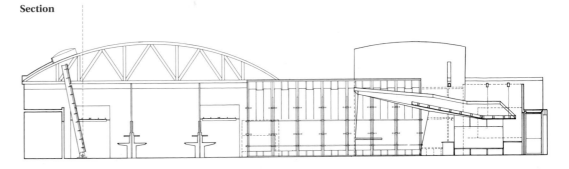

Jestico + Whiles
20-22 Stukeley Street
London, UK

20 – 22 Stukeley Street in London's Covent Garden is a six-storey Edwardian warehouse building on a right-angled site close to High Holborn, which for most of its life has served as a furniture repository for the nearby Savoy Hotel. Its deep plan form – two rectangular blocks split by a narrow lightwell – presented an unprepossessing conversion challenge. Nevertheless, architects Jestico + Whiles, who refurbished the building, were able to create a speculative office block with 2,500 square metres of eminently useable space from its raw material, adapting it so that users could enjoy maximum natural light and good ventilation.

This building type is distinguished by few exemplars, even in this fashionable, high-premium area of Central London, and the harsh economic climate has led to a glut of empty spaces in the capital as companies pursue cautious rental policies and carefully scrutinize their future needs. Instead of following a conventional, commercial path and producing oppressive interiors which perfunctorily acknowledge users' needs, the architects, whose 'green' approach to architecture dates back fifteen years, have used the opportunity to create a light, uplifting and energy-conscious working environment out of the redundant building.

The refurbishment brief called for a new lift, proper access to individual floor areas, and drastic improvements to main entrance and reception areas, natural lighting conditions and ventilation to internal spaces, together with a general upgrading of the existing fabric and the creation of a new street presence for the building. Externally, the building has been restored with new steel-framed, double-glazed windows inserted into existing openings.

The existing lightwell has been extended to the basement, exposing the original cast-iron columns, and converted into a covered atrium, with new, glazed lifts in a partially enclosed steel-framed shaft. Cutting across the expanse are light, cantilevered walkways made of translucent glass lens block floors supported by a galvanized steel T-section. The office areas have full-height, sliding glass doors with simply detailed metal balustrades, inserted into an enlarged space originally occupied by windows facing on to the central lightwell space. On the ground floor, a reception area with a planar glazed ceiling is a welcoming introduction to this brave new industrial aesthetic.

All these elements are made principally of glass and steel (galvanized rather than stainless), so that light, transparent and durable forms requiring low maintenance predominate throughout the building. The effect is to transform the dark and oppressive atmosphere of the original structure.

The project's energy-conscious qualities did not evolve merely as a response to budget constraints, although the need to make a virtue out of necessity was obviously a strong consideration. They arose mainly from the architects' rejection of energy-intensive mechanical ventilation. Instead of installing air-conditioning, a more resourceful use was made of the building's internal environment. This involved exploiting the natural characteristics of the atrium: rather than sealing this space from the outside, as is the norm in this kind of project, it was left unheated, acting as a kind of lung to the heated, open-plan working space enveloping it and thus allowing the building to 'breathe'.

In winter, warm air percolates into the static air space, maintaining a temperature of around 16 degrees centigrade, even when external ambient temperatures drop to -4 degrees. In summer the 'stack effect' of warm air rising through the central atrium draws fresh, cool air through the adjoining office

Looking down from one of the aluminium sheet ramps crossing the atrium to the ground floor. The reception desk on the right has an etched glass counter with galvanized steel facing and a bird's-eye maple and cherry top.

spaces. This method of ventilation – which undoubtedly operates better when the office layout is open-plan, with large windows on to the street, as in this project – also eliminates the need for the paraphernalia and noise of air-handling equipment. In line with the flexible letting arrangement (from single to five, on a floor-by-floor arrangement), the building is heated by a self-contained, floor-by-floor gas-fired boiler system.

The stack effect is further enhanced by an S-shaped roof-light above the atrium. Its planar glass panels act like a greenhouse, warming the ambient temperature at the top of the space, and accelerating the air current via a radiused, perforated stainless steel reflector panel in the curving roof-light. This is angled to catch the sun's rays and project light down into the central, six-storey space.

The resulting environment conveys a sense of changing weather conditions to occupants.

The design also incorporates a number of innovative ideas which the architects hope can be applied elsewhere. These include the perforated solar reflector, and electromagnetic, fail-safe door closure mechanisms incorporated into the atrium windows to ensure automatic closure in the event of fire. For the offices the architects have also designed light fittings which combine the functions of up- and down-lighting within one unit.

The project is clearly a model for future small-scale, energy-conscious developments derived from old building stock. It also demonstrates that speculative office design can transcend the boxy, energy-intensive spaces so many of us have to tolerate.

The entrance area and custom-designed reception desk.

Ben Kelly Design
Lynne Franks PR
London, UK

Right: The reception with its organically shaped desk in MDF lacquered in 'industrial orange', aquamarine glass-brick partitions, terrazzo floor, purple and white striped columns and vivid artworks.

From the point of view of prospective clients sizing up a public relations consultancy, one very potent measure of its ability to succeed where others fail is the image it communicates through its headquarters. Handled properly, the design of the building can give all the right signals about the company's potential.

Lynne Franks, pre-eminent for keeping her music, fashion and retailing clients one public image manoeuvre ahead of the rest, understood this, and chose long-standing contacts Ben Kelly Design, who designed the company's previous office, to give her new headquarters the right visual combination of art and elbow grease. Adequate space for staff was more important than a ritzy West End location, and the company chose the more economical option of a site on the Harrow Road. A drab, windswept spot, it is now vividly signposted for passing cars by a juxtaposition of orange and indigo dominating a white façade.

The whole building needed to act as a promotional device, so that potential clients on a tour around the different departments could sense the company's energy and panache. It also had to house fifty-five to seventy people, providing open and cellular offices, a boardroom, a showroom and a staff canteen, so it needed to be genuinely accommodating, not just a slick surface. The building has great visual impact. The simple roller shutter entrance has been replaced by clear glazing and an American oak door set amidst vividly toned brick walls.

Originally home to a garage used for spray-painting cars, the vast, 1,207-square-metre space is a rectangle 67 metres long from front door to back wall. Rather than a completely open-plan solution, the client wanted cellular offices for accountants and directors around the perimeter, with a maximum amount of open office space in the centre, around two enclosed directors' offices. There was no desire to create a stuffy hierarchy, and the company envisaged the space as a light, airy environment, enlivened by colour, with easy movement from area to area.

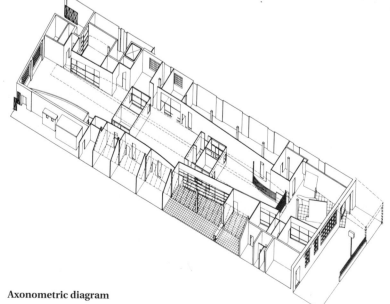

Axonometric diagram

Above: The open-plan workspace, enclosed by blue glass brick wall, and illuminated by light from galvanized steel halide floodlights reflected on the ceiling. The meeting area contains Norman Foster's 'Nomos' glass-topped table and Arne Jacobsen's 'Series 7' chairs.

The building's interior originally had the feel of a 'monster aircraft hangar' according to Kelly, with natural light entering only at either end and via a roof-light running down one side. The BKD design team – Ben Kelly, Elena Massucco and Chris Cawte – felt that it was essential to retain a sense of light and air throughout the depth of the site, and wanted to emphasize the unusual depth of the space. They created a floating, wing-shaped suspended ceiling reflecting light from metal halide floodlights on desks, and introduced bright red linoleum flooring into all the public routes through the length of the building, a path punctuated by green, wall-mounted bulkhead lights.

Solid partitions were avoided where possible in favour of glazed equivalents with

steel frames and, close to the front of the open space, some spectacular turquoise-blue glass block partitions in straight and curved forms. Solar-activated blinds adjust to existing temperatures and levels of brightness to admit or deflect light.

The limitations of the budget (around £500,000) in relation to the scale of the site, meant that materials used for large surfaces like partitions had to be kept functional.

Above: The staff canteen's textured ochre, emerald and indigo walls glisten with light reflected from suspended 'Globe' fittings.

However, BKD managed to vary their repertoire, introducing a range of teak veneer, etched glass and glass blocks in the main office areas which give weight to the stunning brightness of their palette of colours. The designers also ensured that the staff canteen had its own ambience, juxtaposing head-height stainless-steel-clad sliding screens which pull back to reveal the kitchen, with smudge-textured ochre, emerald and dark lilac walls created by fixing pigmented plaster with masonry sealer before it dried out.

The boardroom is given formidable presence by a huge, glass-topped table with a light, stainless steel base structure of pylon-like intricacy designed by Tom Dixon. Ranged around this are Arne Jacobsen's curving, high-backed fuschia red and orange Oxford chairs.

Since the building opened, the staff have customized their open environment with all manner of personal touches (including a row of white flowers in Lynne Franks' office), and their demand for more internal windows to give a clearer view of the interior from front to rear, means that the space is now inevitably not quite as coherent as BKD envisaged it. Nevertheless, the fresh, creative strengths of its design are still apparent.

Eric Owen Moss
Scott Mednick Associates
Culver City, California, USA

In designing offices for Scott Mednick Associates, a design firm specializing in video graphics, Eric Moss has made another intervention in the warehouse complex at 8522 National, a place where he has worked on various adaptive-use projects for tenants and owner, and which eventually, in its next phase of development, will become a 300,000-square-foot mixed-use complex.

The 16,000-square-foot space leased by SMA is spread over four different industrial buildings, and is dominated by a 175-foot-long causeway, conceived originally to meet ventilation requirements. This becomes the primary organizing element, with fully enclosed offices to its south and partially enclosed work areas to the north. Steel angles were bolted to both sides of the building's central wooden beams and their original alignment adjusted by lasers. This dominant design feature, with its arched steel ribs, supports both HVAC ducts and power lines. Its elaborate form shows Moss's interest in the ways in which technology can define structure. Each end of the causeway connects to staircases, a double one in metal leading to a loft gallery and the roof, the other to an executive tower. These provide vantage

points from which the whole studio with its profusion of structural forms can be seen.

The loft gallery provides a long view of the spine, whilst at the opposite end a high window cut in the wall of the executive offices reveals the procession of arched steel ribs formed in the unmistakable shape of a barrel vault. Exposed ducts and box conduits are supported at intervals by chain-hung cross bars suspended from the central beam. Meshed within this busy environment are wooden shed frames defining the semi-enclosed office spaces. Fluorescent lighting is hung horizontally in a sequence of units along the room. Under the central beam is a big hallway, not symmetrical as only the south side is clear of desk space.

At the west end of the office an exercise room is flanked by massive steel columns supporting a wooden deck from which HVAC units are serviced. A metal stair on each side provides access to this level. From the platform a further utility stair leads to the roof. The processional experience here is intended to be one of sensing structural imbalance, particularly expressed via the manipulated geometry of the stair rail.

Moss aspires to create buildings that

'confound your experience of buildings', and his work at SMA, with its intricate support system of rib ducts and box channels, is as considered in its structure as a cathedral. However, his supports, electrical elements, lighting and sprinkler systems, whilst giving the impression of being part of a rational structure and function-led rather than technological fetishes, are ultimately dealt with in a poetic way. His idiosyncratic, questioning attitude to technology brings together a wide range of approaches, some noticeably more refined than others.

The juxtaposition of rational and irrational elements makes for a solution which in spatial terms is highly complex – unnecessarily so from a purely utilitarian point of view. The domination of the main space by Moss's central spine gives it an unmistakable identity and visual interest: its compressed structure is engrossing in its peculiarity. Moss says: 'when you look at it, because of the way it's made, it's not easy to perceive the order, although you get a sense that, somehow, it exists. Part of the reason is that it's above your head. The building is made to have people pick their heads up and look at the world, and not their shoes.'

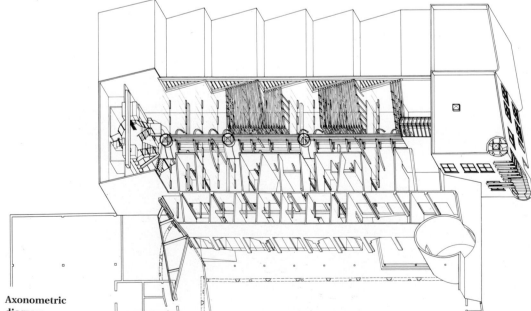

Axonometric diagram

Above right: Views from a second-storey window in the wall of the executive offices of the arched steel ribs over the work areas; lines of exposed ducts, box conduits and fluorescent tubes are supported at intervals by chain-hung cross bars. The layout of the fixtures follows the grid of the original roof joists. Strips of Douglas fir splayed into curves stand over semi-enclosed office areas.

Left: The double stair at the end of the office space, lashed together and to the support structure by the wild curve of the stair rail. Moss has joined another, flattened version to the stair rail to conform to the length of the stair and take the tension cables around in a curve.

Far left: Boxed channels for power and data cables follow the hallway centre line. Where they meet an existing column within the structure, Moss has conducted the wires around it in thick, curved metal casings.

Kazuyo Sejima
Architect & Associates
Saishunkan Seiyaku Women's Dormitory

Kumamoto City, Kumamoto Prefecture, Japan

Right: The building's entrance is on the first floor, leading along a balcony area overlooking the main, communal living space, and linked by a number of staircases to provide a variety of circulation routes. The yellow screen serves as one of the walls of the guest room on this upper level, and can be completely folded back so that the room becomes part of the communal space.

Radically rethinking the dormitory as a place for communal living and working, Kazuyo Sejima has designed a dormitory and study building for employees of a pharmaceutical, cosmetic and Chinese medicine company in Kumamoto City. Up to eighty women are accommodated here, on the edge of the city, in the first year of employment, during which time they also study their trade.

Japan currently has a sizeable labour shortage, and competition among companies for staff is fierce; this has led to a developing trend for the provision of high-quality residential facilities for young members of staff, and Sejima's client, being a firm adherent to principles of communal living (most young people in Japan live on their own, if not with their parents), was keen to 'educate its employees about the concept'.

Instead of offering purely private rooms, the building, which cost 550 million yen to build, is a communal one with 1,254 square metres of floor space. This is focussed around a huge, double-height central living room, with two dormitory wings of bedrooms. Each bedroom measures 20.8 square metres and accommodates four people on either side of the long axis. Access to the building is via a first-floor entrance which leads the visitor on to a wide balcony. Here, above the main space, is one large guest room, the communal bathroom and dressing room areas, the manager's room and spacious roof terraces on the periphery.

Sejima explains that from variations worked out by studying the relationship between private and communal space, she was able to plan a layout dominated by larger, predominantly communal spaces in which the intimate, psychological qualities of private space were maintained. In spite of the formidable scale of the public space, its architectural forms create a lively but relaxing environment which does not throw its inhabitants together in a regimented, institutionalized fashion.

The building's structure is reinforced concrete with round steel posts supporting the main space, and wall posts and

Above: The manager's office 'hovers' at the first-floor entrance level, a large, oval-shaped space which Sejima felt would be less obstructive than the cubic form. To the right, acid-etched sliding doors lead to the bedrooms.

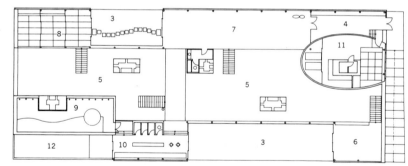

First-floor plan

1 Living space
2 Bedroom
3 Terrace
4 Entrance
5 Void
6 Lounge
7 Hall
8 Guest room
9 Bathroom
10 Dressing room
11 Caretaker's room
12 Machine room

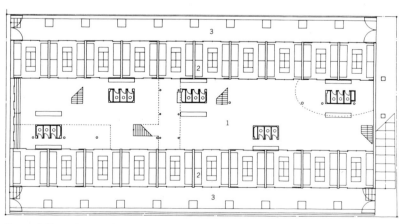

Ground-floor plan

Side elevation of the dormitory with opaque bands screening the main double-height living area.

The opaque, banded towers provide the main lighting for the space and house air-conditioning ducts, and toilets at ground-floor level. As well as being load-bearing, they take all the lateral forces, so that the perimeter columns need only take vertical loads.

Sejima wanted to create
one large but intimate
room housing various
environments, so some
women could talk and
relax while others
studied. The main glazed
areas are curtain-wall
system; other areas are
clad with aluminium
panels, with perforated
aluminium used for
screening.

aluminium slashes partitioning the
bedrooms. Five towers rising from the first
storey support horizontal loads, and act as
the main lighting for the space as well as the
vertical ducts for the air-conditioning. These
elements give the main living space the
purposeful air of a workspace, but one which
is also a light environment full of strong forms
and strategically positioned strips of colour.

The bold curve of the manager's office,
an oval, windowless unit which is clad in
ribbed aluminium, hovers over the space.
Translucent polycarbonate panels cover the
lift towers and diffuse light. Casual groupings
of brightly coloured tables and chairs on
concrete slab floors are set sufficiently far
apart to avoid any suggestion of a classroom,
and there are plenty of staircases so that
movement between floor levels can be varied.

Instead of creating one large, dull void,
Sejima has incorporated many different areas
in which to sit, study or cook, with lots of
storage space. Three kitchen units made up of
a sink, cooking rings and a preparation area
are positioned at intervals along the room,
with small banks of individual basin and
mirror units dotted around the periphery.
While the residents' bedrooms, hidden
behind acid-etched sliding glass doors, are
modern, with wood floors and furnishings,
the guest room on the first floor has a
traditional Japanese aesthetic. However,
even this secluded place becomes
communal when its huge, yellow folding
screen is drawn back. All the wood veneer
tables, storage systems and kitchen units
were designed by Sejima, but she selected
'Arinko' chairs by Fritz Hansen and a few
original designs from Idée for the main
living area.

There is no lighting at all on the ceiling of
the living space: the main source of light
comes from the five towers which dominate
this area, with downlighters within the
ground-floor level. Sejima also lights the
spacious outdoor peripheral area, yet
another space in her democratic design
that she intends to be used freely by all the
building's occupants.

Smith-Miller + Hawkinson Architects
New Line Cinema East and New Line Cinema West

New York and Los Angeles, USA

The 'suspended' conference room at New Line Cinema East, fitted out with an array of technological facilities, seen from the balcony overlooking the nineteenth floor.

New Line Cinema is a rapidly expanding American film company, with bases in both the film heartlands of New York and Los Angeles. Their burgeoning success with film hits like *The Player* has meant a substantial increase in their operations and staff on both East and West coasts, so new offices were needed. New York architects Smith-Miller + Hawkinson's first design for the company was modestly made out of cardboard and plywood; now that New Line is going up in the world, the company wanted environments with a higher profile but also with an unconventional design, in keeping with their image. The architects have cleverly overcome the limitations of a standard office building by applying an innovative design strategy closely geared to, and inspired by, the firm's varied activities.

The New York office occupies a floor and a half of a Manhattan building commanding views of Central Park, Seventh Avenue and the Hudson River. The 18,000-square-foot floor plan was narrow in shape, with an L-shaped perimeter. Instead of creating an open layout or layering the space, the architects introduced an oblique plan with a long, skewed corridor. A range of aligned and non-aligned forms offer diverse impressions and perspectives which challenge the boxy insularity of conventional office design: folding ceiling plates, displaced volumes and glazed clerestory panels along the tops of partitions. The glazed panels bring light to the core of the space and, with ceiling plates sloping towards the windows, this makes it seem larger than it actually is and maximizes views out from the perimeter walls.

The conference room is raised above this floor, a container with windows which looks as though it is suspended in the air. Its thick walls conceal all the technological wizardry that film executives need, and a sliding back wall contains storage racks for scripts.

The architects' design develops an analogy with the film-making process itself, explains Smith-Miller, articulating architectural equivalents to concepts like the 'establishing' or 'set up' shot, the montage, suture and the

Above: The reception area has grey slate floors, and maple and metal-clad walls adorned with posters of the latest releases in glass and steel frames.

Left: A revealing strip of glass floor adjacent to the conference room.

fade. This begins with the 'set up' shot in the foyer, a composition of strong poster images showing new releases, set against a subtle backdrop of metal-clad walls, grey slate floors and a plain maple veneer desk.

In both East and West coast projects the furniture and fittings were custom-designed by the architects in wood, aluminium and glass, and include conference tables, computer furniture, lighting, ceilings and all the partition systems. By exaggerating the thickness of the door and window frames (drawing on Carlo Scarpa and Rudolf Schindler) and separating them from the structure of the building, their own structure and joints become more noticeable.

In contrast to the extroversion of the firm's New York offices, the architects' latest phase of work at New Line Cinema West, based in a nondescript 1950s office building in West Hollywood, has limited fenestration. The clients already occupied a small second-floor

suite that had been designed by the architects four years earlier, and as their presence in Hollywood grew, they took over more and more floors. The latest commission adds new spaces on the third and fourth floors. These are large (22,000 square feet), but their long, rectangular shapes present a more constricted volume, so although the architects do introduce some of their skewed lines, their intervention here could not be as expressive.

The design of the new floors achieves a good contrast with the more conventionally organized second floor, with its perimeter offices and open central core. Responding to the pattern of satellite groups of staff with a more dispersed hierarchy, the architects deliberately created a formal disorder, breaking down clear distinctions between open and closed spaces. The conference room here, for instance, is not a formal space situated in a privileged position at one end of

the floor, but a semi-enclosed volume that can function as a thoroughfare when not in use. The walls have varying degrees of transparency: those closer to narrow windows receive more natural light.

In the New York offices, fluorescent uplighters within recessed troughs in the sloping ceiling give sightlines to the windows at the edge of the space. In the new spaces in Los Angeles, structural columns have been stripped and ceilings exposed, and metal halide and fluorescent fixtures are used.

In these two new office projects Smith-Miller + Hawkinson aimed to evolve similar, yet distinct images for New Line Cinema, which displayed a refined sense of material luxury without extraordinary expense. The sleek materiality and articulation of form within both interiors certainly gives the impression of an assured corporate outfit. At the same time, the off-beat design anticipates the changing needs of the company.

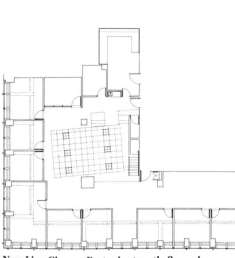

New Line Cinema East: nineteenth-floor plan

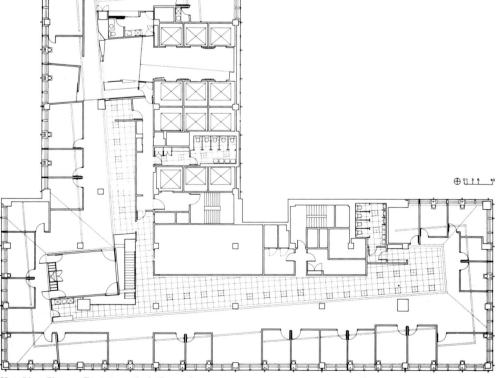

New Line Cinema East: twentieth-floor plan

Plywood panels and filing cabinets line long corridor spaces at New Line Cinema West. Metal halide and fluorescent fixtures inserted along the corridors follow the skewed circulation which marks out the satellite of offices at the far end of the third floor.

James Stirling, Michael Wilford and Associates, in association with Walter Nägeli
B Braun
Melsungen AG
Melsungen, Germany

The B Braun factory complex at Melsungen was completed shortly before Sir James Stirling's untimely death in June 1992. Its opening prompted more than a few architectural critics to observe that the project represented a new development in the work of his practice, a modern building with a subtle, considered sense of history. Sadly, Germany's rich tradition of landmark industrial projects, such as Peter Behrens' AEG turbine hall in Berlin, have not been matched in quality by today's architectural equivalents – it is said that only 2 per cent of industrial buildings in the country are architect-designed. However, thanks to the foresight of Ludwig George Braun, B Braun is an inventive industrial construction with a human scale .

In 1986 B Braun, manufacturers of medical equipment, held a limited competition for the design of their new factory on an idyllic green field site at Melsungen, about two hours' drive north-east of Frankfurt. Stirling and Wilford were amongst the eleven architects invited, and though they did not win, the company decided to build their design, which was done in conjunction with German architect Walter Nägeli and the partners' Berlin office. Construction started in 1988,

and the first phase, providing 81,000 square metres of buildings at a cost of 180 million DM, opened in May 1992.

The complex includes production halls, a distribution and storage centre, administrative offices, a canteen, staff recreation areas and a car park on a 45-hectare site, cleverly integrated within a pastoral valley landscape set against a mountain range. The architects were keen to ensure that the surrounding farmland remained unspoilt. Their solution is a building with different levels for different uses, layered upwards in order to achieve what Stirling termed 'an unmonumental lightness of being'. Instead of having a dull, low-key appearance, it is composed of recognizable and metaphorically suggestive signs, which respond inventively to the Arcadian surroundings, but do not contradict its nature.

Staff arriving by car can enter all parts of the building via a raised timber access bridge across the multi-storey car park in the middle of the site. This connects to an L-shaped walkway on a timber base which, explain the architects, marches across the site like 'a giant centipede' and gives the site a strong architectural image, a bit like a modern road

viaduct, spanning the undulating landscape and a lake. The building itself is compact and vertically planned with packing and storage halls located at the far end of the walkway, a pedestrian spine to which the administrative offices, energy centre, recreation areas and canteen are attached in a non-hierarchical sequence.

At its opening Stirling playfully termed the administration building, raised on stilts, the 'head' of the dinosaur, looming over the green copper roof of the computer centre below. Its grey, concave façade is not plain, but punctuated by windows with brightly coloured, recessed reveals. These reflect directly into the rooms and give the façade a glinting, luminous appearance. The offices here have a good view away from the work zone towards the town.

Internally, the complex is spatially varied: in particular, the canteen with its high sloping roof and wide, curved, glazed façade offering views across the lake and the administration building, is a light, clear space, carefully lined for sound absorbency so that conversations in this communal setting are easy and relaxed. The corridor is not one long, undifferentiated sequence: its treatment and materials vary from stage to stage. At the

Left: The offices of the administrative building, with their coloured window reveals, look out on its concave side, away from the work zone towards the town. The computer centre below is clad in a vivid, reptilian 'skin' of pre-patinated copper tiles.

Right: Corridor light fittings and wedge-shaped clerestory windows along one section of the long, arterial route of the corridor.

Above: The long, sweeping route within the circulation building, a raised timber bridge structure cutting through the site, and providing access at one end to the administrative building.

Above right: A lift within the complex, flanked by bright, treated surfaces, provides a memorable orientation point.

Left: The curved glass walls of the staff restaurant face the landscape and join the sloping lines of the roof to meet at an exterior access point. This provides an easy route to the grass in good weather.

administrative building end, for example, is a dramatic double-height space with an intriguing sequence of horizontally positioned industrial lighting fixtures interspersed with wedge-shaped windows.

The architects have tried to make everything comprehensible to the observer, so that it is possible to reconstruct visually the ways in which it has been built: the load-bearing structures are simplified, for example, and construction and connections are all visible. They have concentrated on simple, technically unambiguous solutions, avoiding 'all that is arbitrary, stylistic ingredients, "design", and personal decisions of taste'. The sparse use of colour emphasizes spatial and functional connections by addition and repetition as a support, but not a primary means of form.

The building phase so far completed allows any block to be extended when necessary, without disturbing the functioning of the completed parts. Most of the surfaces, especially those in concrete and metal, have been left as they were following manufacture, so that they can age naturally and develop a patina. This goes against the grain of much modern German architecture, where surfaces are almost always given a protective layer which stops the ageing process, but it will clearly help the building enrich the landscape.

The client wanted a building that would reflect cultural values. He estimates that a factory constructed purely with utility in mind would have cost perhaps 3 per cent less, but believes it was well worth the additional cost to create a beautiful sculpture which also functions as an industrial complex.

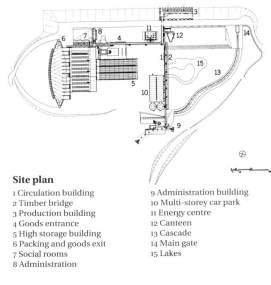

Site plan

1 Circulation building
2 Timber bridge
3 Production building
4 Goods entrance
5 High storage building
6 Packing and goods exit
7 Social rooms
8 Administration
9 Administration building
10 Multi-storey car park
11 Energy centre
12 Canteen
13 Cascade
14 Main gate
15 Lakes

Studio Granda
Reykjavik City Hall
Reykjavik, Iceland

The idea of building a city hall in Reykjavik is almost as old as the city itself. For years it had been discussed by the municipal authorities, and in 1986 designs were invited for a competition. After the City Planning Committee had studied sixteen sites, a prime location on the north-west shore of the Tjörnin Lake in the heart of the old city centre was chosen. The successful architects, Margret Hardardottir and Steve Christer, explain that the project's concept was drawn from 'the fragile, fragmented nature of the site'. By grafting the 'permanence of the city into the delicate ecology of the lake', they aimed to establish a dynamic interplay between the new City Hall's internal and external spaces.

The City Hall is 'designed as a building without a front door' and can be entered by the public from the west, north and across a bridge from the east, each an extension of a walking route within the city. The materials used, illuminated by the cool north light from deep roof-lights, were chosen to accentuate this continuation. The upper levels of the City Hall house executive offices, chambers and meeting rooms in two concrete buildings with aluminium barrel roofs. The City Council, to the north, is a more massive construction housing the chamber; the other, to the south, is a lighter building with a colonnade, housing offices.

The ground-floor areas of the office building incorporate the walking axis, the exhibition rooms and a café. This part of the Hall complex, close to the lake, is intended to be a sociable place to relax in. Initial concern that the lake's ecosystem would be disturbed by the project has been shown to be unwarranted, and this public area, with new basalt steps where skaters can rest, has animated a key pedestrian route. The building's totally glazed south-facing façade overlooks the water, and visitors to exhibitions, concerts, public debates and official banquets can enjoy views of the mountains on the far side of the bay.

The City Hall's office building is arranged in four two-storey units, each providing about 200 square metres of floor space. These are self-contained like housing units, accessible from the pedestrian spine, but with their own internal stairwells on upper floors. The landings house reception counters to the respective departments, and are lit by window walls to the north which give soft light and a view of the City Council building. The stairs and central areas here are lit by giant, elliptical roof-lights which emphasize the change of orientation from the horizontal expansiveness of the ground floor to the vertical density of the office levels above. Two elements help to articulate the office interiors: the closed offices all have full-height doors which, when open, minimize barriers to the core space (communications hub); also, a sway in the plan of the office building in relation to the roof creates a curved perspective along two parallel corridors which connect the two-storey office units. This heightens the contrast between these areas and the communal meeting spaces in between, and assists orientation.

In the City Council building, the 'action zone of city councillors', the main chamber and meeting rooms are separated by the building's central, three-storey staircase and hall. With walls lined in red sandstone, oiled basalt floors and an aluminium ceiling, its ambience is intense in contrast to the soft, open character of the offices. Stairs hewn out of basalt lead to the chamber itself, with one entirely glazed wall overlooking the new corner pond, which forms a backdrop to the head table and lecterns. A large, arc-shaped table in jatoba (a warm, reddish-brown wood) fitted with an array of communication

The City Hall building (left), with the double-height Council Chamber clearly visible through its glazed frontage, next to the longer form of the office building, facing the lake. The rough texture of the wall will allow for moss growth.

Right: Connecting staircase rails and banisters are made of jatoba and perforated steel painted in shades which darken subtly from the east to the west side of the office building.

Below: Reddish-brown jatoba wood was applied to floors, lecterns and arc-shaped desks in the Council Chamber, which features artwork by Kristjan Gudmundsson. On the right, the media balcony is finished in marine-blue wool and jatoba panelling; above this is the giant wing of the aluminium ceiling.

Right: The staff restaurant on the ground floor of the City Council building is an intimate space with a curved, orange-red wall with portholes, and a full-width window with views of the lake. Jatoba features in the flooring and the furniture, which include co-ordinating leather details.

devices, curves across a huge expanse of jatoba flooring. The same wood is used for balcony areas and wall panelling, with an artwork by Kristjan Gudmundsson and areas of marine-blue wool providing a welcome contrast in this cubic space. An aluminium ceiling hovers like a giant wing over the room, a reduced-scale model of the roof above.

The ground-floor staff restaurant has an enclosing curved red wall and a full-width window overlooking the moss-covered side of the Council building. The architects hoped that this 'womb-like' space would calm the nerves of the City Hall staff. Jatoba is also used here for flooring and for some of the furniture. There are no cooking hoods, and the ventilation system is placed at ceiling level, creating a pleasant environment.

The choice of building material gives the City Hall a bright character in all weathers, and the light, sandblasted concrete will retain its dignity as it ages. Throughout the scheme the architects have juxtaposed coarser, natural materials with elegant, manufactured ones, but light, water and vegetation have played as important a role as these solid forms in creating the City Hall's inspired integration of civic presence and local culture.

Above: The giant screen of spruce timber posts positioned across the back of the main showroom, at right angles to a convex storage wall for samples and materials.

Far right: The perforated metal screens around the private offices preserve the sense of transparency between open and enclosed spaces, and hide lighting and heating control panels. The tinted glass door here is designed to pivot with a steel post attached to the glass.

and a screened open-plan administrative area. On the right is a conference room which is given dynamism by an overhanging curved steel canopy. The smaller meeting room adjoining the main display area is a light, semi-cylindrical room close to the window with a steel-wire wall which rotates open and shut for access.

The showroom's most dramatic feature is a large screen made of thick, roughly hewn spruce timber posts set like bridge trestles in a braced colonnade framework of uprights. This certainly pays homage to the primitive power of wood but is more than just a sculptural form. It also creates a boundary between this open area and the rear office spaces, while allowing a degree of transparency between the two so employees

can view activity in the display area through the screen.

The enclosed office and meeting room is created by a series of parallel metal and tinted glass screens threaded off a frame of converging steel beams, elements which are designed to play off concepts of transparency and flexibility. Above, cupola roof lights admit natural light; recessed ceiling fittings give off a subtle blue glow. Sueberkrop and his team integrate structural, dividing elements into the space using understated materials and colours, and the result conveys a strong sense of a cohesive working unit: 'one world, not two', say Knoll.

WORKSHOP
S-Lattice
Sendagaya, Tokyo, Japan

WORKSHOP are motivated by the 'poetry of minimalism', adopting a strategy in their architectural work which, as architect Koh Kitayama explains, employs the minimum amount of words to describe the maximum number of things. It is an approach which connects them with the European ideal of early modernism, but it works well as a dynamic and flexible response to Tokyo's constantly changing cultural environment. It is also commercially competitive, using economical resources to the maximum effect.

S-Lattice is an office building for St Vermeer, a fashion company whose clients include department stores and boutiques. It is sited in the heart of Tokyo, an environment crowded with parks and sports facilities. The client's head office is located elsewhere, and the programme devised was intended to be flexible, with its precise use left unspecified. This gave the designers the opportunity to create an eye-catching edifice incorporating their particularly innovative approach to technology.

S-Lattice is 6.3 metres high, with five double-height floors and a basement; its

structure is a concrete lattice frame. Dark stainless steel panels on this exposed frame create a large, curved surface. With its white steel sashes and transparent glass, the front façade looks particularly open and indirect lighting angled to highlight white panels on the ceilings emphasizes the sense of transparency between interior and exterior.

An exposed concrete penthouse at the top of the frame has glazing on all four sides up to a height of 1.2 metres which makes it look as if it is floating. Positioned on the line of the axis of the road to the east, and protruding from the frame, the box has quite an impact when viewed from the south. Inside, this cuboid space offers a 360-degree wraparound perspective. As with most buildings in Tokyo, the service equipment is located on the roof, which is cheaper in construction terms.

The penthouse – which was conceived as a venue for entertaining clients – has very little furniture, but the presence of a long sink, which seems to continue on the other side of the glass, gives it a wonderfully surreal atmosphere. WORKSHOP's balcony, with its stage-cum-table and small catwalk through

frames, encourages enjoyment of the entire building, as well as offering a magnificent vantage point from which to view the local firework festivals over in Shinjuku.

Internally, the layout is very simple, yet it avoids the repetition with which most office developers in Japan are happy. 'An interior landscape can be viewed as a park', explains Kitayama, with 'extraordinary elements'. The building's light frame structure allows for a variety of spatial configurations and lighting sources, and each floor has been given a distinct identity. The low cost of the structure enabled the architects to put the staircase and lift shaft on the outside of the building, making them a visual feature. This maximizes the space available on each floor.

Cost is now a crucial factor in architectural projects in Japan, and designers compete fiercely for projects. The budget overall was kept economical, mainly due to the light and inexpensive frame, and the use of simple materials and as few details as possible. This made it comparable in cost with a normal four-storey office building, whilst offering much more volume and variegated space.

The light, concrete lattice frame which gives the building its name, with its externally positioned lift shaft. Above the four double-height office floors is an exposed penthouse with glazing on all four sides from the floor and up to 1.2 metres. The roof is designed to be used as an extension of this dramatic corporate entertainment space.

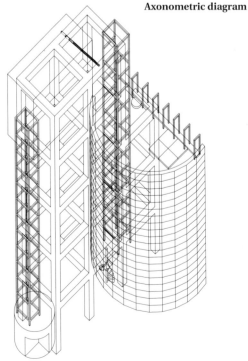

Axonometric diagram

Above: A corrugated metal bridge runs through the double-height space on the third floor.

Right: The fifth floor is designed, like all the others, to be used in a variety of ways. WORKSHOP's simple and effective use of plain materials and combined function design – suspended white panels on the ceiling are used as a reflective board, the lighting is hung off the white steel sashes of the structure and there are no taps in the washrooms as light-sensitive switches activate the water – obviates the need for cluttered, enclosed interiors.

Restaurants, Cafés, Bars, Clubs & Hotels

Allies and Morrison Architects 100
Stephen Bull's Bistro and Bar
London, UK

Jeffrey G. Beers Architects 104
Zoë
New York, USA

David Bentheim Interior Design 106
Minema Café
London, UK

Pepe Cortés 110
El Tragaluz
Barcelona, Spain

Lynn Davis Architects 114
The Ministry of Sound
London, UK

Stefano Giovannoni and Guido 118
Venturini, King Kong Production
Bar Maddalena
Prato, Italy

Peter Glynn-Smith Associates 122
Santini
Milan, Italy

Christian Liaigre 124
Hôtel Montalembert
Paris, France

Alberto Lievore & Asociados 128
Bar Rothko
Barcelona, Spain

Rick Mather Architects 132
Now & Zen
London, UK

Afra and Tobia Scarpa 134
Nexus-III
Kyoto, Japan

Philippe Starck 136
Paramount Hotel
New York, USA

Shigeru Uchida, Studio 80 140
La Ranarita/Guest Room
Tokyo, Japan

Jean-Michel Wilmotte 142
Hôtel du Cheval Blanc
Nîmes, France

Allies and Morrison Architects
Stephen Bull's
Bistro and Bar
London, UK

Stephen Bull is situated towards the city end of St John's Street in Clerkenwell, squeezed between building façades into a poorly lit space once fronted by a Georgian shop. Narrow in width and height, it is bounded by a panelled door and timber fascia above. Its glass entrance door is set back 1.5 metres behind a gridded metal gate, drawn aside when the restaurant is open. This traditional vestibule heightens the sense of arrival, allowing, as the architects Allies and Morrison put it, 'a moment's grace between the two worlds' of the space within and Clerkenwell's congested Victorian fabric.

Allies and Morrison are experienced at dealing with the challenges of inserting new uses into established, historic contexts. Here, the client's desire to give his bistro and bar a lively, accessible atmosphere, gave them the opportunity to rework a neglected space with imagination – but no unnecessary elements. Their design cannot be categorized easily, being neither in the slightest bit frivolous, nor an austere Corbusian shrine, but something in between that is definitely warm and purposeful – but not driven by fashion. An important aspect of their approach, says team architect Robert Maxwell, is that 'the interior is an assemblage of parts – everything is needed'.

The main floor area of the restaurant is set back from the street in a rear Victorian warehouse which, as an extension to the original building, is generous in floor to ceiling height. It is also simple in its structural frame of two cast-iron columns supporting main steel floor beams at mid-span on each floor, with timber joists and boards between.

The client's brief was to produce a large eating room to seat up to a hundred people. The architects set about creating a suitably non-hierarchical environment, where the design would work as a backdrop, not as a distraction. They initially united the ground and first floors in a double-height space via a new staircase, and then removed part of the timber floor between the two at first-floor level. Kitchens and ancillary spaces occupy one side, and on the other, linked by a simple

Left and right: Simple bentwood seating on the mezzanine, reached by a cantilevered steel staircase, and set behind a minimal metal balustrade. A metal ring encircling the column, with hanging meathooks, provides a visually appealing coat-hanging system.

Right: The linear 'causeway' from the gridded metal entrance gate to the white double-height restaurant space is paved in red Spanish sandstone, with saffron-yellow walls to give an immediate sense of warmth.

Left: The cantilevered stair and papier mâché sculpture are both simple, light and cheap solutions.

Above: Flat planes of solid colour, applied with restraint, are a strong element of the architects' repertoire and accentuate the walls, with the help of concealed lighting. Sarah Williams' papier mâché sculptures add colour and wit.

bridge, seating is set behind a minimal metal balustrade. The original plan to site the toilets close to the entry vestibule was financially unfeasible, so instead this area is hidden away behind a curved screen wall on the first floor.

Stripping back the wall linings of the existing interiors to expose the original brick box, Allies and Morrison inserted a new white box within this carcass, rotated to provide the optimum volume needed. They then cut into these walls to reveal the original enclosure behind. The new elevations are given further accentuation using concealed lighting and flat colour panels – in saffron yellow, giving warmth to the entrance, sky blue to provide reflected light, and up on the first floor, walls in subtle shades of blue, cerise and maroon.

The materials which form the backdrop are restrained: wood, glass, metal, terracotta and stone. There are set pieces of a more detailed nature: the cantilevered bent-steel staircase with wooden steps; 'floating' rows of metal coat-rails hung with meathooks encircling the pillars; and dual-purpose maple screens at mezzanine level screening diners and holding coats and bags.

The room is connected back to the street by a causeway of coursed red sandstone, which extends a strong linear axis from the pavement to the rear wall of the restaurant. This maximizes the perspectival volume in contrast to the airy double-height space. The combined effect of the restaurant's carefully planned elements is a restrained elegance as informal as its handwritten logo.

Jeffrey G. Beers Architects
Zoë

New York, USA

SoHo's profile has metamorphosed in recent years from hip, avant-garde locale into a more mainstream, residential district keen to preserve its architectural heritage. Streets are being recobbled for the first time since the 1930s and copies of original lamp posts have been erected. The new mood of gentrification has been accompanied by a fresh wave of commercial and cultural enterprises which have animated this mercurial district of New York City, providing a range of local resources for both occupants and visitors. Giorgio Armani's new A/X clothing shop has opened; also on Broadway is the new downtown Guggenheim satellite, designed by Arata Isozaki. The freshly renovated Mercer Hotel on Prince Street brings 'upscale' respectability and new life to a cast-iron building dating from 1888.

Zoë, a new 6,500-square-foot restaurant on Prince Street, is part of this changing pattern. Like the Mercer, it occupies a nineteenth-century, copper-topped landmark building on Prince Street, between Broadway and Mercer Street. Owners Thalia and Stephen Loffredo aim to avoid the vain and self-regarding 'attitude' which has characterized too many trendy 'downtown' restaurants. Instead they embrace a West Coast approach where food determines all the other elements of a restaurant, and their bistro-style outfit, designed by Jeffrey Beers to a budget of $850,000, returns to the basics of comfortable service and a convivial atmosphere.

Zoë (which is the Greek for 'life') was designed to 'evoke the timeless ambience of a classic European café', Beers explains. 'My primary design challenge was to develop a complementary relationship, both visually and functionally, between the creative cooking techniques on view and the environment of dining room and bar areas.' His aspiration has been translated into a tall and stimulating ground-floor space which mixes old and new motifs and materials, part southwestern, part Mediterranean in origin. This casual, eclectic exuberance suits the Loffredos' ethnically diverse American cooking, which puts technique on show.

Tables and chairs for 125 in cherrywood and granite are laid out between two vivid, angled focuses: an open kitchen at the end of the long room and an equally accessible bar close to the entrance providing a further twelve places. A row of four 14-foot high, roughly grouted, terracotta-covered support columns punctuate the space. The kitchen, with its wood-burning stove and large rotisserie grill, is a flurry of culinary activity, providing constant visual drama against a backdrop of turquoise glass mosaic. Beers acknowledges New York's time-honoured, shoulder-to-shoulder dining style, providing a long cherrywood and greenstone counter with room for twelve places.

The bar is designed to form a key part of this intimate room, not a separate area. It has a simple structure with three different kinds of marble and a base in cherrywood veneer, overhung by delicate hand-blown Murano glass lighting fixtures in contrasting colours. Decorative mosaic tiles retained from the original shell share wall space with yellow, gold and green sponge-painted and glazed surfaces which have a rich, tactile quality evoking American Indian blankets and basket weaving. It was important to Beers to retain a sense of neighbourhood history, and blocks of geometric colour above the tiles recall turn-of-the-century subway station walls.

During the day, light floods in through the tall, folding wood and glass doors of the façade, enriching the glow of Beers' layered details, which at night are highlighted by accent lighting. The restaurant's artful authenticity works: whilst so many new restaurants which have opened in the last few years sacrifice substance for style, Zoë is endowed with an abundance of both.

Left: Hand-blown Murano glass lights overhang the bar, against a backdrop of sponge-painted walls.

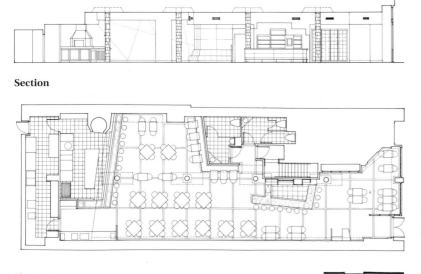

Section

Floor plan

0   5   10   20

Left: The kitchen, with Beers' customized heat lamps, has all the accoutrements for serving Californian-inspired cuisine. All table and counter surfaces in Zoë have greenstone insets, apart from the bar, which is made of three kinds of marble.

Above: Terracotta-finished columns form a line of distinctive totems through the restaurant's bright space, with its warm and earthy Mediterranean tones.

David Bentheim Interior Design
Minema Café
London, UK

'One is accustomed to architectural contributions to the urban landscape, but for interiors to achieve this is a much rarer phenomenon.' David Bentheim's observation underlines the private, enclosed nature of so much of the urban environment. On the Continent, he feels, it is the café which most frequently and forcefully breaks down the division between the interior and the outside world; London, mainly for climatic reasons, has always lacked cafés whose interiors offer intimacy, but are nonetheless linked to the street. The Minema Café, designed by Bentheim, with its dramatic, double-height glazed façade, is a rare exception. It animates a characterless stretch of main road frequently engulfed by traffic half-way between the Lanesborough Hotel on Hyde Park Corner and Harvey Nichols' windows near Knightsbridge tube station. Addressing both the road and the park opposite, it offers an upbeat environment that people of all ages find welcoming.

The owners are the Savoy Group who have long-established credentials as clients with an informed and enlightened approach to design (demonstrated by the Riverside Room at the Savoy, and other hotels including Claridges, the Connaught, the Berkeley and the Lygon Arms). They wanted to open a café on this site alongside the established art house cinema of the same name, and did not want a retro tea-shop or an exclusive, intimidating 'design café ghetto', but an interior that was firmly 'of today', a challenge Bentheim and his collaborator on the project Ferry Zayadi attacked with relish. The Savoy, who had envisaged a relaxed café environment where meals and snacks were served all day, duly 'backed all their decisions' with confidence.

The site was previously occupied by a florist on the ground floor, with a first-floor balcony that the designers have transformed into an upper eating level. Early on, they decided to give the façade a glazed frontage covering its entire 45-foot length, thereby guaranteeing its dramatic impact on the street. At night the design elements become barely visible, and the façade takes on the

Right: Meticulous detailing is evident in the steel balustrades which guide the white, reconstituted marble stair, winding around the wooden toilet cube.

Above: The dramatic scenography of the glazed façade, with the rear dining bridge anchored on a steel frame and suspended by steel rods. The cornet-shaped sculpture over the entrance and the tilted toilet cubes are playful, eye-catching elements.

Right: Ice-cream parlour meets modern architecture: Enzo Mari's aluminium and leather chairs and the 'Tutti Frutti' composite marble table tops.

appearance of a shadow puppet theatre.

The interior is a rectangular space, 5 metres high and 15 metres long, with a narrow depth of 4 metres which makes the occupant feel close to the movement of traffic outside. A goldfish bowl effect is avoided by the use of vertical panels which screen parts of the café. Bentheim considered mirroring the back wall, but decided that this would ruin the open box effect. The café was originally intended to connect with the cinema, but problems over licensing regulations prevented an internal link being made. The narrow depth of the space made it essential that the toilets and kitchen were situated at either end of the café, and these elements are stacked to maximize the space in between.

On the upper floor, above the tiny bar, there is an angled preparation area made from durable stainless steel, rather than laminate, to survive the wear and tear of daily use; there is no attempt to screen this away, and its smooth finish reflects car lights at night. At the other end of the space the designers have positioned two free-standing boxes, the lower in wood, containing compact, custom-designed wooden washrooms and toilets. Given their size, these could have created a monolithic column

structure, but the cubes are angled so that they assume an enigmatic appearance.

Between these two elements runs a mezzanine bridge with high glass sides that is wide enough to accommodate a second eating area with a line of tables down the street side. This steel structure, which appears to be suspended, has been shoehorned into the void, giving views of the park, with the floor below also visible. It is reached by a stair running around the back of the cubicles.

Bentheim admits to being strongly influenced by the economy and efficiency of boat interiors, where everything is reduced to small component parts with the aim of avoiding claustrophobia. The café, with its bridge and carefully sited services, shares this compactness, and its forty seats can be filled to capacity with ease. Bentheim also sees the café as 'a veneered box', making good use of robust and versatile materials that perform to high functional and aesthetic standards – stainless steel, marble, glass, aluminium, leather, rubber and wood. The furniture includes beautifully proportioned 'Tonietta' aluminium café chairs with black leather seats and backs (designed by Enzo Mari), and bar stools with timber seats.

The surfaces of the space have a warmth to

them; the designers felt that white-painted walls would have been 'too cold and hard'. Plaster was chosen which aided the acoustics, and this is enhanced by concealed fluorescent lighting and some downlighters. The materials are predominantly neutral in tone, enlivened by patches of vivid colour (the servery counter base, and menus whose shapes contribute to the graphic composition of the interior). The table tops are made of 'Tutti Frutti' stonit, a material which is not often used. A composite marble inset with tiny, coloured glass fragments, it effectively blends the playfulness of a period ice-cream parlour with the architecture of the space.

The café's detailing has been done with dexterity and wit: a wavy rubber mat at the entrance, the menu holders, adjustable mirrors in the men's toilets and a striking graphic identity scheme for the signage, china and dual-colour menus. The colourful sculpture hanging off the façade just above the entrance hints at an exuberance kept in check by the necessity of making the scale of the café work. The fact that it does is attested to by the clusters of customers, clearly visible from Hyde Park, a sight that makes Bentheim proud: 'the public have understood what we were trying to do'.

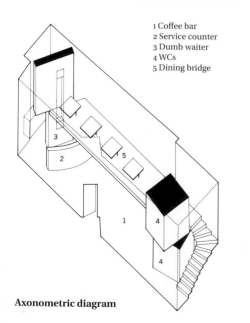

1 Coffee bar
2 Service counter
3 Dumb waiter
4 WCs
5 Dining bridge

Axonometric diagram

The brushed steel coffee bar and chrome-surfaced servery area, below the dining bridge. The 'Tema' aluminium and wooden stools are by Juan Ortinez.

Pepe Cortés
El Tragaluz
Barcelona, Spain

El Tragaluz (which means 'skylight' or literally 'swallow light') 'has a funny history', says Cortés. He originally wanted to buy the house that occupied the site, so he took its measurements and began designing a projected studio there. Conversion work had already begun when, one day, he met the client in Mordisco and invited her to look at the site. The client fell in love with it and, although she knew the age and condition of the building would make it an expensive job, persuaded Cortés to sacrifice his studio for a new restaurant and bar. The result is a fine and accomplished environment which won first prize in the 1990 Spanish FAD interior design awards.

Both Cortés and his client wanted a tranquil design that would contrast with the plethora of extrovert styles which have characterized restaurant design in the city over the last few years and would appeal to discerning restaurant-goers of all ages. The division of the building into two eating areas, Tragaluz and Tragarapid (for a 'fast swallow'), and a bar was intended to accommodate 'different clients in both areas, or the same clients in different moods'.

Azulete, Cortés' earlier restaurant for Victoria Tusquets, wife of the architect Oscar, had featured a very light glass roof structure, and this same principle was applied to Tragaluz's upper restaurant spaces in order to maximize the space available. Cortés did not want heavy cast iron or 'hard-edged metals' to cause friction in the juxtaposition between old and new necessary for the conversion, and the fine metal roof is simply painted, not highly lacquered; even its automatic blinds protect without swamping the calm and classic design. The effect of patinated bronze varnishes on the frames of the restaurant's suede chairs is just one reminder that Cortés likes to mix the appearance of new and old.

There was no overwhelming general

Above: A staircase in Iroco wood and aluminium leads up from the bar past the cylindrical screen of the cloakroom to the upper-floor dining areas.

Left: The restaurant at mezzanine level, with cast-iron columns supporting the roof, a curved wooden canopy, and stairs leading up through an aperture in the terrace of the original building. Automatic blinds deflect the heat of the sun by day, but open at night to give views of the sky.

concept: the designer simply aimed to highlight particular objects without making them excessively elaborate. The overall effect demonstrates a very confident blending of materials and colours. The central tree-trunk structure of the spiral staircase in the double-height restaurant is New Guinea wood intersected by individual metal stairs. Upstairs, two large metal fireplace fittings slice down on either side of the ceiling bracket; this bold detail is set against a subtly toned backdrop: chairs in muted green and blue suede, Arcadian murals by Isabel Esteva on biscuit and ox-blood plaster walls. Throughout the two-floor main restaurant space, old carpets, traditional armoires and eccentrically scaled parchment floor lights give El Tragaluz a lived-in, human aspect, which interacts well with Cortés' functional approach to space.

Tragarapid, reached via the ground-floor bar, has leather banquette seating and the relaxed air of a club restaurant which works just as well in the evening as by day. Its layered and padded suede back wall features a strip of mirror just big enough in which to view diners across the room. Other playful features include shades fastened with wing nuts, and the adjoining basement toilets with almost identical stainless steel doors, divided by a curved wall.

The bar has an aerofoil-shaped lighting gantry, traditional mosaics and Oscar Tusquets' wooden stools and, high behind the counter, a section of old roof peeps through. Back at the entrance, automatic glass doors provide a rare high-tech feature, an aesthetic which is shared by the cylindrical, punched metal cloakroom niche. Both elements are designed to introduce modern functionality without fuss into an old interior whose history is enhanced by a new, versatile type of restaurant.

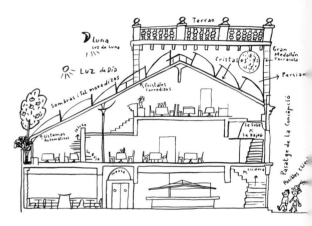

Above: Javier Mariscal's sketch of the project.

Left: Tragarapid is more of a café-restaurant than Tragaluz, where people of all ages come to eat snacks but enjoy the same eclectic mix of materials and forms. Oscar Tusquets' anthropomorphic wooden chairs and stools face leather banquette seating and African wood tables, continuing the rich brown colour scheme.

Above: The restaurant exists on three levels: a spacious lower floor with two dining areas, a cantilevered mezzanine (seen here) and upper floors.

Left: Part of the first-floor dining area, with leaning floor lamps and hanging parchment lamps by Pepe Cortés, graphics and china by Javier Mariscal and murals by Isabel Esteva.

Lynn Davis Architects
The Ministry of Sound
London, UK

The polished concrete bar is fronted by ribbed steel shuttering and stretches 50 feet along the warehouse-sized lounge area. It is enhanced by atmospheric lighting effects and decorative images on overhanging banners. Stairs in the background lead to the mezzanine VIP lounge.

The Ministry of Sound is one of the first legitimate all-night 'rave' dance venues of its type to be established in the UK. In line with 'rave' practice, it has no liquor licence, but a 'juice bar' serving soft drinks – everything from water to herb cocktails – to hydrate its energetic clientele. Its establishment follows the increasing crackdown by the police on impromptu parties held from the late 1980s onwards in low-key, mostly derelict industrial locations in and around London. The antithesis of a high-profile, hard-drinking venue, the club is virtually invisible to the outside world, a bunker-style space occupying an old converted garage/storage depot in Elephant & Castle, south of the River Thames.

The site found by owners Humphrey Waterhouse, a property developer, and DJ Justin Berkman, is located between a railway embankment and a car park, a good distance from local housing. The 1,300 square-metre club is geared towards the over-21 party scene and allegedly attracts clubbers prepared to queue for hours to get in. It holds 1,200 people in a markedly low-tech space which captures the raw spontaneity and clandestine quality of the warehouse 'rave' venue. However, instead of all the drawbacks of a disused building, it boasts superlative sound facilities, a huge purpose-designed dance floor, bar/lounge, cinema and a VIP lounge.

Although the architect, Lynn Davis, had to work with a very modest budget, and to a 12-week construction schedule, she managed to create the right balance between practicality and creativity. The clients were drawn to a futuristic industrial aesthetic; they quoted films like 'Alien' and 'Blade Runner', but were fairly open-minded in spirit. Davis has responded by giving the bunker-like spaces of the old building a creative image using metal, banners, graffiti art and lighting effects, which works with the industrial clutter of the original space – 'old lights, heaters, pipes and gubbins up the ceiling'. A large proportion of the budget was spent on soundproofing and conforming to stringent safety regulations. These features do not dilute the raw, improvisational feel of the club.

Heavy-duty security admits the chosen few through a roller-shuttered entrance with heavy steel fire doors into a small foyer. A long tunnel, with walls and ceiling clad in galvanized rib-deck steel shuttering, stretches ahead. Davis uses this material extensively, and although it is normally covered up by services, she decided that its raw, shiny, functional qualities were best left exposed. It also proved easy to work with, so rib-decking features around the front of the bar, pay desk, duct covers, check-in and cloakrooms.

In the bar, tall decorative banners, which are changed monthly, hang from the ceiling,

Above: The walls and ceiling of the long tunnel from the entrance to the lounge are clad in galvanized rib-deck steel shuttering.

Left: The cavernous dance box, a heavily soundproofed 'building-within-a-building', is deliberately isolated from the bar.

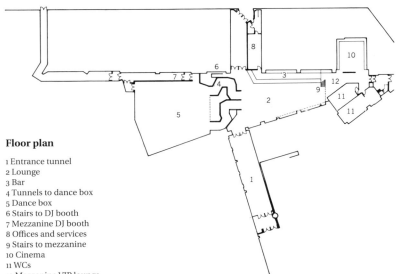

Floor plan

1 Entrance tunnel
2 Lounge
3 Bar
4 Tunnels to dance box
5 Dance box
6 Stairs to DJ booth
7 Mezzanine DJ booth
8 Offices and services
9 Stairs to mezzanine
10 Cinema
11 WCs
12 Mezzanine VIP lounge

concealing the old walls and bricked-in railway viaduct arches, as well as an array of old pipes and conduits from the original building. At night the ceiling becomes invisible, and high banners enhance the room's sense of height. The bar top extends 16 metres, a long slab of polished concrete made with silver sand and white cement to create the appearance of marble – but with a specially crumbled front to give the right rough and ready profile. Sound from the dance floor – the loudest part of the club – can hardly be heard in the bar, thanks to two soundproof tunnels leading to it via snaking routes from one end of the room.

The dance space was constructed as a soundproof 'building-within-a-building', explains Davis, in line with planning requirements so that music could not be heard outside the club. Its solid 190-millimetre concrete block walls are set on a resilient strip roofed with 17-metre-long lattice beams. The beams are covered with screeded wood-wool slabs, and topped with 150-millimetre solid concrete; the top and side walls are covered with a sound-

deadening 'quilt'. High galleries house the DJ and sound engineer away from the sprung maple dance floor, and the lofty ceiling allows room for lighting rigs and air-conditioning. The plain walls create a 'canvas', says Davis, for reflected, sound-synchronized lighting, housed in Perspex units.

Grouped at the other end of the bar are a mezzanine VIP lounge, a small cinema and toilets. The lounge is sparsely furnished with white drapes hanging in tent-like swathes amongst the metallic glint of defunct heating pipes. The improvisational, almost post-apocalyptic character of the space is given a touch of low-life glamour by a huge, spidery fifties chandelier. The nearby cinema is sited in a railway arch, past an entrance showing outlines of original decorative mouldings. Inside, the walls are painted black and hung with dark drapes. A projector screen looms out of the darkness, its ornately gilded frame bringing a Baroque element to the club's industrial aesthetic.

The brief for the toilets was 'to deter drug taking', so Davis designed cubicles providing the minimum amount of privacy. Thin, steel

sheet partitions are held in place by chains above, hanging from the ceilings, and below, holding them in a vertical position, a solution which also reduced the area taken up. Soft, translucent PVC doors which show the shape of a body within are held shut by an ordinary bath plug and a chain. Urinals and basins in the men's toilets are simple troughs made of grey PVC roofing, rolled and solvent-welded to make a pocket over each long edge. This was then threaded with a rod hung from the ceiling by chains. Davis' improvised elements blend with curling ceiling ducts, and the interior is given a comic fantasy treatment with spray-paint murals by graffiti artist Goldie.

London's club culture is lacking in all-night venues, and the immediate success of the Ministry of Sound has given it cult status. Davis has handled its spatial and technological assets with considerable imaginative energy, if not a lavish budget, creating an improvisational, sense-orientated environment that for the moment – as 'a response to modern life and how we feel about it' – strikes a resonant note.

Stefano Giovannoni and Guido Venturini, King Kong Production
Bar Maddalena
Prato, Italy

Bar Maddalena Loveburger, to give King Kong's new café-bar in Prato its full title, is 'for children aged 3 to 80', says designer Stefano Giovannoni. It attracts people of all ages, including the local mayor who enjoys its ambience. Founder members of the Bolidist movement (a loose network of Italian designers whose collaborative projects were inspired by movement and the concept of the 'fluid city'), Giovannoni and his partner Guido Venturini are innovators in image creation. They devise original pop-culture environments with iconographic elements drawing on science fiction, comic strip, robots and film culture. To work in three dimensions, this heady formula requires an underlying rigour which Bar Maddalena possesses along with all its other charms.

Maddalena is an established bar and fast-food café owned by Prato's Cavicchi brothers, who wanted it to be a fashion leader with a strong image that would 'stimulate reactions' from the public. Prato does not boast as many eating places as the big Italian cities, but nonetheless the bar had to have an enduring charm to survive scrutiny from the spiritually young residents of the small town.

The café-bar occupies 220 square metres on one floor; the structure of the existing building has been left unchanged, but the walls have been restored. Here King Kong created a playground made up of many elements. The rooms are differentiated by colour, giving each a distinct atmosphere, but are connected via passages and cut-out walls which offer intriguing vistas.

The environment is 'a bit pop and a bit punk', and pays homage to the surrealist, outsized interior scale that Alice found in Wonderland. Drawing wildly but not slavishly on the last three decades, King Kong's creative gestures are firmly fixed in the present, and they manage to establish a welcoming, non-élitist atmosphere.

King Kong do not believe in architects talking shop through their work, 'lost in the game of style and techniques'. Their expressive interiors are based on a multiplicity of gleaned and reworked pop-culture imagery. 'It is a matter of working with signs that belong to an imaginary world within everyone's reach', says Giovannoni. However, his great passion for fiction and the contemporary imagination meets commercial demands because King Kong's easy, communicative style is also accessible, and is based upon a spatial rigour and simplicity of form.

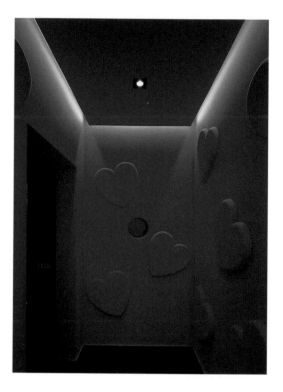

'Maddalena' is projected on to the barrel-vaulted ceiling of the bar, along the disembodied eyes and mouth of the woman herself. The glass and chromium-plated bar top follows the line of the room.

Above: The source of the hearts: a tiny, cell-like pink room lit by concealed lighting, with space only for a table for two.

Right: A hole cut in the wall of the café revealing a glimpse of semi-relief hearts.

Above: King Kong's floating scenography: shiny green lozenge forms in a dancing pattern around the walls of the green room resemble bubbles rising up towards light seeping from the edges of the suspended ceiling.

Left: Dark blue walls are punctuated with painted and projected words and are dominated by a mural of the heart-eyed 'loveburger' King Kong created for Maddalena's distinctive logo. Black glass table tops pick up reflected light.

Right: Blue neon lighting in graphic constellations shines down on slowly revolving polyurethane forms – wide-eyed, friendly aliens, their antennae raised exultantly – which, as they turn, create an alternately open and closed space.

Christian Liaigre
Hôtel Montalembert
Paris, France

According to hotelier Grace Leo-Andrieu, 'a lot of hotels look very dramatic, but don't feel comfortable. A hotel has to have a soul – this comes from its atmosphere.' Her latest project, the Hôtel Montalembert, is situated within the chic and affluent environs of the Rive Gauche. Meticulously renovated and redesigned, it was 'an expensive venture, so it has to last. If a hotel pleases everyone then it's often completely banal. We were ready to take a risk.' It was an $8 million gamble she took, together with her husband Stephane Andrieu, and one that has certainly paid off, for in spite of opening during the Gulf War, when trade in the hotel business fell, the reborn Montalembert has established its credentials as an outstanding place to stay.

Originally owned by Count Montalembert, a politician and writer, it had been a retreat for writers and artists since 1926. Today, 85–90 per cent of the clientele are businessmen and women. Grace Leo-Andrieu anticipated their need for a warm, unintimidating environment which retained a cultural presence by choosing a designer of tried and tested ability and not, like many hoteliers, bringing in a famous name who might not really understand her desire for comfort as well as style, and soul rather than splendour.

Rather than compete with the Ritz and other palatial but traditional Right Bank establishments, she 'wanted to create something that eloquently speaks of its time and place'. She had worked with Christian Liaigre, who originally trained as a furniture designer, on another hotel of hers, the Guanahani in the Caribbean, and felt she knew what to expect. Although she looked at other designers' work, Liaigre was chosen for his classical approach to design, and his ability to fuse pure and sober forms with rich materials like ebony, sycamore and hand-stitched leather. Liaigre believes that a sense of geographical and historic context is essential to design, and his confident mix of classical, contemporary and baroque styles, and imaginative design and renovation has given the elegant framework of the old building a luxurious yet simple aesthetic.

Although the hotel's renovated limestone façade retains its original grandeur, the 390-square-foot ground floor is intimately proportioned. The foyer, with a reception desk to one side, adjoins a small restaurant and a bar, with a living room and a private dining area at the rear. Two lifts and a staircase provide access to eight floors with fifty bedrooms. Six further living and bedroom suites were created by converting twelve former bedrooms. The basement is simply fitted out with toilets and two small meeting rooms.

Whilst the relatively small scale of the hotel makes for easy circulation, the modest size of the bedrooms and bathrooms obliged Liaigre to adopt a functional and thoughtful approach. His creative hand is visible everywhere: in the bed-heads, with their ingenious chrome metal and brass lights in slits that you can screen by adjusting a lever; bedside lights; solid furniture in ebony, sycamore or leather; and in the bathrooms, with their Cascais marble washstands, chrome basins and pivoting mirrors, all compactly composed within tiny spaces lit with diachroics. The only slip-up is the fixed basin tap which makes washing difficult; in all other respects the bathrooms are exceptionally efficient.

The owners wanted to use natural materials which 'aged well and gave off warmth'. Liaigre's design fulfils this requirement and is also sensitive towards the possible needs of the guests, incorporating practical desks, capacious wardrobes (which also house a mini-bar and an extendible TV and video unit) and adequate storage space in

Right: The 'Rive Gauche' spirit brought back in a new guise at Hôtel Montalembert: the renovated limestone façade reveals its original grandeur, with a curving canopy and blue banners announcing its entrance.

Far right: One of Eric Schmitt's bronze and wrought-iron 'pixie hat' hanging lamps.

Right: The inscribed carpet leads to the reception desk, a low form, enhanced by Bruno Taconet's fresco in gold leaf on linen.

Below: A private dining room at the rear of the restaurant and lounge space, which is also used for functions.

Left: Function and comfort are combined in the compact modern bedrooms, with their striped bedcovers, 'Jupiter' bedside lamps and Liaigre's robust, well-designed furniture in ebony, sycamore and leather. Reading lights in chrome metal and glass, with dimmer switches, are set in slits in the smoke-tinted sycamore bed-heads: with the tent-shape created by the curved curtain rail, they evoke medieval references.

the bathrooms. For those requiring a more traditional aesthetic, some bedrooms contain period furniture recovered from other hotels in the district and renovated. This has been blended with elements of Liaigre's modern style, and clients specifically requesting a 'Louis Philippe' room find that the delicately restored inlaid marquetry of its traditional bed is combined with a smart, navy-striped duvet.

Blended with Liaigre's detailed design is the more playful style of Eric Schmitt, a young sculptor recommended by Liaigre's daughter Virginie, and now regarded with admiration as 'the new Giacometti'. His bronze and wrought-iron wall lights in the central reception area, positioned at intervals along the marine and taupe carpeted corridors and on staircases, punctuate the traditional fabric of the building with an elegant wit. Other details in metal – a wrought-iron banister and cast-bronze door handles – continue the theme throughout the hotel.

The reception desk is a straightforward, informal affair, avoiding the pigeon holes so loved by hotel establishments far and wide. Bruno Taconet's gold-hued frescoes adorn the side walls, and a bold taupe carpet laid in a wide strip on pale stone floors greets the

visitor with the elegant, marine-coloured scrawl of the Count of Montalembert.

The central reception and restaurant area is screened at seating height by opaque glass panels covering the windows that overlook the street. Initially unconvinced that a restaurant would be a worthwhile element, the owners later relented, and the result, set in an open space on the left of the reception, has the informality of a modern bistro, with light wood-panelled walls, oak floors, photographs by Jean-Pierre Godeaut and lots of natural light. A warm and unpretentious place, its presence animates the ground floor, drawing customers from the local publishing houses and antiques firms as well as those staying at the hotel.

The bar to the right of the restaurant is spotlit from fittings in the coffered ceiling. Its front curves along the side of the room to a pantry area enclosed within a bold wooden frontage, itself like a piece of furniture. Staff in uniforms designed by Myrène de Premonville work from here, despatching restaurant meals to the tables, but it is also used as a serving area for the living room where guests can sit on leather armchairs around a modern stone fireplace and have tea. These adjoining areas share the same

standard of comfort and, whilst the bar is a fixed element giving the room a strong identity, the furniture can easily be adjusted to accommodate special receptions held by the local business community.

No major modifications were made to the building's structure, but certain elements have been preserved and renewed: the stained-glass window seen from the top of the lift, the staircase and the ornate Louis Philippe furniture in the 'traditional' rooms. The hotel does not provide a business centre (though it offers equivalent services via the reception management). However, the bedrooms are furnished with beautifully designed desks, and their comfortable but efficient atmosphere and restrained colour schemes offer an easy environment in which to work.

Grace Leo-Andrieu shares with Liaigre a commitment to design as an ongoing, reactive process: 'there has to be an evolution – this allows you to think of new ideas'. The success of the Montalembert relies heavily on consistently good service; together with the client's clear vision and Liaigre's thoughtful design, this gives the hotel the 'harmonious atmosphere' Leo-Andrieu aspired to – and thus its distinctive soul.

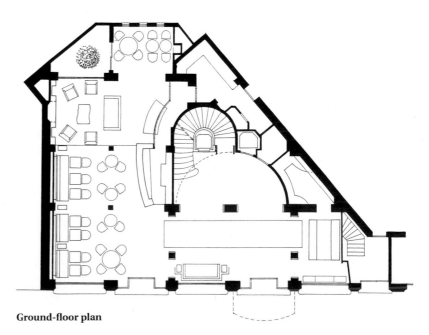

Ground-floor plan

Alberto Lievore & Asociados
Bar Rothko
Barcelona, Spain

Bar Rothko, designed to function as a relaxed bar-restaurant by day and an intimate, but never precocious, bar rendezvous by night, was, says architect Alberto Lievore, inspired by the nuances of colour in the works of the American painter Mark Rothko. Colour, lighting and a narrow selection of materials were combined to create a quiet and sober atmosphere, markedly different from that of the many exuberantly fashionable, but often ephemeral, 'design' bars to be found in Barcelona. Lievore's intention was to break with the trend, followed by other drinking establishments, for a strong but superficial visual identity. His attention to detail, use of materials and subtle handling of natural and artificial lighting have produced an interior with a resonant and robust design of subtle spatial, tonal and luminous qualities.

Lievore has defined two very different areas, each with bars, of 378 square metres in total, giving each a different chromatic treatment and linking them by a two step change of level. On a functional level, both the bars are conceived as low-key meeting points, with the larger central area offering space for relaxed conversation. The large bar, by day also a restaurant, includes a semi-circular glass curtain wall looking out to a

patio garden with a pond. This connection with the outside world brings in natural light and helps to create a peaceful atmosphere. In the evening the glass wall transmits the dying light into the space, until at night it becomes an artificially lit box with the water of the pool reflected on its surfaces. As in the architect's earlier furniture showroom interior for Perobell, designed with Alberto Arola, artificial lighting highlights the space rather than dominating it.

The walls are plastered and painted a warm, sultry Rothko red by the entrance, which changes to soft grey within the central area. Low voltage under-lighting accentuates, but does not drain the subtle tones of the bar's periphery. A similar graduation in texture and colour occurs at floor level, with stone tiles at the doorway being replaced within the entrance by polished and varnished oakwood, whilst the central area is covered with black, fine-grain granite tiles.

The bar was not an easy project, partly because its restricted location made it difficult to get opening permits. Moreover, the building had been empty for a while and had not previously been a bar-restaurant, so there were some technical problems to do with connecting water and electricity, and

Right: The bar was intended to have something of the intimate and moody atmosphere of an English club and Viennese coffee house combined. The lighting throughout is designed to enhance colour and texture.

Above and right: The bar contains Lievore's award-winning Rothko chairs and tables in veneered beechwood, with a dark chestnut dye and a high-shine, lacquer-look varnish which gives the wood a deep finish. The tables have cone-shaped legs and anodized aluminium bases, and the long banquette seating is covered in soft leather. Lievore intended the lighting to be very soft, illuminating the vivid red walls, with their subtly evoked nuances of Mark Rothko's paintings.

Right: Natural light coming down into the courtyard, with its small pond, floods through the glass curtain wall into the bar, across the varnished oakwood floor. To increase the intimacy of the meeting space, some tables have individual floor lamps. The area to the left has two different identities; a café/lounge area by day, it later becomes part of the bar/club; these functions are each defined by a specific combination of natural and artificial lighting.

Above: Tables without floor lamps are lit by fixtures embedded in the wall with curved metal covers which hide the bulbs. To balance the red areas, sections of wall were given the 'Rothko' treatment, but in soft grey.

structural deficiencies in the existing building meant that an independent steel-beam structure had to be added; as a result, the bar took a year to complete.

All the furniture and fittings were designed by Lievore – an accomplished furniture designer in his own right – in conjunction with his studio (architect Eduardo Campoamor and designers Jeanette Altherr and Irene Coll). These include the distinctive round-backed 'Rothko' chair, tables and bar stools, and the 'Alban' armchair, as well as leather banquette seating, bronze floor lamps with simple white parchment shades, and other wall lamps. The final result is a mature and elegant interior which derives its power and glamour from the simplest of elements.

Rick Mather Architects
Now & Zen
London, UK

The Zen chain of Chinese restaurants are famous for their high design profile and currently number three in London alone. The flagship restaurant, Now & Zen, is one of the most extrovert in the group, a dramatic design which makes the most of modern glass and heating technologies. Much of the building's existing internal structure has been removed, reducing the external wall to a transparent, double-height glass façade, with the first revolving door made entirely from curved and laminated glass (no steel frame, just metal supports at the top and bottom).

This highly visible interior provides 5,933 square metres of floor space within a recent mixed development on Upper St Martin's Lane at the edge of Covent Garden. What started as an unpromising concrete shell with an almost unusable basement has been completely transformed. A new steel structure was inserted to create a curving mezzanine, and to open the basement and ground floor into one big space. The basement area is now visible via a clear, double-thickness glass pavement in front of the restaurant, bringing daylight down to its kitchen areas, and drawing the eyes of visitors crossing this transitional zone, for whom an angled, slate-covered bridge is laid across the transparent pavement.

Linking this visible lower level of the building with the main space is a tall 'dragon waterfall', a spectacular string of water-filled glass bowls and connecting tubes snaking through an oval void close to the front of the ground floor and right up to the ceiling. The gentle flow of water catches reflected light from a circular roof-light above. This ethereal feature, linked by a light steel suspension system, visually unites the basement, ground floor and mezzanine level.

The tall yellow back wall, red and purple columns and the blue-green staircase extending through the whole space create almost unbroken lines of colour. Strategically placed rear mirrors – an old but good trick, and not so easy to do imaginatively – give the impression of a doubly deep space. The curving balcony of the new mezzanine floor, the roof-light with a telescopic view up seventeen storeys and the hole in the floor to the kitchen give the restaurant a wide range of dramatic and unexpected views.

The detailing is minimalist, using exquisite materials to create an impression of luxury without layered decoration. The glass tiles on the bars and screens had never been used before in Britain, and were imported specially. All the furniture – with its slim-limbed stainless steel frames and black leather upholstery – was designed by the architects. The balustrades throughout are sleek, light constructions with stainless steel uprights and fine horizontal rods.

Mather's desire to 'bring the liveliness of the street into the restaurant' aimed at creating a relaxed, unselfconscious ambience. Now & Zen has survived its first two years in a tough climate, and the dramatic greenish glass façade is still an impressive and welcoming sight, brightening this less than lively stretch of St Martin's Lane. Sadly, for the moment, the views out into London's recession-weary West End are somewhat grimmer.

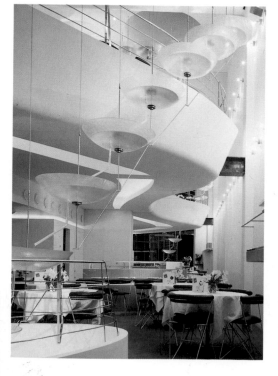

Far left: The 'dragon waterfall' ascends in a sinuous curve from the basement, via an oval opening, past the undulating edge of the mezzanine floor to the ceiling.

Left: The glass-topped, stainless steel-fronted bar.

Afra and Tobia Scarpa
Nexus-III
Kyoto, Japan

The Nexus-III bar is located in Shinbashi which is part of Gion, a historic district of Kyoto along the Shirakawa River with many bars and restaurants. The area had been rapidly deteriorating, but Gion has at last been designated a preservation area, and the Nexus-III bar had to maintain its image as a traditional '*machiya*' house on the exterior, whilst inside providing a new facility to help draw visitors to the district. The Italian designers Afra and Tobia Scarpa were asked to design the interiors of two long, narrow rooms, and they have imaginatively applied their strong sense of colour and detail to this unprepossessing space.

The tiny (42.7 square metres), bunker-like interior of the basement bar is dominated by zinc panels sprayed in banded colours, which recur in an orderly pattern, and at intervals even pile up on each other. The boundary between walls and ceiling merges, giving a sense of height, and the non-uniform grids of colour set up by the coloured bands partition the room, so that it also feels longer than it is. A long mahogany counter runs through the bar, the only fixed element in the room. It has a contrasting grain, but for the designers it signifies 'order and stability' in 'a place of rest and relaxation'.

In the upper bar the solid forms of the Scarpas' leather armchairs fill a wider room with stone floors, curved walls and a vaulted ceiling animated by twinkling star lighting which is reflected on the table tops. Uneven and randomly placed walls, each individually coloured, give the impression of a minute piazza surrounded by small buildings. The doors are differently styled on each side, suggesting, say the designers, 'that upon leaving one is, naturally, not the same as upon entering'. The enigmatic artifice of the design has a peculiar charm, no hint of which is suggested by the bar's traditional, low-key exterior. Crossing a small plank over a stream, the visitor can safely leave all preconceptions and Kyoto's centuries of tradition with his shoes at the door, and enter a vibrant, idealized environment spiritually transported from Treviso.

The long, shed-shaped volume of the basement bar, an environment enlivened by vertically aligned zinc panels sprayed in a variety of warm colours which give depth and rhythm to the walls. Regimented rows of seats and gridded shelving on either side of the mahogany counter emphasize the room's horizontality.

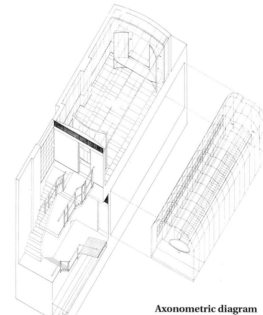

Axonometric diagram showing the basement and upper bars.

The upper bar is a wide lounge area furnished with the Scarpas' olive green and grey leather armchairs. The walls are covered with chalky textured bands of colour. The ceiling lighting is partially concealed behind a gridded metal plane.

Nexus-III inhabits a traditional wooden '*machiya*' house on the banks of Kyoto's Shirakawa River. A fabric banner shields its more modern entrance area.

Philippe Starck
Paramount Hotel
New York, USA

According to Ian Schrager, entrepreneur and owner of New York's Paramount Hotel, 'nightclubs and discothèques were the center of social activity in New York in the '70s; restaurants served this function in the '80s; now, hotel lobbies are the definitive social hub of the '90s'. They provide, he believes, a new, atmospheric kind of gathering place with the spontaneity of a European plaza: the embodiment of 'hotel as theatre', animated by a constantly changing cast of characters. By enlisting Philippe Starck, who by his own admission is 'a professional dreamer', Schrager could bring this not so far-fetched concept into being.

The multi-million dollar, 610-room hotel, the third within the 'luxury' category that Schrager has developed in New York, was from the very start intended to draw New Yorkers as well as visitors, and designed to appeal to a 'vertical market' defined by attitude and lifestyle rather than financial considerations. Morgans, Schrager's first hotel project, designed by Andrée Putman, revolutionized the industry with the concept of the boutique hotel, offering personalized service and a strong ambience based on innovative design.

This second quality was refined with the opening of the Royalton, designed by Starck and one of the first projects to realize his work on an environmental scale. The crucial difference between these earlier hotels and the Paramount was the scale of Schrager's undertaking, which aimed to provide the standards and service associated with a small luxury hotel at under $150 per night.

The Paramount's predecessor, the Century Paramount, located on West Street at Broadway in the centre of New York's theatre district, first opened its doors in 1927 at the height of the swing era. Designed by Thomas Lamb, one of the architects behind the Ziegfield theatre and original Madison Square Gardens, it was a palatial affair behind a fine white Carrara marble façade, which Schrager has had restored to its original grandeur. He got a bargain, buying the hotel for $31.3 million. The cost, including renovation, of each of the 610 rooms broke down to $100,000, way below the usual cost per room in New York of $2–700,000.

The new hotel exudes a playful decadence. Starck greatly enjoyed developing the hotel's

Above: The restored Carrara marble exterior of the Paramount with a new glass façade set 3 feet, 2 inches into its arches.

Left: The balcony bar overlooks the double-height lobby, with its retail niche and postcard stand. Jasper Morrison's 'Thinking Man's Chair', to the right, is one of a host of chairs by notable designers to be found in this intentionally sociable space.

A pod-shaped rubbish bin/toilet-paper dispenser mounted on harlequin tiles in one of the toilets.

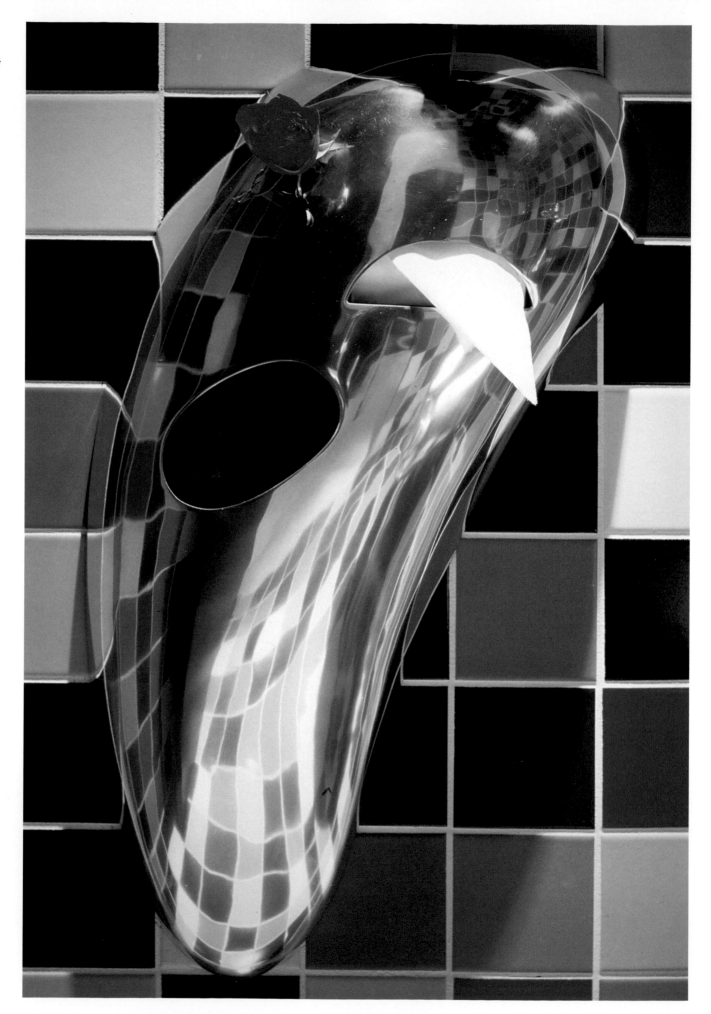

non-élitist idiom, carried out in conjunction with a team of US architects, lighting and colour consultants, many of whom worked with Schrager on his previous projects. In line with Schrager's famed reliance on word-of-mouth publicity, the hotel has no sign on it, just a laser light running the full height of the façade. The marble entrance foyer beyond acts as a kind of decompression chamber from the energy of the city to the relative oasis of the lobby.

The lobby itself defines the theatrical element Schrager wanted. A huge, cavernous, square vault, at least triple height, it resembles a dramatically austere living room. The visitor enters regally via a gold-leafed, gravity-defying staircase, asymmetrically wedged into one corner against a white gold-leaf wall. Details draw the eye: ceiling lighting, inspired by Joan Miró; reproduction Venetian plasterwork made in Italy; and, filling the central space, a collection of furniture by designers of international renown, old and young, alive and dead, including Marco Zanuso, Franco Albini, Jean-Michel Frank, Antonio Gaudí, Carlos Riart, Marc Newson and Jasper Morrison. Their bright, jewel-like colours are particularly vibrant in this strange environment, finished largely in a dark grey, matt-surfaced plaster.

The lobby is other-worldly, a *mise-en-scène* with an almost atavistic simplicity of composition and form. Overlooking it there is a wide bar and brasserie at first-floor level running around the edge of the room, with tables and chairs arranged in little alcoves. The toilets situated directly off the lobby are engrossing environments in which to linger. Starck enjoys redefining functional objects, and even the metal sink fixtures are customized with engravings.

The aim of the Paramount was to offer an all-purpose interior incorporating such a range of facilities that visitors need hardly step outside. The lobby houses a newsagent and shops with gourmet food and souvenirs. Leading off this cavern at ground- and first-floor levels are a restaurant, another bar and grill, a rather small play room and crèche designed by Gary Panter, rooms for working out, film viewing and video games, a business centre and, below, a basement cabaret club.

For lifestyle-weary visitors, the bedrooms themselves are furnished in style and comfort, providing a whimsical atmosphere that Starck hoped would be at once 'restful and humorous', to 'distract as well as comfort visitors'. In the diminutive 12 x 14 foot single rooms, guests are greeted by an oversized version of Vermeer's painting *The Lacemaker* hanging over the bed. Starck chose this image because he thought it evoked the right aura of soothing security for single dwellers. (The double rooms feature instead a simple matt-black square.)

When the Paramount opened in 1990, tourism in New York had begun to slacken off after the heady days of the late 1980s, and business in the industry had already dropped by 10 per cent during the previous year. The ability of design to add value to commercial operations like hotels was still endorsed by many without close analysis of the ways in which it had to work with other factors to produce enduring success. The Paramount's euphoric mixture of atmosphere and accessibility worked, and the hotel has so far survived the deeper troughs of recession; but, as Schrager observed back in 1990: 'hotels are not about design. Design is just one of the elements. It's part of the total equation.'

Far left: The overscaled, doll's-house world of the single bedrooms, each of which features a print of *The Lacemaker* by Vermeer.

Left: Starck's compact, conical basin, mirror and shelving unit in one of the hotel bathrooms.

Shigeru Uchida, Studio 80
La Ranarita/Guest Room
Tokyo, Japan

La Ranarita is one of Tokyo's new Italian restaurants, designed in fine style by Shigeru Uchida. Rather than being hidden away at street or basement level, it is elevated way above the traffic jams at the top of the twenty-two-floor Asahi Beer headquarters downtown at Azumabashi. From its vantage point, visitors can look across the city and see the Sumida River stretching into the far distance.

The top-floor space is not wholly devoted to Italian cuisine: Uchida was asked to design two additional spaces contributing to the company's catering facilities. These are not purely for company use: La Ranarita, like Sky Room, a centrally positioned observatory café, is open to the public. On the opposite side to La Ranarita is a third space, Guest Room, a spacious bar identical in shape to the restaurant, with room for music performances, and an entertainment space for the brewery's executives and their guests.

In La Ranarita, Uchida tried to create the kind of ordered design he achieved in one of his earlier projects, Hotel Il Palazzo in Fukuoka, which featured a lobby of symmetrical columns, and a strong red and grey grid motif in the public areas. However, although the concept for the 339-square-metre restaurant is also based on a grid of vertical and horizontal frames, his choice of materials and colours differentiates it from the more stately Italianate forms of the hotel. Uchida chose orange as the predominant colour for the ceilings and upper walls at La Ranarita because it evoked the vivacity of the Italian temperament and the warmth of the country's climate. The aluminium column, wainscot cladding and lighting fixtures also help to underline the modern, youthful image the client wanted to present.

The dining area is a long, narrow space running parallel to an adjoining bar of similar proportions. With its nine-metre-high ceiling, the restaurant has an airy spaciousness, and Uchida's design also makes the most of its panoramic aspect, with extensive glazing along the length and sides of the room. Deep triangular notches in the pitched ceiling contain skylights which allow geometrical patterns of light to play on the orange stucco walls. A wall of columns interspersed with tall glass windows at the rear of the restaurant gives diners a sense of openness akin to the experience of eating on a bright terrace. Uchida reinforces this feeling of being out in the open, using the restaurant's high level to dramatic effect. On one side of the room, the zig-zag line of angled windows, which jut out at the far corners, create small niches which push more than half of the tables out towards the periphery, so that they enjoy the maximum amount of natural light.

Guest Room is slightly larger than La Ranarita (376.7 square metres), and is positioned on the other side of the Sky Room café. It too is divided by a succession of columns and windows into an inner core space running parallel to a long room edged by angled windows, with light-filled niches into which tables are set. At one end, an open performance space for music concerts breaks up its horizontality. Away from the lighter environment of this terraced area, the entrance and bar areas are dominated by a curving bar in smooth Chinese quince veneer. This material was heavily used at Hotel Il Palazzo to give surfaces a rich, lustrous appearance, and applied in Uchida's simple forms, it helps to give Guest Room an ambience which is smart, dignified but not stuffy. The columns and grid configuration of La Ranarita are carried through to this second, more select area, giving a fluidity to the sequence of spaces.

Uchida manages to create two very distinct atmospheres within the similarly proportioned, parallel spaces. Guest Room's calmer, more sophisticated atmosphere is matched by the use of richer materials such as wood veneer and leather. There are graduated areas made up of sections of veneer in contrasting shades of warm brown and travertine, also used for the columns. La Ranarita's warmth, informality and durability is underlined by large terrazzo tiles with contrasting marble inlays which create a dynamic visual effect within this spectacular urban observatory space.

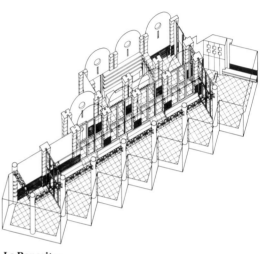

La Ranarita: axonometric diagram.

Fluted, aluminium-clad columns dominate La Ranarita's subtly lit bar.

La Ranarita's long, light-filled dining space, with its bright orange ceiling, has the warm, vibrant atmosphere of an Italian terrace.

Right: The Guest Room lounge-bar, occupying a space on the other side of Asahi's top floor from La Ranarita, has striped Chinese quince veneer floors, travertine columns and narrow, gridded window frames.

Jean-Michel Wilmotte
Hôtel du Cheval Blanc
Nîmes, France

The Hôtel du Cheval Blanc, a converted medieval inn grandly sited on Place des Arènes in the centre of Nîmes, is Jean-Michel Wilmotte's first hotel project, although earlier commissions such as the Technal showroom in Toulouse and the Grenier à Sel in Avignon, demonstrate his skill at historic building conversions. At Nîmes, working to a budget of 9,600 francs per square metre, he aimed to emphasize the links between the town's heritage and its contemporary art activities, and the hotel's simple, sober interiors respect and complement the building's original fabric, whilst offering all the creature comforts and facilities appropriate to its four stars.

The inn had to be totally stripped down to its foundations to preserve original structures established over a huge span of years, such as the basement and ground-floor area – a sixteenth-century cloister – the stone walls and beams of the upper levels which date from the seventeenth and eighteenth centuries, and a monumental central staircase kept as the main access route. These original forms determined the layout (over three floors) of the hotel's twenty-six bedrooms, each of which has a different shape. Some are positioned in a line along the front façade of the building; the rest are fitted into a triangular floor plan around the curve of the stairwell.

Most of the hotel's facilities are situated on the ground floor, including a sixty-seat restaurant, a bar, wine bar and office. Here the stone floors and gritty textures of the building's old vaults are subtly illuminated by halogen lights. A footbridge runs across the double-height stone-walled entrance hall, and this balconied area links two conference rooms on the floor above, also reached via the main stair.

The bedrooms, six of which are suites with a mezzanine, have a tranquil and austere atmosphere, somewhat redolent of a monk's quarters, with simple, custom-designed furniture in chestnut and canvas, plain white table lamps, new oak floors and new white stone walls superimposed on to the old structure. However, the asceticism of the rooms is tempered with comfort, which makes them at once warm and elegant. All have a good aspect, with natural light and many superb views of the huge Roman arena across the street. Fragments of the old building – masonry, wooden beams, stone staircases – have been preserved and combined with new details, such as rolling window shutters in strips of chestnut and varnished metal guardrails.

The designer also invited local artists to create works to be strategically placed around the hotel. A red blot attracts the eye amongst the rough stonework: not a tablecloth but a vivid bullfighter's cape casually thrown over an upper balcony – a work by the artist Claude Viallat and a symbolic reminder of the bullfighting activities in the arena close by.

Wilmotte's aim was to bring the building back to life. In the process, instead of introducing elements which negate its past, he wanted to maintain something of its medieval allure, and to create a dialogue between his sober aesthetic and modern building technology, so that it was easy to use as well as to look at.

Above: The stone walls and beams of the original building, subtly illuminated by halogen lighting, are complemented by Wilmotte's simple wooden furniture, shown here in the hotel's bar.

Far left: The bedrooms have a tranquil, almost monastic quality. The conversion handled the original fabric with care, and discernible traces of the old building remain visible, with masonry, wooden beams and stone staircases preserved and combined with oak floors, chestnut wood shutters and metal guardrails.

Stores, Showrooms & Retail Centres

Ahrends Burton and Koralek   146
John Lewis
Kingston upon Thames, UK

Branson Coates Architecture   148
Jigsaw
Knightsbridge, London, UK

Antonio Citterio and Terry Dwan Architects   152
Fausto Santini
Paris, France

Michael Hopkins and Partners   154
David Mellor
London, UK

Shiro Kuramata   156
SPIRAL
AXIS Building, Tokyo, Japan

John Lum/Reid & Tarics Associates   158
Urban Eyes
San Francisco, California, USA

Torsten Neeland   160
Uta Raasch
Hamburg, Germany

Boris Podrecca   164
Mazda Lietz
Waidhofen, Austria

Fernando Salas   166
Roberto Verino
Barcelona, Spain

Wickham & Associates   168
Fifth Floor, Harvey Nichols
London, UK

Ahrends Burton and Koralek
John Lewis
Kingston upon Thames, UK

Although the last twenty years have seen a huge increase in the amount of retail space built in the UK, new, purpose-designed department stores – in particular distinctive buildings with memorable interiors – are rare. The availability of cheaper land and greater space at the edge of cities has attracted scores of developers and retailers away from town centres and their communities. Ahrends Burton and Koralek's commission to design John Lewis's new store at the entrance to Kingston upon Thames – first mooted by the client in 1970 – was an opportunity to create a good building within reach of the pedestrian, and at the same time, as architect Paul Koralek puts it, to 'draw on the rich tradition of department store design', interpreting its dynamism in a modern form.

This tradition was exemplified by grand nineteenth-century buildings like Bon Marché and Au Printemps in Paris, which Koralek describes as 'huge daylit spaces, exuberantly employing newly developed engineering techniques in cast iron and glass, which in turn took their inspiration from earlier market halls and large covered halls'. Both architects and client regard the elegant and spacious Peter Jones in Sloane Square, built in 1936 by Spedan Lewis, as the twentieth-century equivalent of these pioneering stores. The ambitious brief devised for John Lewis at Kingston proposed an updating of this tradition with a 'Peter Jones' for the 1990s.

The new store clearly demonstrates that John Lewis's reputation as retailers of sound, reliable goods and their strong commitment to the well-being of staff, is accompanied by a discerning approach to the built environment. The sizeable, prominent site between Kingston's town centre and the River Thames – with a footprint big enough to contain St Paul's Cathedral – gave them the opportunity for a high profile. The choice of warm, sand-coloured brick, glass and mild steel finished with metallic paint was a judicious one, and the new dual-carriageway relief road which gives diagonal access to the site is visually stimulating.

Right: The sales floors are planned in the form of stepped terraces linked by lines of escalators. Their visual connection within one huge, top-lit central space, is impressive and offers an easily negotiated circulation. The horizontal aluminium louvres give the effect of a continuous ceiling and conceal the large glazed roof supported on a tubular steel structure.

Left: The partners' dining room has good river views. Blinds reduce glare from the extensively glazed ceiling.

Below right: A view of the store from the north bank of the River Thames: its site adjoins the Kingston town centre conservation area.

1 Storage
2 Second-floor sales area
3 Administrative offices
4 Plant rooms
5 Lettable areas

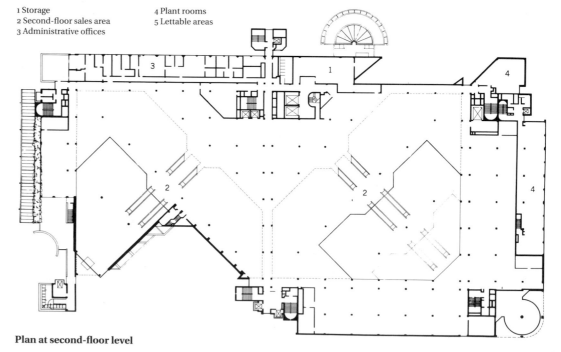

Plan at second-floor level

The store has a very large, daylit central space, around and within which five sales floors (with a total area of 40,000 square metres) are planned in the form of stepped terraces linked by lines of escalators. These rise towards the centre and lead from the main entrances, up through the building over the relief road to riverside spaces and the Kingston Bridge entrance to the west. Instead of a forced, strategic orientation – frequently so disorientating to the customer – the cascades of escalators rise through the tiered shopping floors allowing a clear pattern of movement, with the five floors exposed to view on entry.

The huge, 3,500-square-metre glazed roof is a striking construction which allows the majority of the selling floor to be under direct daylight, a welcome change from low ceilings laden with fluorescent light-fittings which distort colours. Its transparent double-glazed units, interspersed with bands of clear glazing, are supported on a tubular steel structure and screened internally by specially extruded aluminium louvres. This structure has a strong diagonal rhythm which complements the layout of the large open concourses with their wide shopping aisles.

The store's interior finishes are deliberately subdued to focus attention on the merchandise. The main materials used are cream-painted plaster, grey-painted structural steelwork and stainless steel. The customer coffee shop is a pleasant, naturally lit area with high ceilings and hanging lamps. It is simply furnished in natural tones, with bright silk wall hangings by Lucienne Day providing two areas of vivid colour. This clear, functional aesthetic is continued in the partners' dining room, with its handsome river views and substantially glazed façade with white blinds to reduce glare.

Branson Coates Architecture
Jigsaw
Knightsbridge, London, UK

Jigsaw's Knightsbridge branch – the largest in this high fashion chain – occupies a prime site near Harrods. Approached from Hyde Park Corner, its bold exterior, with a double-height glazed façade divided by a glinting, copper-clad column, steals attention from the department store behind. The 350-square-metre flagship shop's exuberant, show-stopping qualities contrast well with the more subtle lyricism of the other branches designed by Branson Coates Architecture. 'Knightsbridge is about splendour, salons and noble interiors', says Nigel Coates. 'We had to rise to the occasion.'

Set back from the pavement, the upper storey is partially concealed behind a vivid orange curtain. The design was intended to create a 'rich spatial experience', and to do this most effectively it plays on the contrast in atmosphere between upper and lower floors. A simple stone-paved floor, low ceiling and soft grey-green tones give the ground floor the look of a transitional space, half-street and half-interior, which leads to something more lively and fully formed. A wall of mirror reflects the approach to the central staircase, the twisting, muscular forms

Left: The design of the first floor, with its inviting salon-style ambience, is characterized by a sense of movement and an intricate craft aesthetic. A spiralling 'Spring' lighting track continues the rhythm of the staircase, with, at its centre, a chandelier with hand-blown blue glass and cast-aluminium pendants made by Simon Moore at Glassworks. Wrought-iron wall display units incorporate matching blue glass fleurs-de-lis.

Below: Changing rooms beyond the grey, padded-velvet walls of the 'proscenium' stage at one edge of the upper floor.

Jigsaw's dramatic double-height façade with its central, copper-clad column and tantalizing glimpse into the partially curtained upper salon.

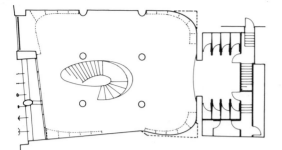

First-floor plan

Left: Nigel Coates' curved-backed 'Tongue' chairs and 'Gallo' console tables are arranged around the swirling carpet encircling the top of the staircase.

Right: Stuart Helm designed and painted the decorative mural which gives a pastoral quality to the light yellow plaster walls of the salon.

of which are like large roots, holding up a sweeping terrazzo stair with cast-iron banisters. A great oval carpet wraps around the stairwell, urging the visitor forward into a warm and inviting boudoir. Here Branson Coates' characteristic sense of movement in form and detail is pitched against a more traditional craft aesthetic to create 'a 21st-century Arts and Crafts approach'. Curving corners make the rectangular space seem more intimate. On the yellow plaster walls, decorative friezes in warm tones encircle the space above display units.

The changing rooms, with their grey, velvet-padded walls, stand on a platform flanked by mirrors reflecting the details of the crafted display systems. This arrangement avoids self-conscious staginess and blends well with the rest of the room. Its warmth is enhanced by oak-timbered floors and Nigel Coates' brickdust velvet 'Tongue' armchairs and zoomorphic 'Gallo' console tables, made bigger for impact.

Jigsaw's clothes represent affordable, modern style, well made with good materials, and this is reflected in the interior; its design deftly translates classic salon ingredients into a relaxed and witty space full of expressive forms and stimulating detail.

150

Antonio Citterio and Terry Dwan Architects
Fausto Santini

Paris, France

Rue du Cherche Midi in St-Germain is lined with up-market shoe shops, but none has been designed with such clarity and assurance as the Paris retail outlet of Fausto Santini, an Italian shoe and bag designer and manufacturer. Antonio Citterio has been in charge of the company's interior design since 1983. Its desire in recent years has been to develop a more classic image of accessible luxury and the shop – which occupies a new 100-square-metre-space – needed an architectural identity which would help differentiate it from its neighbours in this competitive location.

Fausto Santini is a carefully tailored space where something of a rationalist spirit coexists with a more traditional, classical approach. It had to be adroitly laid out because the space was a complex volume broken into two areas by the building's stairwell. The architects made a virtue of a necessity by emphasizing the 'backbone' wall linking the front and rear spaces and introducing two deep wooden steps to mark the transition. They also added an internal glass display unit, reminiscent of a traditional shop window, which 'wraps' the corner of the wall around the stair and gives the illusion of greater spaciousness.

The strong architectural identity of the space is asserted by two 2.7-metre-high solid plaster panel display walls – one in each area – with square, internally lit niches. The use of modern, Italianate plaster structures on this scale gives each part a sense of the solidity and durability one expects from the merchandise.

There are two further types of display system. A plain plinth of Paris limestone pitched at a sensible height at the front of the shop invites you to start your scrutiny of its wares. The sparing use of materials such as mahogany on the top of the cash desk and as a base to the window display underlines the architects' desire to create a modern and approachable image for the client.

Along the left-hand wall, five free-standing cases are set back from the space in wide niches, and there is a pleasing lightness and transparency to their simple, nickel-plated brass and plain glass construction. Their drop fronts express both sophistication and accessibility. These structures are complemented by the solid nickel-plated brass lamps hanging above them, which Citterio designed specifically for the shop. All the display units, including the niche walls, were made in Italy and brought in for the eight-week building phase.

The architects intended the bold, intersecting white planes of the ceiling to make reference to its original, classic, moulded form, illuminated from the cymas (wavy mouldings on the cornice). This is successfully reinterpreted on modern lines, with interweaving strips of plaster dropped in to conceal the lighting system. The wall and ceiling surfaces are very pale yellow, which gives them a luminous warmth and makes a striking contrast to the rich mahogany floors.

The architects have made dramatic use of the length of the space, and a long strip of wide steel net carves through the side of the shop from front to rear, emphasizing the unbroken nature of this perimeter wall. The strip also serves to screen lighting over individual display cases set at intervals along the wall, and extends at the front into the left window of the shop's dark mauve, double-fronted façade.

Citterio remarks that in European cities like Paris where historic buildings predominate, it is always extremely difficult to get permission for new retail façades, even if the designs are in keeping with the traditional fabric of neighbouring buildings. Fausto Santini has a relatively open façade for such a narrow street, and this creates a sense of scale which belies the shop's modest internal proportions.

The front and rear areas of the shop are linked by mahogany steps and a long steel-net surcoat running the entire length of the shop's main wall. A plinth of Paris limestone makes a solid, simple display unit.

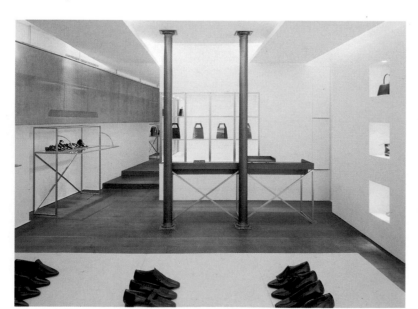

Above: Fausto Santini's double-fronted façade asserts a strong and unadorned presence amongst its more traditional neighbours.

Michael Hopkins and Partners
David Mellor
London, UK

The two-level plan of the shop. Its fair-faced grey concrete walls and ceiling and spare detailing convey a precisely crafted, utilitarian aesthetic. The large back windows provide views of the river and neighbouring buildings.

David Mellor's latest building project is a multi-storey, multi-use concrete building on a tight site, facing on to St Saviour's Dock close to Tower Bridge on the south bank of the River Thames at Shad Thames. It was developed jointly with the neighbouring building on the site of former warehouses. Apart from being the rare product of a process of design and construction shared between the client and architect Michael Hopkins and Partners, it also represents a convergence of interest in the potential of modern architecture to benefit from craft techniques.

The brief given to the practice, which had designed an earlier, award-winning factory for David Mellor at Hathersage in Derbyshire, revolved around his business as a designer and manufacturer of cutlery. Mellor had three shops, in Sloane Square, Manchester and Covent Garden (the last of these was closed to finance the new project), and the new building was intended to be a flexible space at Butler's Wharf, a recently developed area close to Tower Bridge. It was to accommodate a variety of uses: a ground-floor showroom, three floors of offices, a two-storey apartment on the top floor with a double-height hall in the middle, a roof terrace and basement parking. The concrete

structure encompasses all these diverse activities within a neutral framework, as well as providing the potential for other future activities.

The low-ceilinged warehouse occupying the site had to be knocked down and replaced by the architect's scheme for its modern equivalent, a light industrial building, completed to a modest budget. As with the Hathersage project, the client was to be involved in its construction, with Mellor and his son Corin on site from the beginning, acting as part-contractor, part-clerk of work and part-client.

A design led by 'appropriate', rather than high technology, the building has a simple, rectangular, 6 x 3.85 metre floor grid of columns, creating an overall size of 24 x 12 metres. It is deliberately made up of few elements and highly practical materials. The architects found from working with Mellor at Hathersage that he was a perfectionist, bringing, as John Pringle, an architect on the project team put it, 'a combination of the precision of production engineering and the art of the silversmith to the construction industry: he shared our usual preoccupation with bringing out the quality of materials used in building'.

The frame is made of fair-faced concrete

which suits the tough context of surrounding warehouses (as well as possessing inherent fire resistance), combined with fully glazed front and back walls. Above the plate glass walls of the showroom, the offices have full-height horizontal sliding windows, and above these, the top-floor apartment shares the same glazing system, with projecting steel balconies. The lift and stairs are separated from the main structure in a free-standing shaft of plate steel with glazed bridges. Service areas are squashed into the wedge-shaped left-over space between the main frame and the party wall of the next-door building.

The architects had not worked much with concrete before, and used the opportunity to enlarge their expertise in design for concrete structures. Pre-fabricated concrete walls – more of a known quantity within the industry – could have given a roughly similar result, but at twice the cost. Working with Mellor, the architects developed their ideas about the innate qualities of the material. They wanted to let the concrete look like itself, not something it was not – a moulded material which looked as though it had been poured, and incorporated within a seamless structure, with a moulding process to provide profiles for services and lighting. It was also felt that

Far left: The concrete-framed building, with its full-height sliding windows and open interior spaces was intended to be as adaptable as the old Victorian dock buildings along this southern stretch of the River Thames. The separate stairtower is made of mild steel with lead cladding panels.

Left: David Mellor designed the cash desk and stainless steel and glass shelves to meticulous standards.

its internally exposed thermal mass could, in theory, be used as a heat store, providing a relatively stable environment and reducing reliance on mechanical systems.

The construction phase proved to be a learning experience: formwork came to be regarded as a piece of joinery. In the showroom Mellor's parallel line light fittings are cast into ceiling slabs as reinforcement supports fixed to the formwork, with electrical conduits fixed at the same time. The architects took up the advice of that master of concrete forms, architect Tadao Ando, regarding the surface finish of the concrete, and literally used sandpaper to ensure that the compacted dense texture was left intact, smoothed into a surface of sand and cement.

Mellor and his son, with their work force,

designed and manufactured the mouldings for the concrete – virtually handmade craft objects – as well as the soffits, and sheets of lead cladding on the front of the building. Although McAlpine built the structure, Mellor's team did much of the rest of the building work, including the lead-faced wall panels, steel lift tower and all the metalwork.

The designer has always been closely involved in the fitting out of his shops, and as well as lighting, he designed elements in the ground-floor showroom/shop (originally intended to be a workshop but changed mid-scheme) such as the cash desk and stainless steel and glass shelves, which form a well-crafted setting for larger household items like wooden bowls. The shop's transparent façade enables the passer-by to see the whole space

with its meticulously formed 'forest' of vertical shelf supports and light fittings. As one moves through the strong, symmetrical layout, the river bank's older warehouse stock can be glimpsed, a suitable backdrop for the beautifully crafted utilitarian aesthetic of this modern light industrial building.

Shiro Kuramata
SPIRAL

AXIS Building, Tokyo, Japan

SPIRAL was one of the last interior design projects of Shiro Kuramata who died at an early age in 1991. A clock shop, it has much in common with his other tiny, imaginative projects, such as the Yoshiki Hishinuma shop, and the Oblomova bar which uses Perspex forms and OSB, a wooden chipboard treated to look like marble. However, whereas these earlier interiors have a wonderfully calm sense of artificiality and dematerialized form, SPIRAL demonstrates a more exuberant, but equally surreal creative temperament.

The context of the AXIS Building in Roppongi is perfect for a Kuramata project. Its eclectic group of design shops include CHAIRS and Nuno, respectively selling furniture by Shigeru Uchida, one of Kuramata's peers, and Junichi Arai's exquisite 'functional textiles'. The products sold at SPIRAL do not need much display space, and Kuramata has given them five rows of wooden shelving around three edges of the space, leaving the rest free for his own purposes. The shop has a glazed façade and entrance, punctuated by two futuristic dumb-bell handles in Perspex and metal. Not content to fit in with the rectangular dimensions, Kuramata introduces an angled expanse of lemon-yellow rubber matting over the terrazzo floor.

Slicing diagonally across the room are two wooden slab structures with softly curving sides, with the side facing the shop front covered with blue-tinted metallic material. These are hung from the ceiling allowing just enough room for people to pass between them. In the compact space the effect of this reflective screen is to draw attention to the small-scale items which adorn the shelves. To the right of these structures are five reed forms, three of which bend forward like strange, mutant flowers growing from acrylic troughs; the other two reach over to the wall, climbing hoops strung with clear Perspex discs. Two squat Perspex chairs, a table in OSB and an enigmatic mushroom-shaped feature complete the design.

This tiny esoteric environment, which masterfully combines the transparency of Perspex and the warmth of wood with vibrant colours, takes on the appearance of a stage set at night. In his quest for de-objectification, Kuramata, who has been called 'a poet of evocative vacancy', did not like to leave any traces of handwork, preferring to work with hard, synthetic materials. With their less tangible qualities he could conjure up a dream-like metal world, free from rational thought.

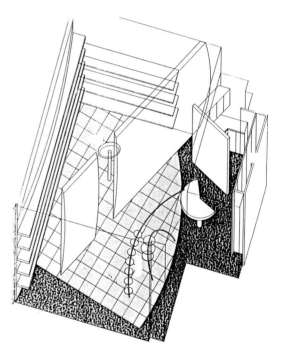

Axonometric diagram (1:60)

The metal and Perspex dumb-bell door handles are the only details punctuating SPIRAL's clear glass façade. A terrazzo floor leads on to an expanse of yellow, reinforced rubber matting.

Left: The ethereal
transparency of
Kuramata's objects
contributes to the
stage-set quality of his
interiors.

Above: Kuramata
divides the space
diagonally by means of
two hanging screens
faced with steel, their
front sides a tinted
mirrored surface, their
backs covered with a
textured paint which
gives a wood-like finish.
The left wall is enlivened
by reed-like forms made
of acrylic sticks and
discs. Feathers 'float',
suspended in time,
inside Kuramata's clear
acrylic block chairs.

John Lum/Reid & Tarics Associates
Urban Eyes

San Francisco, California, USA

Looking through the entrance past the three-foot-wide door with glass panels and 'eye' logo, a support column decorated with the imprints of hands and optical equipment provides a strong visual focus.

Optometrists traditionally come from the medical profession, but if they can combine good health care with retail flair they provide a more satisfying one-stop service. The enterprising Dr Lee, owner of Urban Eyes in San Francisco, sells distinctive, 'upscale' face jewellery, whilst providing all the health-care facilities that even fashion victims need. With its clever lines of perspective, his tiny 450-square-foot boutique and consultancy makes the most of some very modest ingredients.

Urban Eyes was John Lum's first retail project and 'a labour of love' for the associate architect of Reid and Tarics. It has already won three design awards from the American design profession and media. Much of the shoestring budget of $100 per square foot was used to attract the visitor in from the workaday building lobby outside to the triangular space which opens out into a bar-style consulting area with an examination room at the rear. The venerable Chinese *feng shui* masters brought in to pronounce on the space's potential, approved of Lum's telescopic perspective, and the balance they advocated between the man-made and natural forms is wittily asserted by the presence in the window of a single manzanita branch supporting a tiny display case.

Lum includes plenty of deftly scaled visual stimuli to create the illusion of depth: jutting out from the left is an imposing cube-shaped restroom and storeroom with a built-in display unit framed by ash veneer panels (its curvy metal forms are like letters that cannot quite be made out). Facing this, a curved wall carves into the room, studded with rubber-coated lag bolts on which various arrangements of aluminium shelves, mirrors and stock can be set up. Diagonally brushed and scratched walls and work surfaces enrich the space's minute proportions. Lum and Lee also personalized it by pressing hands and optical instruments into the terracotta-toned joint compound covering a structural column. This rises up to the cutaway plane of the ceiling like a totem pole.

Working in Florence a few years ago, Lum explored the architectural possibilities of fashion show sets and window displays for designer Enrico Coveri. In the 'small town big city' of San Francisco, Urban Eyes' discernibly European sensibility makes spatial drama out of a few elements.

Above: Urban Eyes mixes geometric and organic forms. A spotlit, custom-designed display case hovers on its manzanita branch support. In the background a gridded cube of ash-veneered panels frames a recessed, back-lit display unit animated by metal arabesque forms.

Timothy Harris designed the 'come hither' logo at the entrance.

Right: The curved wall studded with rubber-coated bolts provides a simple and compact display system. There is a sense of movement in the surfaces: ash-strip floor, hand-painted tiger stripes on the wall and the brushed aluminium apron of the reception desk, with its concealed cash register. The backs of the painted steel and aluminium stools echo the distorted letterform display unit.

Torsten Neeland
Uta Raasch

Hamburg, Germany

Fashion designers are fond of stretching one strong interior design identity to suit all their own retail outlets, with perhaps a more economical, popularized look for diffusion outlets. Whilst this strategy provides an instantly recognizable environment for customers, it does not often give the interior designer involved much creative freedom to evolve varying interpretations of the client's personal style. Working to a tiny scale, Torsten Neeland's latest shop in Hamburg for the German fashion designer Uta Raasch, demonstrates that one approach can be broadened by applying subtle new ideas which enhance the client's products.

Uta Raasch's small shops stock only her own designs: simple and stylish off-the-peg creations. Neeland, who prefers a similarly understated approach, designed an earlier shop for the fashion designer in Düsseldorf. His brief for the new outlet was to embody a similar philosophy, and whilst some fitting elements are common to both shops, he was keen to develop new ways of accentuating the formal space of the shop and reducing its details to a minimum.

The tiny boutique is set within a restored art nouveau building on central Hamburg's ABC-Strasse, amongst exclusive fashion shops like Chanel, Yves Saint Laurent and Joop! Not a lover of glitz or decoration, Raasch wanted a calm, modern environment to reflect the style of her unfussy clothes and accessories. Neeland's challenge was to create a new, aesthetically pleasing and comfortable space in which to accommodate her elegant stock, with only 62 square metres to play with.

In contrast to fashion shops where a high concentration of details are amassed to keep the customers visually engaged – if not overwhelmed – Neeland's design plays down the impact of the furniture and display systems. He does this by using light-coloured and transparent materials, applied to mostly vertical forms. Light seeping from concealed sources around the space gives the shop's environment a light and ethereal beauty, based on transparency and minimalism.

Mirrors placed strategically around the periphery in narrow bands give the illusion of a deeper space, and the other vertical elements – cupboard doors and dividing walls – are made of frosted glass, and so reflect and diffuse light. Instead of symmetrically positioned downlighters, Neeland has given

Right: Neeland conceals all the light sources behind glass walls and cupboards, from which diffused light seeps, giving the tiny, cream and grey cast terrazzo floored space defined areas with an ethereal glow. To make the room look bigger, all cupboard doors and dividing walls are made out of glass.

Above: Facing the changing-room door is a tall, swivel mirror framed in burnished steel.

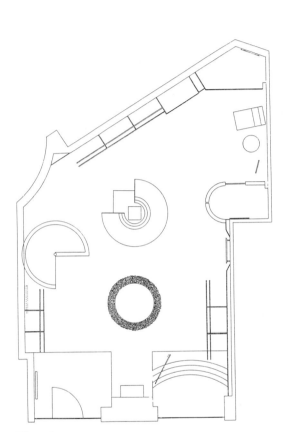

Floor plan

the shop several distinct areas of lighting; their sources are not obviously visible, and the light pours in tall, concentrated lines from openings between and behind the walls and cupboards. Some of the fittings have tinted blue tubes, which helps to wash the space in cool tones. Apart from in the window area, there are no spotlights, so no single elements are picked out. Instead, small ceiling fittings illuminate the space in wide swathes.

Neeland's furniture and fittings for the shop have clear, uncluttered forms with an unobtrusive presence. Two free-standing circular elements alone create islands to be navigated: cream banquette seating backed with frosted glass curls round a pillar; and a low ashwood and glass display case is positioned in the middle of the room. Their shape is echoed by a white wall at the edge of the room encircling a spiral staircase to the

basement, and the smaller curve of one of the changing rooms. The colour scheme for these solid elements is white and cream throughout, a combination requiring much loving care to retain its glamorous appeal.

Neeland's bleached ashwood forms are very plain and durable: just a single upholstered chair with a deep wooden base, and a row of wide shelves above display rails made of long bands of burnished steel. Certain details, particularly in a service environment like a shop, cannot be completely subsumed by the desire to create a reduced architectural space, and two further, customized elements underline the personalized nature of Neeland's design (as well as his facility as an industrial designer): curvaceous coat-hangers in untreated cast aluminium, and a sleekly modelled bust made from pieces of sheet steel.

Boris Podrecca
Mazda Lietz
Waidhofen, Austria

The new Mazda Lietz showroom stands in rural surroundings close to the Ybbs river at the edge of Waidhofen. The budget for its design and construction was no more than that of other car showrooms dotted around the periphery of the city; the difference lies in Boris Podrecca's approach which provides an interesting comment on the position of the car in contemporary culture.

Although architects have long found the car a fascinating and inspiring product and a potent symbol of the modern age, Podrecca acknowledged that it would be difficult for his building to rival its efficient and beautiful use of technology. The building could not be mass-produced; it had to work on a one-off basis. He made no attempt to forge too narrow a stylistic connection between the two, particularly as his building was designed to hold a large number of cars and had to be functional, as well as carrying Mazda's corporate identity. Instead, the building is a container, with a form which neither suggests the anonymity of a huge shed, nor simply a homage to the automobile. Podrecca calls it 'a contextual building'. There is little architecture around the site to relate to, so he was relatively free to develop an independent design language. Its Italian-style loggia at the front is a slightly incongruous classical element which underlines his playful, heterogeneous use of materials and forms.

There is a shed element to the showroom in the form of a rear workshop, but it is hidden away, fronted by the main showroom hall and reception, a curved segment applied to an otherwise rectilinear form. Podrecca's arrangement of the periphery is his key planning device: by creating a ramp (out of an earth mound) which runs through the entire showroom up to the front of the first-floor hall and extends out of the building as a small display space over the forecourt, he gives his design a backbone on to which other elements can be built. This structure – the public front to a basic shed form – is lightweight, with steel columns, corrugated metal sheet, plastered pillars, large doors, and an extensive glass skin.

The showroom is a container aesthetically equipped to stand empty or full without losing its identity. It also has a provisional quality, for even quirky elements like the reception desk, the stick insect-like forms of the staircase rail and the curved glass panel fronting the mezzanine office floor look

Offices are incorporated into the upper floor behind a curved transparent screen, leaving the ground floor free of obstructions; only a boldly defined information desk is set in the middle of the space.

mobile and easily disassembled, like the car itself. Waidhofen's outskirts lack the historic identity of the city; their large buildings are predominantly commercial centres for out-of-town shopping, and the lacklustre environment provides few compelling reasons for most businesses establishing a base here to break the mould in any way. But Mazda Lietz's creation of an architectural focal point in this no-man's-land, one that is clearly visible from cars passing to and fro, represents an investment in the area. Ironically, its success in this location depends heavily on the car allowing customers access. A major departure from the ubiquitous shed-style showroom, for critic Dietmar Steiner Mazda Lietz is a 'cultural and aesthetic symbol of today's relationship between the car and architecture, between mobility and place'.

More than just a shed in no-man's-land: Mazda's 'signboard' display hall on the fringes of Waidhofen, with its forecourt and extended ramp.

Fernando Salas
Roberto Verino

Barcelona, Spain

Right: The entrance to the main corridor with its flagstones of oxidized brass and walls clad in soft-toned Jurassic marble and interlocking maplewood panels. A navy-coloured wood and stone slab (which Salas sees as the sky, to the sea of the floor) lines the ceiling of the passageway.

Roberto Verino's new fashion showroom in Barcelona is located away from busy shopping streets in a nineteenth-century building in the most select part of the Eixample. Close to Barcelona's industrial district with its bustling textile industry, it also benefits from the quiet seclusion of the district's many patios and garden terraces. What used to be a notary's office has been completely remodelled to encompass a showroom, sales offices and styling rooms. All the non-structural walls and divisions have been taken out to create as great a sense of transparency as possible within a calm and serene environment, intentionally detached from its urban context.

Two massive wooden doors open into a hallway with walls made of maplewood sections arranged in a jigsaw pattern. Soft-toned Jurassic marble walls lead the visitor towards a central corridor. Their plainness provokes the impression of an interior stripped down to its essentials – Salas even hides the light sources, switches and doors.

This main corridor, with its strong axis through the entire space, acts as a central spine, connecting the different rooms of the showroom. The showroom floors are covered with smooth Canadian maple parquet, but this route is paved with flagstones of oxidized brass with a greenish patina, marking it out as a transitional zone. Salas has inserted a navy-blue ceiling slab in wood and stone, slotted into brickwork at each end and hiding the services. At opposite ends are larger spaces for the workshop and sales area.

The showroom itself has windows opening on to a balcony. However, Salas does not really make much of this feature, preferring to focus attention on the interior space. Garments and fabrics are stored in a bank of aluminium cabinets on castors incorporating large mirrors, which also serve as screens. When these are moved, a photoelectric cell is triggered, and ceiling spots automatically light up their interiors. At the other end of the room there are fixed units, finished with more 'appliquéd' maplewood panels, which hold air-conditioning units. The suspended,

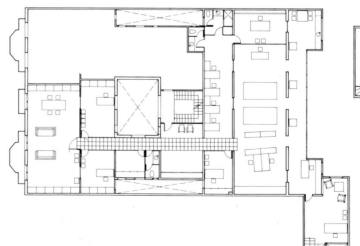

Floor plan of the showroom and the upper floor of the executive suite.

Above: The working spaces of the executive suite, with burnished teak stairs leading to living areas. A 'Tolomeo' lamp stands on the desk in front of the lightwell.

Far right: The showroom walls are clad with maplewood panels arranged in a jigsaw pattern below aluminium cabinetry.

anodized aluminium ceiling has electrified rails (for hanging projectors), fire detection units and loudspeakers.

The offices on either side of the corridor are open, glazed spaces, lined with grey Jurassic marble and bare of all but the most restricted amount of furniture, including elegant teak worktables, anodized aluminium shelving and Richard Sapper's 'Tizio' lamps. An old gallery is used as the prototype and styling room, a utilitarian space without curtains in which Salas felt the presence of people would be the main animating force. An executive suite at its rear consists of a two-storey apartment reached by a winding staircase. Continuing the theme of the showroom, this private territory is again graced by 'a few essential items to help create a refuge from the scene below'.

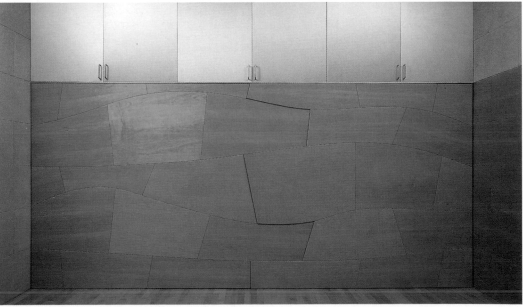

Wickham & Associates
Fifth Floor, Harvey Nichols
London, UK

Department store design in London has at last taken a leap into the future with the conversion of the Fifth Floor at Harvey Nichols, which brings *haute cuisine* to the fashion store. The new, naturally lit space is organized like a village, with panoramic views of Knightsbridge. The brief to architects Wickham & Associates called for the complete refurbishment and fitting out of this top-floor space, to create a host of new facilities: a food hall, wine shop, café, bar, restaurant, kitchens and office areas.

This new retail/eating environment does not follow custom with caution and indifference: on the contrary, its well-organized design opens up the floor to the outside environment, bringing light streaming in through a spectacular glazed roof. Instead of a dull, regimented or maze-like retail area, a varied environment of linked spaces brings eating and shopping together in a user-friendly foodie paradise which manages to be spectacular without relinquishing the underlying orderliness of its design. Dominic Ford, director of the Fifth-Floor operation, selected the architects and was the 'guiding light' behind the project.

Although it is rare for London stores to be distinguished for their catering facilities, the newly activated floor has a celebrated chef (ex-Bibendum, to whose specifications the architects designed the kitchen). By extending the opening hours into the evening, Harvey Nichols has drastically added to, and reshaped its identity, putting considerable funds (£5.4 million) into the design of the space.

The original building was developed over a period of more than one hundred years, with the last changes taking place in the early 1970s, when the lightwells were filled in, and new lifts and escalators were inserted. By stripping the top-floor space right back to its bare structure, the architects have enabled the interior to be perceived as an open one, free of any obstruction. Where the old northern lightwell had been was an existing roof structure of triangular steel-lattice beams. These were retained and restructured

Above: The ceiling of the restaurant is washed with diffused light from fixtures on the sides of long coves which, with their metallic paint finish, recall the sweeping lines of plane wings. The coves provide a neutral backdrop to Julyan Wickham's custom-designed furniture.

Right: An external view of the department store's Fifth Floor, with its restructured steel lattice beams and glazed roof.

1 Kitchen
2 Restaurant
3 Bar
4 'Market square'
5 Café-bar
6 Food hall
7 Wine shop
8 Food preparation
and serve-over units
9 Escalator access
10 Lift access

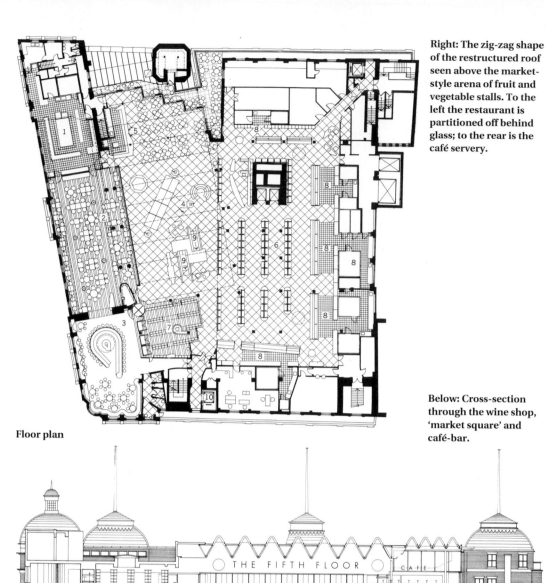

Floor plan

Right: The zig-zag shape of the restructured roof seen above the market-style arena of fruit and vegetable stalls. To the left the restaurant is partitioned off behind glass; to the rear is the café servery.

to create a large, saw-tooth-shaped glass roof. This zig-zag form has been covered with cladding in ascending lines of soft yellow, pink, cream and white polycarbonate panels and transparent Perspex.

The northern section of the space on the Knightsbridge side, which has four large cupolas, was completely gutted, and a new roof constructed, with an extensive steel structure to support the cupolas. This formed an open space connected to the fifth-floor interior, providing views out into the street. To the east of the old main lightwell a new structure has been built, incorporating a café, which in summer will extend out on to a roof terrace close to one of the cupolas.

The result is a light, lively environment, and a most unusual space to find at the top of a large store, for as Julyan Wickham observes, 'London department stores have traditionally developed as closed internal spaces without much relationship to their environments. Here we have opened up the interior such that it relates back to the street below, and receives natural daylight and good visual and functional contact between the individual departments.'

The long views to be had between the restaurant, bar, café and food hall make the most of the spacious 3,000-square-metre floorspace, and prevent any one area developing a sense of exclusivity. The decision to install glazed partitions between restaurant and café/food hall was a judicious one, avoiding an enclosed, élitist restaurant space. Good lines of visual communication are set up within the restaurant, and the circular glazed partition the architects designed to grace its far wall reveals at least some of the considerable effort being put into the food. Overall, the floor is an environment with a great sense of flow, in which the visitor feels free to wander from section to section (including right up to the periphery, in the deep spaces behind the charcuterie counter) – all of it open-plan – without experiencing the sense of confinement controlled circulation gives. The floor is reached by an express lift with its own lobby, easily

Below: Cross-section through the wine shop, 'market square' and café-bar.

Above: Table lamps in the bar are crowned with fluted beechwood fins.

Left: The crafted furniture and fittings in the circular bar include high stools and walnut table tops designed by the architects.

accessible from its Sloane Street entrance, so the rest of the floors can be bypassed if desired. However, it is also linked by centrally positioned, neatly accommodated escalators to the floor below.

All the furniture and the vast majority of the fittings were designed by the architects. Top-quality fittings have been specified and incorporated with care: the servery counters were made in Italy; the 'Metro' metal shelving system is American, and the architects have adapted its light structures by adding glass backs and rails, and circular end units. The absence of standard shopfitting units – ungainly gondolas and the like – is commendable. Distinctive, crafted items were developed for areas such as the curved walnut tops at the window in the bar, the central bar unit, also topped in walnut with grey, bird's-eye maple facing, and the custom-designed bakery display units with tilting shelves.

However, for surfaces which need to be high performance or are large scale, basic and easily machinable materials which take a variety of finishes are used. The wine shop, adjacent to the bar, is a heavy duty cellar-style area with bottles displayed on its periphery behind glazed partitions. It looks like metal, but this would be an impractical solution, clanking against the bottles, and instead 'Trimrite' hammer-finish paint has been used on MDF. The long coves like plane wings running the length of the restaurant on its far sides also have a metallic paint finish. The architects have used second-hand wood blocks for the restaurant's floor. Huge, chequered vinyl floor tiles throughout the shopping and café areas should withstand the crowds, and provide a softer touch than the harder, more shiny and slippery surfaces often found in food retailing outlets.

The food hall ceiling was very low, and adding a suspended ceiling would have made it two feet lower than the existing roof, so the architects left much of the ceiling's services exposed here. 'To make the ceiling disappear' the architects painted wide bands at this high level in four different colours, each becoming visible at a different 45-degree angle.

Extensive natural light filtering into the space is backed up by distinctively designed fittings. Lamps in the bar are made of veneered beech stems crowned by a swirl of overlapping beech plywood fins. Above the café, discs holding bulbs on hoop-shaped metal tubes form modern chandeliers.

The architects' ingenious solution demonstrates the potential that buildings possess for adaptation to new uses. Although it includes numerous successful restaurant and bar projects, their track record is not narrowly retail-oriented, and this enabled them to bring to the project some fresh thinking about the use of top-floor department store space.

Cultural & Public Amenity Buildings

Roser Amadó and Lluís Domènech 174
Fundació Antoni Tàpies
Barcelona, Spain

Architekturbüro Bolles-Wilson 178
and Partner
Kita Griesheim-Süd
Frankfurt am Main, Germany

Esteve Bonell and Francesc Rius 182
Badalona Sports Palace
Badalona, Barcelona, Spain

Eduard Bru 184
Museo del Juguete
Ibi, Alicante, Spain

Henri Ciriani 186
Historial de la Grande Guerre
Peronne-Somme, France

Antonio Cruz and Antonio Ortiz 190
Santa Justa Railway Station
Seville, Spain

Foster Associates 194
Stansted Airport Terminal
Stansted, UK

Sir Norman Foster and Partners 198
The Sackler Galleries,
Royal Academy of Arts
London, UK

Tony Fretton 202
Lisson Gallery
London, UK

Beth Galí, Màrius Quintana and 204
Antoni Solanas
Joan Miró Library
Barcelona, Spain

Gwathmey Siegel & Associates 206
The Guggenheim Museum
New York, USA

Hans Hollein 210
Museum für Moderne Kunst
Frankfurt am Main, Germany

Toyo Ito & Associates 214
Yatsushiro Municipal Museum
Kumamoto Prefecture, Japan

Carlos Jiménez 218
Lynn Goode Gallery
Houston, Texas, USA

José Antonio Martinez Lapeña, 220
Elías Torres Tur
Monastery of Sant Pere de Rodes
Port de la Selva, Catalunya, Spain

MacCormac Jamieson Prichard 224
Fitzwilliam College Chapel
Cambridge, UK

José Luis Mateo 226
Can Felipa Cultural Centre
Barcelona, Spain

John Miller + Partners 230
The Stevens Building,
Royal College of Art
London, UK

Enric Miralles 234
Circulo de Lectores
Madrid, Spain

Kiko Mozuna Architects 238
& Associates
Notojima Glass Art Museum
Noto Island, Ishikawa Prefecture, Japan

Akiko & Hiroshi Takahashi/ 240
Work Station
Sakamoto Ryoma Memorial Hall
Urato, Kochi City, Japan

Yannis Tsiomis 244
Académie Musicale de Villecroze
Villecroze, Salernes, Var, France

Roser Amadó and Lluís Domènech
Fundació Antoni Tàpies
Barcelona, Spain

The Fundació Antoni Tàpies is handsomely housed in a spacious, early *Modernista* building on Calle Aragó in the heart of Barcelona's commercial district. Originally designed by Lluís Domènech i Montaner in 1879 as the headquarters of the Montaner i Simon publishing house, it was a key industrial building within the city's Cerdà Plan. Its conversion by the architect's great grandson, Lluís Domènech i Girbau, with Roser Amadó, maintains a purposeful, rational atmosphere conducive to serious activity. However, it now functions as a public cultural amenity, and the airy, transparent spaces are home to a centre for the study and understanding of modern art and culture – not just the work of the celebrated Catalan artist and founder Antoni Tàpies, but other contemporary figures.

Tàpies first proposed the Fundació in 1984 when he announced that he would be donating 300 paintings and 3,000 graphic works to the city of Barcelona. The artist's blueprint for a study centre was the subject of protracted negotiations with the local autonomous government and the Ministry of Culture in Madrid, who provided the 700 million pesetas for the purchase and conversion of the building, now on loan to the Fundació for fifty years. The Fundació opened in June 1990.

Gracing the roof of the building, which is shorter than its neighbours, is Tàpies' wiry 'Cloud and Chair' sculpture. The high-profile position of this semi-transparent, metal-mesh structure caused a frisson in the media when it first appeared, but it undeniably forms an eye-catching 'crown' above the sober façade. When back-lit at night, the metallic tangle animates the rooftop, emphasizing the new identity of the building with panache.

The original drawings of the building were a Domènech family heirloom and gave the duo a headstart in their conversion. Their practical solution introduces a double façade to soundproof two floors of light-filled gallery spaces, a basement gallery, library, offices and seminar rooms. The old publishing house, with its tall rooms punctuated by slim, six-metre cast-iron pillars, had a grand spatial quality and the project emphasizes this. A central feature is the great, glass-roofed 'lantern', originally a storeroom. The architects have also adjusted the upper part of the exterior to meet the higher level of later buildings in the vicinity, by reconstructing the profile of the cornice and adding long, projecting beams holding Tàpies' roof artwork.

New stairways connect the building's various areas, and their positioning and materials make spaces which were once static and solemn, dynamic and accessible. The architects decided to make the semi-basement the most busy and public floor, as it could be easily reached from street level by a few steps and had the largest spaces for temporary exhibitions. A patio was opened at its rear, creating a convenient access route to the summer terrace at the back of the galleries. The first floor had less space because it houses the library, with shelving retained from the original building, and the floor area was reduced further to bring in more light from the central lantern.

Lighting in the large exhibition halls was given great consideration, and as well as the modification of the floor area, a dome-shaped skylight oriented towards the north was introduced over the central lightwell, replacing the original glass roof. Its vertical plane and large reflection-diffusion surfaces of white-painted corrugated sheeting not only reduce ambient lighting in the ground-floor galleries to 300 lux, but give better fire and humidity control and make cleaning easier.

Looking across the first-floor balcony from the library to the gallery walls. Star cutouts show the stained-glass windows of the façade.

Left: Antoni Tàpies' 'Nuvol i cadira' steel and wire-mesh sculpture provides a swirling 'crown' to the restored *Modernista* façade. As an extension of the order of internal pillars and girders, its form enhances the building's height in comparison with its neighbours, and announces the new identity of the former publishing house. Internal lighting shows off the polychromed stained-glass windows and floodlights the sculpture.

Above: For the first-floor library, the architects reused the old pine shelving structure left in what was a paper store in the publishing house, removing some units in the centre of the space to create a reading area and office for the librarian.

Section prior to remodelling

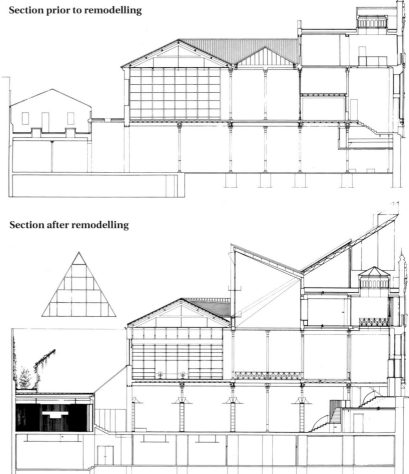

Section after remodelling

Above: View of the spacious lower gallery with its removable display structures, and of the upper gallery spaces opposite the library. The neutrality of textures and colours is intended to facilitate contemplation of the exhibits.

Right: Detail of the rounded main staircase descending from the entrance. Curved, free-standing walls of banded wooden panels screen the information desk and bookshop on either side.

The old octagonal skylight in the entrance to the building was also reconstructed, so that visitors can see Tàpies' roof structure from the inside.

The first-floor library contains a narrow grid of wooden floor-to-ceiling shelving, with only a small central aisle. Housing a rapidly expanding collection of books, its rational design, restricted sightlines and intimate quality give it the atmosphere of a historic interior, reanimated for the study of modern art. Smaller spaces on this floor house administrative offices, while the basement area contains a set of galleries below the auditorium which are suitable for smaller works and for video works requiring darkened spaces.

It proved a considerable challenge to create a close relationship between design

elements that solve one or several problems, such as those associated with acoustics, lighting and air-conditioning. The architects have largely succeeded in their aim to emphasize the transparency of the airy spaces, although the double soundproofing screens on the main façade (necessary to stop reverberation) somewhat reduce the brightness from this south-facing side. This is in spite of little star-shaped holes which reveal the *Modernista* decorative glass features of the façade.

Regulating the temperature and humidity of the interiors – one element which, for the sake of the artworks, could not be stinted on – proved to be one of the major problems because of the difficulties of installing the outlets in the required zones without damaging the original architecture. The

section at the top of the building had to be modified to accommodate the equipment and conduits installed in the chamber created between dividing walls.

As well as its functional importance, an architect's approach to lighting and acoustic control helps to give a gallery or museum its character. Amadó and Domènech point out that acoustics is a less overt, but no less important, contributor to the overall impression produced by a gallery than the quality of light. Their inspired attention to the sensory dimension of their conversion, while demonstrating due respect for the building's fabric, is a commendable achievement.

Architekturbüro Bolles-Wilson and Partner
Kita Griesheim-Süd
Frankfurt am Main, Germany

This project, designed by Peter Wilson and Julia Bolles-Wilson with Eberhard Kleffner, is a 'kita', the shortened word for *Kindertagestätte*, meaning children's day-care centre. It is part of an extensive and enlightened programme for new building in Frankfurt, involving eminent architects including Toyo Ito, Future Systems, Hans Kollhoff and Arup Associates who, in anticipation of future needs, have been invited by the city's Building Department to work on a series of sites within its bounds. The 'kita' centres fulfil an important social role, combining a kindergarten for pre-school children with a *Kinderhort*, a care facility providing lunch and activities for older children when school finishes at 1 p.m., while their parents are at work.

The long, narrow site is in a low-income housing area on the edge of the green belt between Frankfurt and Hoechst, with an autobahn close by. Its shape dictated a linear building with a basic form and orientation, closed on its northern, road-facing side and open to the south, with outdoor play spaces to which there is direct, controlled access from classrooms. The architects responded to the amorphous nature of the site's context by creating a clear, unambiguous, wedge-shaped form. Blank on its north side, the building's south elevation is full of lively geometric detail.

The 1,850-square-metre, two-storey building includes three classrooms for small children on the ground floor, with two group rooms above for older children to use for a variety of activities, including homework. The project also houses an office, staff rooms, kitchens (one each for adults and children), a general purpose hall and workshop.

Stringent cost control by the public authority (the project was actually completed under budget) meant that the pedagogical and safety requirements had to be creatively interpreted with plain materials such as plywood and steel. The project has a simple layout: at the entrance, the interior is divided into small rooms but these become progressively bigger as one moves through

Above: One of three ground-floor classrooms with adjoining toilets. The windows facing south, away from the road, have sections which can be opened at various heights.

Right: The upper floor can be entered from a steel access bridge in the playground, through the red door into this foyer space. The wooden staircase leads up to a bright lightwell and loft area.

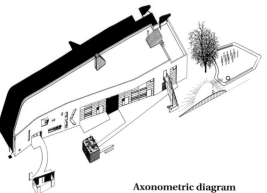

Axonometric diagram

the building until the large hall is reached. As the plan expands, the roof gradually rises in a slope. The building is full of distortions of scale, not wilfully applied but imaginatively interpreting a theme of the 'growing object', based on a child's developing perception of gradual changes in the scale of things.

The three ground-floor rooms open directly on to the play space. Two first-floor group and homework rooms also face south, connected to playgrounds by an external steel stair. At the upper level, dividing walls meet the ceiling as glass, which allows light to penetrate the entire depth of the building. Ancillary rooms fit into the corridor space like giant building blocks. At the centre, a giant green building block contains washrooms at ground level with azure-blue glass block windows that have an appealing 'fishbowl' quality; above, on an upper gallery, there is a 'hanging about' corner for older children.

The playful element, essential in a kindergarten, is introduced within the design through small details: windows in the south façade arranged to form a giant 'K'; paired doors, at child and adult scale; child's-height windows in the double-height passage. Both the children's kitchen, a volume of glazed bricks accessed via a light steel bridge at the end of the hall, and their washrooms, with blue glass block windows and irregular doors, have an expressive geometry, stimulating the imagination without overwhelming the user. Throughout the building, strong references to De Stijl are apparent in the abstract compositions of horizontal surfaces. Shapes in the linoleum floors encourage games and define territories.

The concept of the child's development has been interpreted allegorically throughout the building with both imagination and practicality, reflecting the architects' evident enjoyment of the way in which forms are put together, and their sensitivity to perceptual and physical growth. All the elements cohere into a harmonious composition which is easy to negotiate, creating a welcoming and lively environment which should inspire future 'kita' schemes.

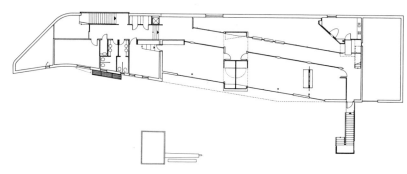

Ground-floor plan

Above: The calm colour scheme of the upper-floor classroom is conducive to homework and other quiet, creative activities. Washrooms at the end of the room feature azure-blue glass block windows.

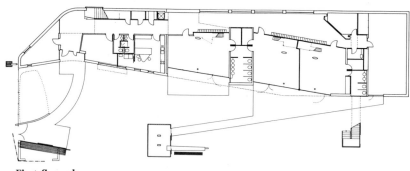

First-floor plan

Esteve Bonell and Francesc Rius
Badalona Sports Palace

Badalona, Barcelona, Spain

Right: The fluid circulation of the generously proportioned public spaces around the arena is enhanced by the robust and handsome industrial materials used.

The Badalona Sports Palace, conspicuously sited near a motorway out of Barcelona, is designed to hold 12,500 spectators at regular high competition basketball matches. Whilst the 150 x 120 metre project meets the functional and programmatic requirements of a sports building, the architects have also been motivated by the concept of a cathedral, in the sense of a building on a large scale for specific activities. The grand antecedent of the sports building, the arena, was kept very much in mind. However, its spatial power has been effectively translated into a strong, simple form appropriate for the 1990s.

Establishing a relationship with the surrounding urban structure was a priority for the architects, although the immediate context is, they admit, not ordered but lacking in expression or emblems, a heterogeneity 'provoked by economic speculation and urban vulgarity'. In such an environment it was important to create a very precise and bold building.

The structure of the Palace consists of two parts, one formalizing the central arena, the other organizing access and communication with the exterior. The arena is ellipsoid and two huge side elevations extend from the circular façade around this central shape, creating a graduated avenue, a strong visual focus which invites visitors into the building from the surrounding plaza. Changing and training rooms, press suites and stores are situated beneath the front steps, linked by two corridors which in turn are connected to the arena in four places. The entrance at one end faces the city, and the building's strongly directional nature and clear, autonomous form gives it a monumental quality.

The interiors reflect this clarity. The spectators walk along a circular ambulatory and a succession of corridors to reach the arena itself where, the architects hope, 'his emotions are aroused by its dimensions, proportions and light'. Two unbroken rings of plain concrete run horizontally around the expanse. To position some seats closer to the game, the ellipse was made into a shorter, broadened form, and four straight rows were

Left: Despite the massive scale of the sheet-steel trusses of its roof, the arena is magnificently ordered. The sprung, wood-strip sports floor, incorporating removable areas of seating, is surrounded by a plywood wall, and the two blend visually into each other, creating a strong nucleus.

Below left: The strong, simple, elliptical form of the sports centre reflects the arrangement of its interior – a central arena with facilities laid out rationally around it. The entrance is positioned at the open end of its longer axis, facing the city.

Below right: A wooden door between the basketball practice area and the dressing room shows the building's fine detailing.

inserted at right angles beneath the lower tiered ring and the sports floor. These are backed by a plywood wall. Bonell and Rius wanted to ensure that the arena had a strong identity, even when there was no competition taking place; when games are in progress, the geometry and pared-down detailing of the arena helps spectators and players to form a

bond. For the architects, each person is 'a unit within the space's grandness'.

The long corridors around the arena form an ambulatory which, with its generous proportions and fine views, is more like a street than simply an access route. Short ramps give access to the lower tier of seats, but also provide good views of the action. All the arena's public facilities, such as bars and toilets, are situated in a ring between the ambulatory and the arena itself. Access to the upper tier of seats is via regularly spaced series of stairs; openings with stairs to the plaza below also occur at regular intervals. The ambulatory is simply finished, with ceilings rising quite dramatically on the outer side, and from landings on the route to the upper tiers, panoramic views can be had of the open spaces beyond. Overall, the design demands a fair amount of climbing, but the visual compensations are many and access

from the ambulatory to the outside is made relatively easy.

The building's structure enables the visitor to engage with the game in progress, without drawing undue attention to itself. The roof lacks the light structure of Arata Isozaki's larger Olympic Palau Sant Jordi indoor sports arena on Montjuic – the scale of its huge sheet-steel trusses is massive; the arena, ambulatory and foyer spaces below are not seriously compromised, however.

This is not the first sports building the duo have designed: they won the FAD Architectural Prize in 1985 for their Horta Velodrome outside Barcelona. Badalona needed to be a 'low cost, quick construction' project. By giving the building good access for natural light and a clear construction using robust, industrial materials, the architects were able to 'control the internal ambience' of their sports palace for the masses.

Eduard Bru
Museo del Juguete
Ibi, Alicante, Spain

Toy-making has been one of Ibi's principal industries during the twentieth century, and an initiative by the City Council in the mid-1980s resulted in the creation of a local museum dedicated to toys – one which explores their social context and their evocative power, in a dramatic labyrinth of colour and light. This permanent display, which was designed by Eduard Bru with Neus Lacomba, and made by the Expografic design collective, is intended to provide 'a tour between reality and dream'.

Six hundred tin toys – many of them related to transport – were mostly gathered locally, with some exhibits from overseas, and their display emphasizes both what they represent in social-historical terms, and their manufacture. A lack of information about the dates and origins of the toys themselves meant that a chronological order was rejected. By stringing together a series of small geometric enclosures within semi-enclosed spaces linked with transitional display areas, Bru instead provides a developing sequence of thematically linked figurative environments, exploring subjects such as nature and rural life, mechanization, travel, speed, the city and the domestic world. This guiding thread is established via a series of economically constructed windows, display cases and niches inserted at a variety of heights.

The design is not simply an evolved, three-dimensional exercise in colour and abstract form: Bru's ordering of the interiors relates each room to the theme presented. In the section related to the natural and rural environment, for instance, dozens of types of horses and other means of farm transport are suspended from the ceiling of a green room within mesh cages of the same colour. For Bru, the green mesh and grid structure recalls the irrigated and cultivated plains of the Levant in the early twentieth century.

As it progresses, the sequence reflects the growing artificiality and mechanization of the world, with photographic images of expanding Levantine cities, and the noise of trams, cars and conversations in the background. These areas are intercut with rooms conveying social change in a more abstract way. One darkened, turquoise-hued room is animated by long, illuminated niches cut into the walls at diagonal angles which look as though they are jostling for position. Tiny rows of automobiles ride bumper-to-bumper along these slashed, perspectival channels of light. From within the subdued light of a room like this, another, much brighter chromatic environment in bright yellow or red can be glimpsed, a vivid rectangle framed by darker planes, beckoning the visitor forward.

The design of rooms showing larger and more powerful forms of transport draws on strongly lit, open-plan effects, such as a large glass cube with suspended aeroplanes casting shadows on an ice-blue backdrop. Finally, past a transitional zone with an acoustic backdrop of telephone conversation, warmer colours, soft textures and more enclosures signal the world of domesticity, with a room padded in vivid cerise velvet. Here exhibits are not immediately visible and have to be sought out, by exploring rectangular flaps on the walls which lift up to reveal the displays.

Left: In the room devoted to urban life, semi-relief vignettes of life in the expanding Levantine cities were created using blown-up photographs. The pink walls of the adjoining room convey privacy or the domestic scene, with tiny models of furniture and other household items hidden in wall niches, and faint sounds of telephone conversations relayed as an acoustic backdrop.

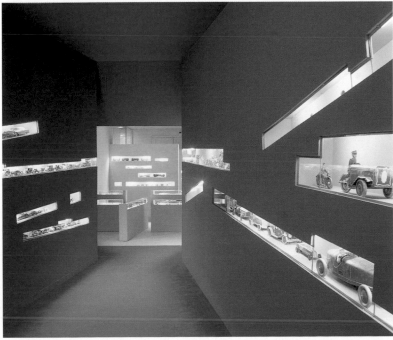

Left: Long lines of light shoot from the room displaying trains along more moodily hued walls which present the rapid development of the motor car. The long funnel-shape of the space emphasizes its speed-orientated theme.

Above: Looking past the glazed panels of the blue aviation room into the yellow room devoted to trains, with its linoleum floors, diagonal block display units and horizontal back-lit display niches. Bru's simple repertoire includes chipboard for the structure and floorboards, chicken wire and methacrylate for the display systems, and plastic swimming-pool flooring.

Henri Ciriani
Historial de la Grande Guerre

Peronne-Somme, France

The Historial of the Great War in Peronne is a historical and cultural museum designed to present its subject as a world-wide social phenomenon. A permanent committee of some forty expert historians representing over twelve countries was responsible for developing the museum's ambitious concept. Their aim was not to put on show a parade of military objects from one country, but to present museological displays with a widely gathered range of visual documentation and artefacts illustrating the events, myths and consequences of the war and incorporating the various perspectives of the countries, civilians and soldiers involved. This comparative approach to cultural history demanded a modern building capable of presenting the museum's narrative, whilst acting as a lively international study centre in the heart of the Somme. At the same time it was essential that the design expressed a sense of gravity and feeling in keeping with its theme.

After some years of discussion, the Conseil Général de la Somme decided in December 1986 to build the museum at the site of a medieval château close to the Lake Cam in Peronne, a location with a strong historic and symbolic significance. Two competitions were held, one of which was won by the architect Henri Ciriani, and one, for the museographic design, won by the firm Repérages. The project – Ciriani's biggest to date – cost a substantial 95 million francs, and was funded jointly by the Conseil Régional de Picardie, the French Ministry of Education and Culture and the European Regional Economic Development Fund.

'Architecture cannot symbolise or represent the absurdity of war', comments Ciriani. 'To represent a work of peace, architecture must draw on its own values to identify and display gravity ... and to achieve depth of feeling'. The white concrete and spare forms of his museum give the project a resolutely modern and distinctive style which expresses these qualities. From across the lake, the façades with their calm horizontal lines, flooded with light, look like petrified chalk rising from the water. They bear metaphorical traces: faint lines across the stone evoke trenches, while its bleached whiteness recalls the chalky soil of the area, punctuated at regular intervals with cylinders

The white concrete form of the museum, elegantly supported on stilts, reflected in the lake.

Beneath the raised structure of the museum there is a pleasant lakeside walkway.

of marble planted like crosses.

The new museum, barely touching the château next to it, sets up a respectful dialogue with the older building, which in turn helps to form its framework. The museum's presence completes the medieval layout, extending the building to the rear and providing a striking elevation on its western side. The picturesque surroundings include a community hall, a garden next to the lake, lakeside paths, a nature reserve and a banked open-air theatre.

The museum is built on a raft supported by stilts, with the reception, technical areas and a research centre on a lower level close to a lakeside walk. A long access ramp leading into the main foyer does not dramatize the entrance, but keeps it architecturally very simple. Ciriani did not want to create a 'musée-labyrinthe'; on the contrary, he wanted the visitor to know where he enters

and leaves: architecture's role, he feels, is to help us escape from our mental labyrinth.

Within the raised building are the galleries, an audio-visual gallery, documentation and research centre, restaurant, cafeteria, lecture hall and shops. Ciriani responds to the difficult challenge imposed by the brief, of organizing the museum's interior thematically, by creating the figure of a four-branched spiral surrounding an open axis.

At the centre of the plan is a portrait gallery, with three of its sides overlooking adjoining rooms; an opening on the fourth side provides access from the first museum hall. The areas around this dramatic central hall cover five main historical phases in turn, from before the war to its aftermath, in galleries occupying a total of 1,800 square metres. Around the walls of the rooms the chronological sequence of showcases presents themes and developments on a

The segmented shape of one of the main galleries provides a spacious environment in which to show documentation and artefacts related to the war. This room, with its strong curved wall, shows the acceleration of the conflict.

187

Right: Upper-floor plan, showing the access bridge from the château, and the four main exhibition galleries surrounding an open axis.

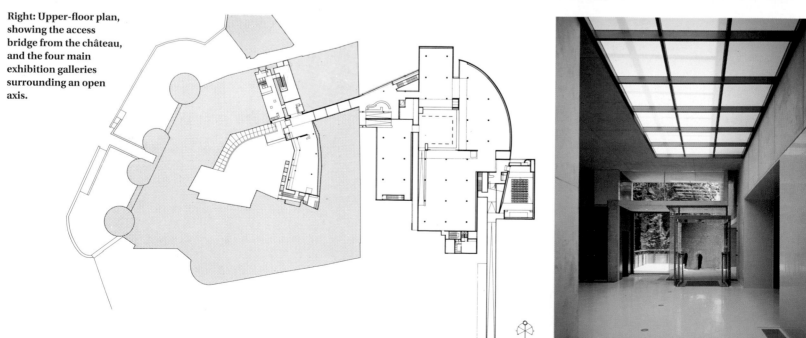

Above left: The rough brickwork of the château's old walls next to the gallery windows.

Left: The entrance foyer with its glazed ceiling panels. Internally the layout is simple, and Ciriani's spare aesthetic language respects the gravity of the museum's theme.

Above: The luminous light of the portrait room. The design firm Repérages took charge of the museological design, and their displays present a comparative, humanist approach to the war.

horizontal axis, with the nations co-ordinated vertically, enabling the visitor to compare their various attitudes.

At the heart of the open spaces, white marble settings for military clothing, equipment and personal possessions are displayed on a cutaway floor. Small display units punctuate the space with 'news from the front' and silent documentary films. Overhead lighting reinforces the territorial aspect of the Front, framing the exhibition spaces from behind and emphasizing items relating to the soldiers' lives.

The presence of slim support columns (43 centimetres in diameter) within the interiors gives a gallery such as the pre-war area, with its lateral rows, its own sense of stability. This is reflected by the presence at the windows of the rough brickwork of the château's perimeter walls. The close proximity of these old walls brings rays of light down into the

large gallery windows, an effect Ciriani describes as 'a tableau of transparency'. He aimed to give the openings around the façade a solid, shaded character, so that the visitor could look straight out of them. Light comes from above much of the time via roof-lights.

At the Historial, the architect has avoided the feeling of visual density and enclosure which, for more than just practical reasons, so often makes a museum interior a limited kind of space: like Le Corbusier, he treats the museum concept as an evolving one, not as a finished project.

In the same illuminating way that the museum treats the phenomenon it studies, Ciriani, instead of hiding his building away within its historic surroundings, raises it up close to the old château, allowing diffused light to enter its calm spaces.

Antonio Cruz and Antonio Ortiz
Santa Justa Railway Station

Seville, Spain

The Santa Justa station is one of the most important buildings to be constructed in Seville in recent years, and its location is equally significant. In spite of its relative proximity to the city centre, the area selected for the new project between the old inner city and its estates had hardly been touched by urban developments, with just an old abandoned goods station standing alone in a huge pocket of land. The city's railway networks were disorganized and obscured views across the river. As EXPO '92 was to be situated opposite, there was an opportunity for RENFE, the Spanish railway company, to create a new urban asset which, with railway tracks repositioned underground, would allow a clear view of the city's river front from the EXPO site.

The building of the new station was intended to trigger the conversion of the rest of this deserted area, a process which will be helped by new streets being constructed around its perimeter, linking adjacent but previously separated areas of the city. The architects' proposal to create a layout for the whole station block was accepted, permitting a series of three-storey buildings – railway company offices, a city bus stop, town council offices and housing – to be constructed close by. This would help to make sure that the station's immediate surroundings were appropriate neighbours in terms of their character and materials, even if the rest of the masterplan for the area was scheduled to be implemented at a later stage. The architects felt that the outward character of these perimeter buildings (not yet built) would also help ensure that the identity of the station complex related to, and helped extend, the surrounding urban fabric.

Cruz and Ortiz decided to give the station the grand identity of a traditional terminus translated into a modern idiom. The clarity in layout demanded of a terminus building was, they felt, better able to accommodate the variety of functions proposed by the clients (including retail outlets). Although the station is not actually a terminus (a small percentage of trains pass through a tunnel under the station on their way south to Cadiz), the architects nonetheless wanted to 'endow it with a certain metaphor or analogy of movement and arrival'. This is reflected in the U-shaped composition of the building, introduced visually by a huge, curved glass canopy over the main entrance.

The streets surrounding the station are built at a higher level (11.00 metres above ground level) than the tracks coming from the north (+8.40 metres). However, as tracks to the south go under the middle of the building, the main entrance and passenger hall were elevated even higher (+14.65 metres) above street level. The building settles on this large plaza, with escalators, staircases, ramps and elevators providing routes down to the platforms.

The downward thrust of the ramped escalators in particular gives the whole building a wonderful sense of movement which so many newer stations, with their clogged waiting spaces of indeterminate shape, seem to lack. This transit area leading to the platforms has a tremendous simplicity, with long, oval-section vaulted roofs which run above the tracks, tall lift shaft columns, and along the sides, brick walls pierced by secondary thoroughfare routes. So that access is not just from the top, gates opening from lateral streets are positioned at a mid-way point (+11.00 metres) on both sides of the station yard. These lead to an east-west walkway positioned transversally to the tracks, from which one can watch the movement down the escalators and beyond.

Six long, oval-section vaulted 'sheds' sheltering the railway platforms, each with its own character, are gathered together in this single, magnificently atmospheric space. Its suspended roof connects the passenger hall and entrance canopy. Structure is played down: the ways in which the huge spans of ceiling are supported is never made explicit, allowing the traveller to enjoy wide, unimpeded views. The building's large structures are covered either by sheet metal or panels of glazed concrete, which gives greater emphasis to other features of the

Top: Long platforms are sheltered by a vaulted metal roof. Filtered light enters the sweeping spaces via metal latticework at the sides of the vaults.

Above: Long, ramped travelators leading down from the concourse. The circulation spaces from the concourse to the platforms display great clarity, and the downward-thrusting routes give the whole U-shaped building a sense of movement.

Cross-section through the platform area

Below left: The high-ceilinged concourse, with light entering from above, provides a calm but uplifting atmosphere.

Overleaf: A wide view from the transversal walkway at the rear of the concourse. The oval-section vaulted sheds above the platforms are covered in sheet metal, part of a simple repertoire of functional construction materials which includes red Seville brick, concrete and slate.

design – the play of light and the simple palette of construction materials (red Seville brick surfaces, concrete walls, slate floors, light metal vaults). For the latter, the architects' choice was guided by the need for durability and low maintenance costs in a building subject to intensive and rough use.

The architects introduce daylight into the station in a number of ways, differentiating its spaces and providing a sense of sequence from one to another. Filtered light is allowed in via the lightweight vaults over each platform through their metal latticework at the sides rather than at the crown. At the front of the station, the high ceiling of the main hall with light entering from above creates a calm and sober atmosphere, and a wonderful sensation of raised space, after the more modestly proportioned entrance areas reached via the portico at the front of the station.

The main hall (at level +14.65, and accommodating ticket offices, passenger information offices and shops) is a large, prismatic space with a more static character than the rest of the station, appropriate to its role. Its natural lighting is carefully handled, and its open volume, with clear vistas of the platforms beyond, avoids any sense of being disorientated or hemmed in. Some of its porches and exterior galleries repeat the circulation pattern, providing passengers with either direct access to a given spot from the street, or rapid exit from it.

The shopping areas on this floor are easily accessible, but juxtaposed to the main passenger routes in order to retain the station's functional identity. More compact shopping areas are sensibly positioned on higher levels (+19.15 and +23.65 metres), partially hidden by brick walls, and add to the facilities provided, without conflicting with the building's main function. The clarity of the design, its exceptionally well-conceived layout and restrained use of materials are exemplary features of the station, enabling it to function as an attractive hub of activity within the city.

Foster Associates
Stansted Airport Terminal

Stansted, UK

In recent years airport terminal design has become so dominated by commercial considerations that the jaded traveller frequently wastes precious time negotiating a maze of shops, cafés and bars. Even when these consumer services are presented in a restrained fashion, dozens of cardinal sins continue to be committed in the name of rational planning (wearisome artificial lighting; confusing signage; hopelessly attenuated corridors to gates, to name just a few). It is refreshing to see a return to basics at the new terminal at Stansted, the third London airport, which fits its advertising image of 'the world class airport', and contrasts with the less successful adjustments at Heathrow.

The project is situated at the south-east end of the runway (exceeding 3,000 metres in length), 32 miles north of London, with a new direct rail link. It provided the opportunity to reconsider the configuration of an airport terminal building from first principles. The masterplan has orderly and clearly defined zones for its various activities, and the terminal design matches this rational layout, aspiring to a simplicity and convenience which characterized the earliest flying era.

The brief called for a solution that would be cheaper than previous BAA terminals at Heathrow and Gatwick, provide better passenger convenience and allow flexibility for future change and growth (there is enough land within the terminal zone to expand from 8 million passengers a year – over 700 flights per week – to almost double that amount). It was also important that the building did not intrude on the gentle Essex landscape.

All public amenities are provided on a single concourse floor, with arrivals and departures facilities occupying the east and west sides respectively. This creates a compact building and reduces walking distances for passengers, enabling them to take simple linear routes of no more than 160 metres through the building. To give the airport the required degree of flexibility for development, all the passenger facilities on the concourse, such as shops, banks,

kitchens, left luggage, toilets and medical facilities, have been designed as free-standing enclosures or cabins which can easily be dismantled. The simplicity of the interior has been achieved by banishing services usually contained within the ceiling to an undercroft containing the baggage handling and environmental plant.

The structural columns at concourse level are set on a 36-square-metre grid defined by the needs of the terminal, in particular the check-in. This also makes the layout of the passenger floor level as flexible as possible. The supports for the tree-like roof form structures are made up of clusters of four interconnected tubular steel columns and are angled 4 metres above the concourse in order to reduce the structural spacing at roof level to an 18-square-metre grid. The light appearance of the roof was achieved by using lattice shell domes rising to a height of 15 metres above the concourse; in this way the need for heavy roof trusses or beams was avoided. All services distribution equipment for the concourse is contained within boxes at the base of the clusters of columns. The sides of the boxes act as focal points, displaying all the travel information passengers need.

An abundance of natural light enters the concourse via the fully glazed cladding of the walls and via roof-lights in the lattice domes, giving the space a welcome sense of calmness and airiness. After dark, it is lit indirectly by a lighting system designed in collaboration with Claude Engle. This concentrates on light reflected from the internal surface of the roof and, as a result no harsh light sources can be seen from the outside: the building just glows gently. The same indirect lighting system is used to illuminate the landside passenger set-down area on the forecourt and track transit stations positioned under the roof canopies.

The 15-metre-high terminal has an assertive, easily recognizable but low profile from the exterior. The main floor level is set on the existing ground-floor at the top of a natural rise in the ground, and 12-metre-high eaves match the height of trees in the surrounding landscape. The two main

Above: An exterior view of the entrance forecourt of the shed terminal.

Right: Detail of a services pod with information system.

The baggage reclaim hall. The visible structural system is made up of central spans and cantilever supports in the form of tree-like structures with clusters of interconnected tubular steel columns. The design of the roof-light shades in this passive solar energy building break up individual areas of light into mobile patches. The east wall is constructed with translucent white glass, giving a calm and subdued visual effect.

elevations are fully glazed, with deep canopies providing sun shading and eliminating reflections in the glass walls. The side elevations are made of translucent white glass above pale grey metal panels, with a low horizontal band of transparent glazing separating the two at concourse level. The building is not just superficially attractive: it was substantially cheaper to build than any other airport dealing with the same capacity of passengers. It is also said to be about 33 per cent more energy efficient than any other British airport terminal.

The flexibility required within the scheme did not prevent the architects from paying attention to the design of fittings. The check-in desks are solid structures incorporating polished granite and stainless steel. They have removable elements, so that they can be coverted for use as car rental booths, immigration or information desks. The cabins

forming the offices, shops and cafés adhere to a similar 'kit of parts' principle, and are sensibly scaled so that sightlines across the concourse are not impeded. The signage – which was developed in conjunction with Pentagram – makes for swift, confident circulation.

Materials are noticeably high quality and robust, with wide use of stainless steel, and polished granite floors (in the landside area). The café, with its Arne Jacobsen chairs and Brian Clarke's stained glass column and wall panels, is a tastefully attired space. A few evident compromises forced upon the architects – including the jarringly mixed signage now appearing in the shopping mall running through departures at the centre of the concourse – stand out amidst a highly logical and impressive public building which thoughtfully reassesses the needs of international travellers.

Right: Detail of a roof-light. Suspended triangular metal panels filter and cut off the glare of direct light which is reflected from the shallow, lattice shell domes, and bounce light back on to the ceiling to create a halo of reflected light.

Below: Information pods are housed in the structural 'tree trunks'.

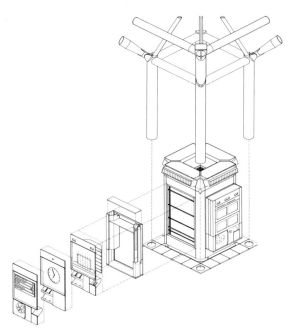

1 Departures concourse
2 Check-in
3 Security/passport control
4 Departure lounge
5 Shopping area
6 Catering zone
7 Domestic channel
8 Arrivals/immigration control
9 Baggage reclaim hall
10 Customs
11 Arrivals concourse
12 Management offices
13 Forecourse: coach and taxi drop-off point with railway station below
14 Track transit platforms to satellite
15 Airside coach stations
16 Track transit system
17 Short-term car park and coach station

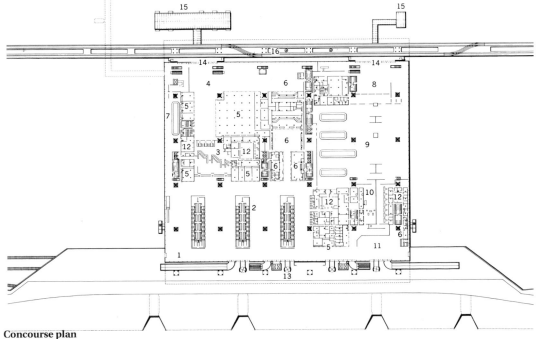

Concourse plan

Sir Norman Foster and Partners
The Sackler Galleries, Royal Academy of Arts
London, UK

Burlington House on Piccadilly has been home to the Royal Academy of Arts, one of Britain's finest exhibition venues and a unique art institution, since 1869. It is actually not one building but two, one behind the other. When the Academy moved into the seventeenth-century building, its lease stipulated that another storey be added and a new gallery be constructed behind the main building on the site of an old garden. This main gallery was started in 1867, and three Diploma Galleries were also added to Burlington House as an extra floor to house Diploma shows.

Visitors were unaware of the 4.2-metre gap separating the original house and the main galleries, since the grand staircase rises up from the entrance hall to the main galleries at first-floor level, bridging the two parts of the building. Together with a new scheme for the Diploma Galleries, it is this mysterious area, bounded by the two external façades, which has been reanimated by Sir Norman Foster and Partners' intelligent masterplan, a project which combines conservation with new construction.

Access to the original Diploma Galleries has never been very practical or pleasant: a small, winding staircase and antiquated

lift to the right of the entrance hall made them unappealing as a venue for special exhibitions. In addition, poor environmental controls made them virtually unusable during the summer months. Lord Burlington's suite of rooms on the first floor has been used in preference, but these important, historic interiors were equally unsuitable as exhibition spaces, lacking the robustness and flexibility needed for a busy programme of events. Their location also made it necessary to move the works up from basement storage areas through the crowded entrance hall.

By the early 1980s, dramatically increased attendances, rising expectations of exhibition presentation and a need for better environmental controls to conserve valuable works of art had made expanded, modern facilities essential. Roger de Grey, who became President in 1984, made it a priority to bring the Diploma Galleries back into regular use by some form of conversion. As it receives no government support, the Royal Academy had to raise money to finance this latest alteration, and the initial brief to the architects was accordingly quite modest in scope, with remodelled galleries, and a new lift to improve circulation. Sir Norman Foster and Partners began work on the building

in 1985, and during the same year Arthur Sackler, an American philanthropist, became involved with the project. His funds made it possible to expand substantially the brief for the Galleries, which became the Sackler Galleries, bearing the name of Sackler (who died in 1987) and his wife Jill.

The architects' scheme transforms the unseen gap between the original house and the main galleries into a brightly lit fulcrum. Doorways now open on to a new staircase and lift which link all five floors of the building, with direct access to the Sackler Galleries and the library at the top, and to the restaurant at ground level. The new construction in the gap is free-standing, with a glazed edge at each level which brings light down on to two previously hidden façades: the classical garden front of the original Burlington House (remodelled by Samuel Ware in 1815), and the stone parapet of Sidney Smirke's main galleries, notable for its blind arcading, carved ropework and *oeil de boeufs*.

A glazed lift car and a glass staircase, with a distinctly modern, late-twentieth-century character, give the space a new lease of life. As Foster puts it, one is 'made aware of the new so that one is more appreciative of the old'. Their construction involved the removal of

Right: Sculpture positioned in the new second-floor reception to the Sackler Galleries.

Left: In the Sackler Galleries, simple, barrel-vaulted ceilings echo the form of the main galleries, and central roof-lights provide UV light filtration. Fin-shaped louvres running longitudinally down the galleries control light intensity and contain tracks for artificial lighting.

the old cantilevered stone stair and lift up to the Galleries. Foster and the Royal Academy were able to convince English Heritage that this was justified on the grounds that these elements had been injudiciously applied to Burlington House in the first place. Their removal would, it was clear, permit the introduction of a vastly improved and well-lit circulation scheme for the movement of people (including vertical access for the disabled) and works of art. The renovation work was also considered essential: the badly damaged wall to Burlington House was restored to its classical form under the supervision of Julian Harrap Architects, appointed as historic buildings consultant.

The architects' masterplan aimed to ensure that the existing building was interfered with as little as possible, and the new lift, stair and floors are structurally independent. The glass hydraulic lift and light, elegant staircase in steel with sand-blasted glass treads, are structures with a strongly transparent character, which do not impede natural light. Extensive use of glass as the margins of the floors further opens up the dark space.

The three Diploma Galleries, the main impetus behind the scheme, have been completely rebuilt. Originally on two levels with flat ceilings and pitched roof-lights, their existing roofs were demolished, and new, simple, barrel-vaulted ceilings with central roof-lights inserted, echoing the form of the main galleries. A uniform floor level has been established to improve circulation, and full controls over temperature, humidity and air movement now provide a sound, robust exhibition environment. Air-handling units are sited on the roof over the lightwell, and the ductwork is concealed behind the ceiling along each side of the gallery. The roof-lights provide UV light filtration, with fritted glass to reduce the overall amount of light transmission. Electronically controlled louvres running longitudinally down the galleries provide a further degree of natural light control. Their light, airy spaces are reached through a new glazed reception area

Above: Long view of the reception to the Sackler Galleries. A glass bridge links the display area for Michelangelo's tondo, which has its own niche, to the meeting space.

Right: The new glazed staircase at the western end of the converted lightwell allows light to spill down through the floors. The Burlington House garden façade was renovated.

On the top floor of the converted lightwell – now the reception to the Sackler Galleries – the parapet of the old building has become a display space for sculpture. At the far end, a glass hydraulic lift shoots up between two lift support columns.

Bottom: Detail showing the steel structure and sand-blasted glass treads of the staircase.

1 New external fire escape
2 Glass bridge
3 Sackler Galleries (originally the Diploma Galleries)
4 Gallery for Michelangelo's tondo
5 Sculpture shelf
6 New hydraulic glass lift
7 Full-height void
8 Library
9 New glass staircase

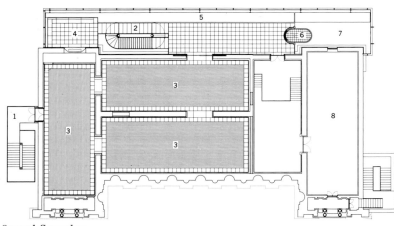

Second-floor plan

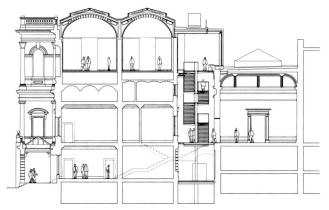

North-south cross-section

at the top level of the gap. They are also accessible via a staircase on the floor below which leads off from the building's main vestibule on the first floor, now the hub of the circulation system, giving access to the main galleries, Sackler Galleries and the restaurant.

The Sackler Galleries' reception space, transformed by Foster's modern aesthetic, is a long, narrow area with side lighting, which reveals itself dramatically to visitors arriving by stair or by lift and encourages informal congregation. The popularity of the new galleries demands a second lift, but limitations of space make this unfeasible. From a position close to the lift at the edge of this level, the full extent of the vertical volume being utilized is visible, crowned by the lightwell closed in by a wall of translucent glass. The quality of detailing is high and in an

imaginative use of space, sculpture from the Academy's permanent collection is displayed along the parapet like a frieze. This display area is linked to the main reception floor by a narrow glass strip which provides a dramatic view through the levels.

In 1993 the project was judged RIBA Building of the Year. The National Awards jury commented as follows: 'It is a pleasure to see an architect at the height of his powers teasing a piece of architecture out of a much needed and eminently sensible piece of micro planning. At the Sackler Galleries, like all the best conjurors, he [Sir Norman] has extracted the maximum effect from a very shallow hat. It is particularly rewarding to produce a late 20th-century gem that dignifies the work of Samuel Ware and Sidney Smirke without artifice or compromise.'

Tony Fretton
Lisson Gallery
London, UK

Below: The building's huge glass windows provide transparent elevations dramatically exposing the artworks displayed within. The lower gallery is directly engaged with the street. The pavement lights can be pulled out to allow works to be moved down to the basement gallery.

Right: The linking of the existing and new gallery spaces provided a versatile environment in which to show differing exhibitions of two- and three-dimensional works.

The new Lisson Gallery at 52 Bell Street in London's Marylebone presents an uncommonly open face to the world, with two huge glass windows fronting ground- and first-floor exhibition spaces. Since the gallery was founded in 1967, director Nicholas Logsdail has successfully promoted many minimal and conceptual artists, including Carl Andre, Sol LeWitt, Donald Judd, Art and Language, Richard Long, and more recently sculptors such as Tony Cragg, Richard Deacon, Bill Woodrow and Anish Kapoor. The new space, designed by architect Tony Fretton, represents a major expansion from existing premises (which he also converted in 1986), doubling the overall exhibition space to create one of the largest purpose-built private galleries in Britain.

The existing premises occupy an eighteenth-century townhouse, whose frontage is next door but one on Lisson Street, just around the corner, and the architect has constructed a pivotal, first-floor link between the two. For Logsdail, new galleries did not mean lavish spending on enormous, daunting spaces like those which sprang up in New York during the art boom of the 1980s. Instead he wanted a building with flexible spaces, possessing some degree of intimacy and continuing the ambience of the existing premises.

The building occupies a 7 x 7-metre site, with its main entrance and staircase to the left of the glass frontage. A narrow passage leads to a front-facing gallery sunk below ground at the same level as the main gallery of the first phase, down to a basement exhibition space, and up to a first-floor gallery and reception, and two rooms above this designated as apartments for visiting artists. The two phases connect at lower-ground and first-floor levels (a long, linking reception room runs across the roof to the existing gallery), but their separate entrances make it possible to show different exhibitions simultaneously.

The staircase which links the galleries, with its functional metal and glass balustrades, possesses the down-to-earth quality of a modern domestic interior. The composition and treatment of the gallery spaces is similarly restrained, with entrances positioned unobtrusively in the corners of each of the concrete-floored rooms, and uplighters supplementing natural light. As with the first conversion, Fretton tried to prevent functional elements like fan heaters from looking like works of art. However, he does not adopt a full-blown 'form-follows-function' approach: details such as framed sky-lights above the reception assert a quiet elegance, while other, quite mundane elements are given an almost surrealist touch.

The exterior is a different story, though still subtle. The upper gallery is only 2.74 metres above pavement level; the sunken effect of the lower gallery at the front (about 90 centimetres below pavement level) makes its relationship with the street a more humble one than that normally asserted by commercial galleries, enabling passers-by to look down on the art on display there. The basement gallery is lit by a row of pavement lights which can be pulled out to allow large works to be lifted into the basement.

From the street, both the structure of the volume and the depth of its interior spaces are clearly visible through an extensive glass

façade. This front elevation repeats the scale of the main façade elements of the adjoining building, imitating its arrangements of shop front and doorways. The presence of so much glass gives the building 'a hollow, diagrammatic quality, resembling a rack', Fretton feels, on which work is displayed 'directly against the street', and this produces a closer visual and this relationship between interior and exterior. Some artists, used to enclosed spaces, find this disconcerting. For the visitor, the overall effect is to link art and the everyday world (a screen system, with studding, has been designed in case it should be necessary to close the gallery off from the street). Fretton's rigorous and durable design comments on the distanced relationship between the art world and the wider community. The building is bold architecturally, without being intrusive or alienating in its composition or outward demeanour. For Fretton the design is an optimistic, forward-looking one and, he feels, contemporary art should share its sense of engagement.

Although the design of the interior, with its absence of detail, has an affinity with some of the minimalist work the Lisson shows (elements such as the floor grid, for example), its treatment and utilitarian finishes strongly reflect Fretton's assertion that 'in an art gallery, architecture mustn't refer to itself'. Neutrality is neither desirable, nor achievable, and instead a priority is the 'need to make strong, coherent backgrounds' which are not rhetorical or sculptural, but which speak qualitatively, with plain materials enhanced by light. This is a restrained solution, which gives art full rein – something of a challenge: 'a gallery should look empty when it's empty, and just-right when it's full,' remarks Fretton.

Beth Galí, Màrius Quintana and Antoni Solanas
Joan Miró Library

Barcelona, Spain

The ground-floor library space has a long line of south-facing windows overlooking the lake in the direction of the park. The bookshelves are arranged radially along an orderly curve, facing this view. Huge perforated steel baffle screens, from which slim rods of low-voltage lighting are suspended, conceal beams, curving outwards over the lake, and inwards above the reading areas. The wooden library furniture was sourced from Gama, and the flooring is a highly varnished industrial parquet made of warm red eucalyptus.

The Joan Miró Park is located on the site of an old slaughterhouse between the edge of the Eixample and the old neighbourhood of Hostafrancs. It was built in 1982, an early step in the urban reconstruction of Barcelona which has been taking place over the last decade. The new 1,200-square-metre library for the city was completed in 1990, the result of a national competition held in 1981 and won by Beth Galí, Màrius Quintana and Antoni Solanas. An island of learning surrounded by a lake, and at the same time a gateway to the park, it lies in a clearing on the edge of the park, in keeping with its natural tranquillity, but at the same time clearly part of the urban hierarchy.

The architects wanted the outward character of the library to denote its role as a container of books, in much the same way that the great public libraries of the nineteenth and early twentieth centuries did, for example, as Asplund's library in Stockholm, Labrouste's Bibliothèque Ste Geneviève in Paris and Boullée's projects for the Bibliothèques du Rois, also in Paris. The blind, north-facing stone façade of the Miró library solemnly reflects this tradition, with solid walls sufficiently robust to support the weight of the book stacks which run its length on the other side.

The main access to the park is on an axis with one of the streets of the Cerdà grid and divides the library building into two symmetrical wings – one for adults and one for children. The two porches are brightened by sunlight reflected on the tall, narrow stone slabs like fins positioned along the approach to the library. A route on the outer sides of the fins provides access to the two library wings and, at an upper level, follows a mezzanine along a glass catwalk crossing the porches. The inner route between the walls is a boarded walk, rather narrow for comfort, which gives access to the park straight through the site, without entering the library. At each edge of the two wings, the roof extends over the building to create porches for reading in the open air alongside reproductions of some of Miró's unfinished bronzes; unfortunately, these idyllic study areas have given the library a few security problems and have been slightly adjusted.

Looking at the building in section, with its north-south orientation, pitched roof slanted on one side and mezzanine, it is clear that the architects have encouraged natural light to enter on both sides. The main reading room, facing south, with its radial bookshelves placed along a curve close to a long glass window, opens towards the park, but a sense of distance is maintained by the reflective sheet of water in between. The wide eaves of the roof protect the interior from the direct rays of the sun and filter the incoming light, which is relayed into the calm workspaces with a shimmering but controlled brightness.

The architects have differentiated the adults' and children's sections: on the right, the front of the gallery allows for a curtained-off area for children, and a bank of stepped seating for story readings is included. However, in general the layout is similar, with both sides benefiting from a rational design, with radiating shelves and good natural light.

The north façade is an enclosing blind wall made necessary by the orientation of the building and placement of the book stacks. By contrast, the south façade, looking on to the park, captures the light via a continuous glass wall along which reading tables are

Above: The entrance to the east wing of the building, showing its pitched roof and the connecting glass-floored bridge for staff to cross between the two wings to the mezzanine study area.

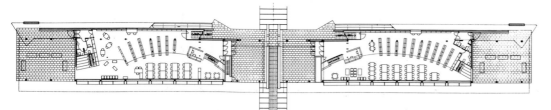

Ground-floor plan

204

positioned. The varied nature of the building in section shows that the architects aimed to create a container for undefined, flexible uses – an interior with a dynamically curved mezzanine which enriches the various vistas.

Galí, Quintana and Solanas have also introduced some unusual small-scale elements which mix the language of art with their architectural forms: hanging metal lighting fixtures have the appearance of mobiles; the chicken-mesh ceiling has 'arte povera' connotations; and the entrance gate depicts children running to the library carrying books. These details may or may not actually enhance the process of learning, but they give the library an individuality that its symmetry can easily accommodate.

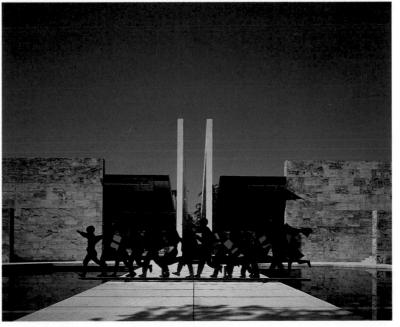

The main approach to the symmetrical library building, surrounded by a lake and sited between the city and the park. Two white stone slabs flank entrance porches to the adults' and children's sections (east and west, respectively). The route between the walls leads to the park behind. A mobile, steel-painted 'gate' at the entrance depicts a line of children running with books.

Gwathmey Siegel & Associates
The Guggenheim Museum
New York, USA

The Guggenheim Museum cost a cool $50 million to expand, and there has been wide debate as to whether Frank Lloyd Wright's masterpiece – which itself was the culmination of a 16-year-long design process and was finally unveiled posthumously in 1959 to a mixed reception – has been saved or compromised by Gwathmey Siegel's new additions, which took two years to complete. The museum felt that expansion was essential: in the early 1980s, no more than 3 per cent of the 5,000 works in the permanent collection could be displayed at any one time; it also desperately needed more space for offices, storage and conservation, but was reluctant to move these activities off the site.

A full-blown Guggenheim expansion has now taken place in Manhattan: a new 50,000-square-foot annexe has opened in SoHo, designed by Arata Isozaki, with a separate facility for support services on the West Side, and 10,000 square feet of offices have been created beneath the streets adjoining the museum. For the on-site expansion of the Guggenheim, Gwathmey Siegel presented a number of proposals, the merits of which were discussed by architects, historians and preservationists before a third, modified scheme was accepted in 1989. This new phase of expansion nearly triples the exhibition space, bringing the total to 80,000 square feet.

The architects aimed to work with the basic formal intentions of the original Wright masterplan of 1949, which included a gridded, rectilinear, high-rise building in the north-east corner of the site, never built due to lack of funds. This contrasted with the seamless, curvilinear volumes of the large spiral rotunda alongside it to the south, and the small rotunda (the monitor building) to the north-west. The 'compelling geometric order' of the two concrete rotundas provided a regulating factor in the architects' new tripartite arrangement. This incorporated their own gridded, limestone-clad, ten-storey high-rise block (a conversion of the storage wing of the 1968, four-storey Taliesin annexe) on the site with the existing rotundas,

Above: The renovated interior spaces of the small rotunda, with Wright's projected cornice encircling the edge of the ceiling. The triangular lighting fixtures are recreations of Wright's originals; the gridded glass wall and bronze railing are new elements designed by Gwathmey Siegel.

Right: The newly defined composition of the Guggenheim Museum, with a gridded high-rise wing behind the two rotundas.

housing staff in its upper floors and creating additional exhibition space on the lower floors.

The backdrop of the new wing (a tactful and refined version, reduced in height to decrease the degree of intrusion into the Guggenheim's visual field) introduces a comparatively prosaic element next to Wright's dramatic rotunda. However, the architects' adjustments to the interiors of the two rotundas have given much more scope for exhibiting art, and have created dramatically ameliorated lighting conditions in the large rotunda. Its seventh-floor ramp, which completes the spectacular quarter-mile-long ascension from the entrance foyer, has been opened as a processional route to and from the new building.

One of the most practical and badly needed aspects of the architects' renovation of the rotunda was the repair of the skylight dome, sealed off to provide storage space even before the building was officially opened. New double-glazed skylights and a refurbished laylight with thermal glass have been installed, and in the 18-inch space between the two there is a new climate control system. The result is an environment washed with natural light. The plaster walls of the rotunda were stripped down to the outer concrete shell, and replastered by hand in dazzling white. Other improvements include newly opened roof decks, allowing visitors to climb out on to a sculpture garden. Also on the agenda are plans to reopen Wright's original exterior ramp down to the basement auditorium, which is being restored.

The revival of the small rotunda, the 'monitor' building, formerly containing offices, is particularly successful. It has created graceful new galleries, an enlarged museum shop and a new restaurant. For Charles Gwathmey, the renovation asserts the connection between Wright's original design and his prairie houses, with glazed horizontal pavilions reaching out towards nature, in this case Central Park. It also provides a new circulation route connecting with the galleries on the lower floor of the addition and the large rotunda. The architects have adapted Wright's designs for oak ticket and information desks and benches.

Using as a precedent Wright's double-height 'high gallery' planned to be sited next to the main rotunda, the architects' own nearly windowless, gridded structure contains two-storey galleries (providing spaces totalling 30,000 square feet) on the second and fifth floors of the new building, from which Central Park can be seen. They may lack the idiosyncratic power of the rotunda exhibition spaces, but their modern environments provide the Guggenheim with a much greater curatorial flexibility, freeing up the original building.

Ever since the Guggenheim opened in 1959, artists and curators have differed strongly in their views of the suitability of the sloping wall heights on the large rotunda's spiral ramps. What for some are compelling, atmospheric spaces, for others provide irritatingly restricted horizontal distances for viewing. The undulating enclosures of Wright's design were judged impossible to qualify within the existing envelope, and thus the onus was on the architects to invest the new galleries with airy, double-height spaces, devoid of mezzanines, which they had proposed in an earlier scheme, but which were rejected prior to construction.

The power of Wright's 'creation', as he referred to it in the 1950s, has not been weakened in the process of the museum's expansion. Brendan Gill, a friend and biographer of Wright, writing in *The New Yorker* of 27 July 1992, asserts that 'the Guggenheim has never before come so close to being the structure that Wright in his last years has hoped to see and never saw', and now 'radiates an inimitable joyous quiddity'. For Charles Gwathmey, 'these new layers encourage exploration and rediscovery of the Wright building in a way that was previously impossible. Moving in and out of the original building varies the spatial experience, while it reinforces the intention and spirit of Wright's masterpiece.'

Seventh-floor plan

Second-floor plan

Below: The wing-like form of the small rotunda's prominent cornice within its intimately scaled galleries.

Far right: Before its renovation, the Guggenheim's small rotunda contained administrative offices. The architects removed interior partitions and refurbished the original skylight.

Bottom: Transitional space between the new galleries and the main rotunda.

Hans Hollein
Museum für Moderne Kunst

Frankfurt am Main, Germany

Neutral space doesn't exist', says Hans Hollein. 'Good gallery architecture acts as the utensil, dwelling – and catalyst of art. The visitor perceives architecture via art, and art via architecture.' Art has broken away from the pedestal and the frame, and is now characterized by more complex installations which frequently involve new media and found objects. Showing these multi-dimensional projects to their best advantage, he feels, therefore requires a 'matrix-like' gallery structure which the visitor can explore freely, rather than 'linear or chronological enfilades' with limited views. For Hollein, the forming of a dialogue or direct confrontation between the work of art and the building is an essential characteristic of a gallery display.

The Museum für Moderne Kunst in Frankfurt, which cost DM48 million to build, was initiated in 1985 after Hollein's design for the project won an international competition. The architect has had a long involvement with museum buildings and with art, and his most recent attempt to produce a *Gesamtkunstwerk* satisfying the needs of both has been largely judged a success.

Because of its triangular shape and complex exterior curves and details, the museum was immediately likened to a wedge of cake, but the design (creating 4,150 square metres of floor space) undoubtedly makes the best possible use of a difficult site. Despite its cramped location, sandwiched between the cathedral and dull blocks of post-war buildings in the old Stauferstadt district, the museum asserts a strong identity.

The main entrance is positioned on a corner, 1.5 metres above street level, with a ground-floor café animating the street on its right. The pale red sandstone façade with its rather sickly rose-coloured granite features (such as the arcaded façade in front of the café) is full of detailing which plays on symmetry and asymmetry, and each side presents a different character. However, the interior spaces within have been deftly handled, producing a dynamic environment of powerfully articulated volumes, full of cross views of the works and carefully framed glimpses of the world outside.

The museum's collection of installations, many groups of work by one artist or single works requiring one room to themselves, makes for concentrated viewing. It aims to show connections between its collections of art from the 1960s and the present day, and stimulating juxtapositions play each other off in the differentiated volumes of the galleries.

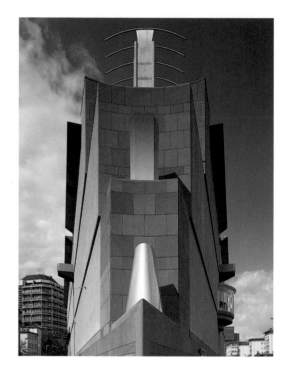

Left: View from the third-floor bridge linking exhibition rooms, above lower galleries accessed by curved staircases leading from the main hall.

Above: The view from the north-east of the east elevation and apex of the triangular, pale red sandstone museum building, between Braubach Strasse and Berliner Strasse, looking up to part of Hollein's aluminium, stainless and copper-clad roofscape.

Right: Level 3: The view from the east, showing works by Andy Warhol and a curved window.

Below: A basement lecture room, seen from the south-west.

Below right: The view from the west into the main hall, with works by Thomas Ruff and a huge, double-glazed roof-light with automatic louvres. The galleries are mostly a combination of light grey marble (Clauzetto) or waxed oak floors,

gypsum plaster walls and gypsum board and acoustic tiled ceilings, with white triple-layer security sandwiched glass.

The elevation of the entrance hall establishes its independence from the café positioned unobtrusively alongside, to which it has access. The hall, with its light grey marble floor and stuccolustro walls, is a small, simply finished area. Hollein did not want to rely on 'intimidating', high, vertical staircase shafts for access, but provides imaginatively inserted access routes which encourage an 'experiential diagonal penetration' of the building.

Service and administration space is concentrated on the ground floor, close to the entrance and next to a square temporary exhibition space. Marble-floored galleries of a variety of sizes are situated at the far corner of the triangle, and on levels above around a central double-height space. There is no fixed circulation around the floor levels (three, plus a mezzanine), but many round walks are possible using alternative staircase routes. The clustering of spaces, interspersed with smaller niches for video works, provides a variety of vistas and interconnecting areas.

The design concept is not intended to accommodate rapidly changing shows, and its strengths are geared to the contemporary nature of the collection and the displays, which are in place for about a year before

1 Collection
2 Installations
3 Main hall
4 Foyer
5 Service
6 Café
7 Temporary exhibitions
8 Administration entrance
9 Main entrance
10 Double-height space

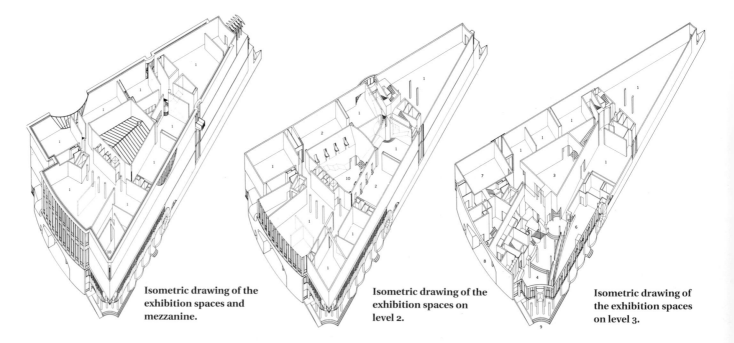

Isometric drawing of the exhibition spaces and mezzanine.

Isometric drawing of the exhibition spaces on level 2.

Isometric drawing of the exhibition spaces on level 3.

they are changed. The way in which rooms are grouped allows curatorial links to be made between works spanning twenty or thirty years, for instance, with the rooms showing works by Bernd and Hilla Becher, Gerhard Richter and On Kawara. The museum's openness also allows interconnecting spheres of activity to become almost an enclosed, 'climatic zone', as with the areas with works by Schnabel, Clemente, Trockel and Balkenhol.

Daylight and artificial light both play important roles in the museum: in the roof-light areas, there is a system which simulates natural light. In artificially lit areas, the structural layout and ceiling thicknesses are designed to provide various lighting effects, depending on the needs of the artworks. New linear wall washers flood the walls with light from floor to ceiling; however, some areas are primarily illuminated by roof-lights or side lights.

The German museum curator Heinrich Klotz, writing at the time of the museum's opening, welcomed it as both 'calm and manifold, neutral and idiosyncratic'. For those who do not find the theatricality of the interior, with its striking views and central staircase with ascending and descending flights, conducive to contemplation, he pointed out the 'contrast between approach and destination' in the museum's design, which allows the 'calming influence and appropriateness of the exhibition rooms' to be felt 'all the more intensely'.

Toyo Ito & Associates
Yatsushiro Municipal Museum
Kumamoto Prefecture, Japan

Yatsushiro is 40 kilometres south of Kumamoto City in a very flat, natural setting with the ocean to the west, mountains to the east and a river running through the middle. Since the Edo period it has been a major cultural centre in the Kyushu area of Japan. The new museum there is one of the first major projects of the 'Art-Polis' programme being sponsored by Kumamoto Prefecture to develop the area as a centre of culture. It has been built to house the city's historic artefacts, previously stored in several locations.

The site is within parkland close to the dilapidated Yatsushiro castle, opposite Shohin-ken, a one-storey, Edo-period villa owned by the family who governed the area at the time. Architect Toyo Ito was initially struck by the horizontal profile of the villa which echoed the flatness of the site. As overpowering volumes in such a landscape were strictly forbidden, he began to plan the building on a low-rise scale, but the programme and ratio of building to site area required a volume at least three storeys high.

Ito was determined to avoid the conventional massiveness of museum buildings; instead he has created a bright ground-floor space with plenty of natural light and a multi-vaulted, steel-frame roof similar to those at two of his other recent projects, Gallery U in Yugawara and Shimosuwa Municipal Museum (one long curve). The architect explains that its theme is the sequence of experience, with two dramatically contrasting floor levels.

The museum's largest space – the main exhibition hall and machine room – was positioned on the ground floor and covered with an artificial hill, creating a spacious submerged level with few windows, and not visible from the street. Access to the foyer, café and other open exhibition spaces on the level above is via a curved ramp running over the hill towards the entrance.

The floor above, a cylinder over the roof of the main volume, is used as storage space. In contrast to most museums where this is hidden away, Ito wanted to stress

Left and below: The form of the museum reflects the low, horizontal profile of the Shohin-ken, an Edo-period villa opposite, and the flatness of the leafy site itself. Ito tried to avoid the conventional massiveness of museums, creating instead a bright space under a light, vaulted roof. The ground floor exhibition space is submerged under an artificial hill.

The exposed technology of the lift is visible as it rises from the basement exhibition hall into the light upper floors, encircled by wavy metal stair rails.

Left: The open-plan entrance level, with its space-age furniture, is located above the submerged ground floor, with good views over the artificial hill down to the street. Its glass border minimizes the barrier between interior and exterior. The floor above, a cylinder hovering over the multi-vaulted roof, contains storage space.

A computerized study
area furnished with
Teruaki Ohashi's
designs.

Section (1:300)
1 Studio
2 Storage
3 Gallery
4 Lecture room
5 Café
6 Office
7 Back entrance
8 Machine room

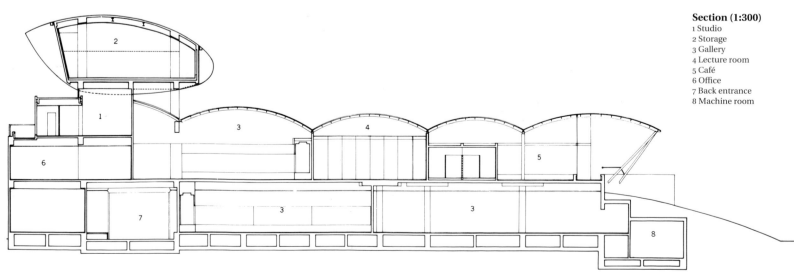

Yatsushiro's role as a collector and conserver of artefacts. Placing this space on a prominent upper level derives from ancient Japanese 'shosoin' (storehouses) where storage areas are located higher than living spaces.

A variety of structural systems form individualized spaces. On the submerged ground floor where a minimum ceiling height was required to reduce the volume, a flat slab is used with randomly placed columns. Over the two floors above is a steel-frame, multi-vaulted roof which covers the whole space, giving the exhibition areas which are surrounded by glazing around the periphery

a light, open atmosphere. Offices at the rear of the museum are housed within a rigid, reinforced concrete frame.

Ito's intention was to create a modest, and even provisional, architectural structure, at the same time ensuring that the exhibition and storage functions of the project were responsibly accommodated. Whilst the main exhibition space is a relatively conventional gallery, smaller details in the museum assert Ito's interest in lightweight structures. The museum's stairs are arranged in a casual fashion: the furniture (designed by Teruaki Ohashi) has a fragile appearance which links it to the human form. According to the

Japanese critic Hiromi Fujii, who distinguishes what he chooses to call the 'feminine sensibility' of Ito's work from the 'chaos' of deconstructivism, this approach to architecture, emphasizing the 'natural instead of the artificial, absence instead of presence', is a growing phenomenon in Japan, clearly visible at Yatsushiro and also in Kazuyo Sejima's Saishunkan Seiyaku Dormitory. In this latest project, Ito uses materials commonly applied within his buildings: translucent glass, perforated metal panels and stainless steel. These underline the simple beauty of the museum, as well as its link with the landscape.

Carlos Jiménez
Lynn Goode Gallery

Houston, Texas, USA

Right: The largest of the ground-floor galleries provides a glimpse of the courtyard. The high, central, cutaway stair and first-floor landing serve as both divider and link between the various galleries.

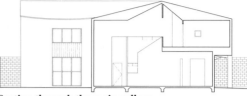

Section through the main gallery

Carlos Jiménez's design for the Lynn Goode Gallery fulfils two closely connected functions of a modern art gallery: to be a public sequence of easily negotiated spaces, but at the same time a contemplative environment – a combination frequently aspired to but not often satisfactorily achieved. The project is located in a mixed-use neighbourhood of Houston known as the 'gallery corridor'. The city's absence of regulated zoning means that the juxtaposition of residential and cultural building in similar sized lots is typical, with neither type assuming a subordinate role to the other. The soft orange stucco façade of the low, rectangular building presents a pared-down, abstracted application of the area's residential typology. Its front elevation is a striking composition, with a two-bay, galvanized steel panel entrance flanked by windows. A high entrance portico protects the foyer from the sun.

The primary challenge Jiménez had to meet, before considering the treatment of interior spaces, was presented by the site itself. Three live oak trees which had stood there since the early 1920s presented a complex geometry and Jiménez responded to this by giving the gallery an L-shaped form. The trees were incorporated into the site with its two-storey, wood-frame and stucco

structure as a design element, the two at the front 'protecting' the building, and the one at the rear within a small garden courtyard.

The building is a relatively open space, with a floor area of 4,500 square metres (two-thirds of which is reserved for offices, the storage of artworks and services). Instead of adopting the undifferentiated volume of a single loft-like space, Jiménez's design is a composition of galleries of different sizes, each with their own character, resulting from varying ceiling heights and light apertures. The galleries accommodate a diversity of exhibitions, with room for very large works in one large-volumed space on the ground floor with clerestory windows.

The visitor does not enter a hermetic container, isolated from the outside world: for Jiménez the presence of nature was indispensable to the viewing of art. One major advantage for him in designing a gallery like this one is that he could allow natural light into the display spaces without fear of excessive exposure to light, since exhibitions last only a couple of months at the most. Visitors experience changing light conditions, and this is made more dramatic by the varied positioning of windows.

Jiménez's design, with one partially open gallery leading to another, offers a sense of

both expansiveness and intimacy. This creates a particularly effective environment for a gallery: one through which it is easy to move, but which at the same time encourages the visitor to linger and contemplate the works. A high, central cutaway stairway and first-floor landing serves as both a divider and a link between the galleries. This allows the stair to function as an observation platform, from which the visitor can see a variety of gallery walls, as well as glimpses of tree branches swaying outside in the courtyard and on either side of the front of the building.

The gallery's low-voltage track lighting systems are made up of manufactured products, laid out to Jiménez's design. His practice also designed the built-in furniture and fittings, using Carlton Cook, a local cabinet-makers, who themselves designed and made some special items of furniture including the main office desk and credenza.

For the same price as most warehouse-style galleries, the project achieves a richly layered sequence of spaces. Jiménez's architectural forms and his framing of nature are powerfully articulated elements, not working independently of the artworks exhibited, but with their changing forms in an active three-way relationship.

Right: The off-centre entrance of the stucco-finished building framed by oak trees. Recessed planes of vertical-seam metal siding provide a contrasting, cooler backdrop.

Far right: The natural world outside and changing light conditions are vividly experienced within the exhibition spaces via generously proportioned windows.

José Antonio Martinez Lapeña, Elías Torres Tur
Monastery of Sant Pere de Rodes

Port de la Selva, Catalunya, Spain

The architects' new wooden entrance. Their intention was to make interventions, using modern materials and construction methods, to enhance and facilitate the circulation, without reproducing the existing architecture.

The ruins of Sant Pere de Rodes, a Romanesque monastery perched high on the mountain of Verdura close to the Costa Brava and long since abandoned by its ascetic occupants, had needed radical consolidation for many years. Under the auspices of the Government of Catalunya's department of culture, it had become a popular but fragile landmark. The historic site is heavily visited, and its fabric was declining rapidly, in spite of numerous inadequate restorations, the last occurring over ten years ago.

Lapeña and Torres' architectural strategy involved a series of interventions throughout the monastery complex, using modern materials and construction methods. The idea was to reinforce the monastery's ancient and unstable fabric, to guide the regular influx of visitors around its impressively scaled buildings and to provide some badly needed facilities. The forms introduced meet these needs in a pragmatic and aesthetically pleasing way, without compromising the historic nature of the site.

Apart from making sure that the walls were structurally sound and adding protective roofs to prevent further deterioration, the architects' main task was to create a new circulation system of stairs and footbridges. The materials chosen are in keeping with the spartan nature of the environment, but not so low-key that they fail to assert any kind of aesthetic presence; indeed, there is a sculptural quality about these access points, which fulfil their functional roles without attempting to reproduce the Romanesque

Above: The Monastery of Sant Pere de Rodes, a Romanesque landmark perched high on the Verdura mountain overlooking the Costa Brava. Lapeña and Torres have renovated this site with subtle new insertions.

Left: Sliding teak doors and one of the wooden benches which appear throughout the monument.

Far right: In the old
refectory a laminated
teak display unit stands
on the polished floor of
a newly inserted teak
platform. New window
frames and mullions in
brass have been added.

Bottom: In the visitors'
toilets the atmosphere is
maintained, with basins
built into the walls and
specially designed
rubbish bins.

Below: The new folded
and cantilevered
concrete stair leads to
the crypt below the main
exhibition area.

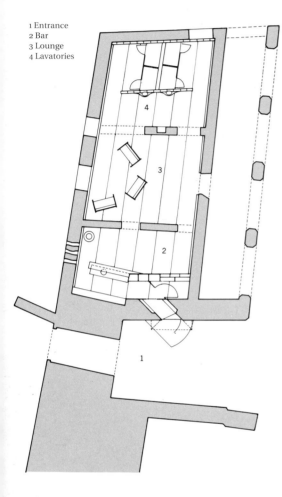

1 Entrance
2 Bar
3 Lounge
4 Lavatories

architecture. The footbridges are metal
structures with wooden flooring; the floors
are teak or San Vicens limestone; the roof
material is wood with copper sheathing;
and the reinforced walls are also covered
with copper.

Two parts of the monument received
specific attention: the entrance building
and the original refectory. In the former
there is a wooden bench, and more of these
placed in other parts of the monument give
the circulation a consistent theme. The
refectory's previous floor levels are retained,
with the addition of a teak platform, free from
the room's perimeter walls, which appears to
float over the space. Between the platform
and the rock below runs a projecting concrete
staircase. Intentionally made slightly too
short to forge an uninterrupted link between
the two, this symbolizes the desire for

intimacy between new and old. A teak display
unit, designed as a slanting structure with a
single fold, stands on the platform.

Identical armchairs in solid marine
plywood punctuate the rooms as sparingly
as the display units; more are positioned at
regular intervals around the open areas of the
site, lending the ancient structure a curious
air of occupation and providing a subtle
uniformity of interior and exterior elements.
New facilities have been introduced,
including a bar, ticket office and toilets.

As the monastery is only open during
daylight hours, natural lighting was deemed
sufficient for the interior spaces, many of
which have new, partially glazed roof
structures. The result, as with the rest of
Lapeña and Torres' clever intervention, is
to bring life and a new perspective to the
monastery's ancient structure.

MacCormac Jamieson Prichard
Fitzwilliam College Chapel
Cambridge, UK

Fitzwilliam College is situated on Huntingdon Road to the north of Cambridge, in three-storey buildings designed by Denys Lasdun. It was originally intended that a nineteenth-century villa to the centre of the complex, owned by the Darwin family and set in its own garden, should be pulled down. When in 1984 Richard MacCormac was asked to design a new residential wing on the south-west corner of the site, however, he also proposed an alternative masterplan which left the old building and garden untouched, and added a new cloistered route at its perimeter connecting all the communal buildings of the college. Although the cloister has not been implemented, the desire to create new social facilities to give life to 'The Grove', resulted in the chapel, a beautiful, modern place of worship inspired by ancient archetypes.

The building stands against the truncated wing of Lasdun's residences towards the middle of the college grounds, but facing the great plane tree at the heart of the garden. Its curved, brick walls, banded with precast string courses, form cusps which open to reveal a gridded metal window on the east elevation, a striking element which seems independent from its brick structure.

The height of the existing wing allowed for an elevated place of worship, and the building – a combination of orthogonal structure and circular enclosure – represents a ship held up and enclosed within two curved walls. The architects explain that the ship form signifies both passage and protection, an archaic metaphor which recurs in a number of ways throughout the building.

The building's plan can be read as a cross, projecting from the residential building, clasped by two arcs. Its main rooms: the meeting room and the chapel itself, are placed on two levels, one above the other. This not only helps it to meet the scale of its three-storey neighbour, but allows the architects to develop a strong contrast between the crypt-like meeting room, 'a kind of underworld', with its rusticated stone surfaces, and the numinous atmosphere in the high-ceilinged open space of the chapel above. The chapel was created by a raised platform structure made of American oak, a timber used in wooden shipbuilding, which is set within the space like a boat within a larger, protective building.

Doors in banded oak are set on the keel-line of the 'ship', leading in at ground level to a vestibule with access to the chapel and the crypt. Here, on both sides, rectangular bays of glazing rise right up to the ceiling of the floor above. Banded, white, rendered concrete walls enclose sturdy wooden staircases which wind upwards around the drum-shaped sides of the curved 'ship' structure to the congregational space. The hull slopes down through the vestibule towards the crypt with its rougher wall surfaces and piers of *in situ* concrete. Their horizontally striated surfaces are intended to suggest geological strata. In this space, the 'underbelly' of the chapel floor produces a floating effect accentuated by 'curtains' of natural light spilling down around the periphery.

The vista opens out dramatically in the intense light of the raised congregational space of the chapel, which seats up to 136 people in an aisled arrangement. It is strongly oriented to east-west with a large, glazed east window overlooking the garden. A cross can be made out from its metal bands, but this is one of few overtly religious symbols in the space. The central, flat-ceilinged area is defined by a high cubic frame of polished, precast limestone columns and supporting beams, separated from the roof itself by polished metal cylinders. The columns and beams were polished to give them a precious appearance. This tall structure blends into the spacious interior of oak, white render and white concrete.

'The Chapel's principal elements are simple, yet they encounter the age-old problem of how to resolve the interfaces of the differing geometries of the circle and the

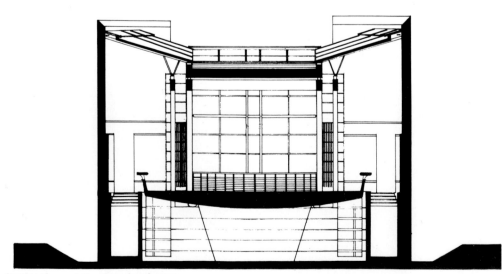

Section through the chapel and crypt

square', the architects comment. They explain that 'light is used as the mediating and reconciling element': at the east window, instead of being able to flood the calm interior through an open area of glazing, it is 'fretted by the modulated tracery of mullions' which 'contain the light as a measured volume'. The curved walls and east window are disengaged from the central square, so that top light falls from apertures in the roof (glazed bays, and from a skylight above the organ) into the perimeter of the chapel, enhancing the sense of separation between the congregational space and the outer walls .

The detailing of the chapel demonstrates a high level of craftsmanship in wood and metal, as well as a confident application of different wall materials which emphasizes the contrast in levels. To the left of the altar, a gate structure in the side of the wooden ship gives the priest access to a narrow, private stair. The structure incorporates a door rest and a raised rail which form a neat, simultaneous opening mechanism, and are barely visible when shut. The thick, black-painted metal structure of the tall bays is also evident as boldly geometric stair rails. In all cases, materials were chosen for their innate qualities, and their flawless application throughout contributes greatly to the creation of a still, intimate and atmospheric space.

Left: Seen from the garden, the floodlit east elevation of the building, with its gridded metal window, clearly shows the raised congregational space of the chapel defined by a high cubic frame.

José Luis Mateo
Can Felipa Cultural Centre
Barcelona, Spain

The recent regeneration of Barcelona has greatly enriched and extended the city's public facilities, providing many new and revived civic buildings with a wide range of uses. The architect José Luis Mateo's inspired conversion of the former Catex textile factory into a civic centre was commissioned by the municipality. A forward-looking development, it builds on the site's historic forms and typifies the hybrid nature of the city itself.

Can Felipa is close to the coastline north of Barcelona at Poble Nou, a rapidly developing location that was previously a down-at-heel, high-density working-class area, and whose old mills and factories are now seen as ripe for conversion to new uses. The old, neo-classical industrial building had stood in a ruined state until the city council took it over in the early 1980s; ten years later, its structure and surrounding site have been transformed by José Luis Mateo into a 1,350-square-metre sports/cultural centre for the local community. (The construction cost was 500 million pesetas.) The architect has also undertaken some rationalization of other areas of the site and created a block of inexpensive apartments for the developer behind the centre.

Mateo explains that the old building was a 'strange construction in a rather Frenchified style, with a construction system of some beauty based on Catalan vaults and a cast-iron structure'. He particularly admired the wooden roof which spanned the massive volume with great finesse. But it was the interior of the factory, virtually in ruins, that he found the most beautiful. Empty, windowless, it was a huge space formed by the vaults and pillars around the periphery. Looking at the 'hulk' of its exterior, Mateo says, 'it was just possible to envisage the palace its builders had once imagined', and his restoration tries to retain something of that image, whilst at the same time managing to accommodate modern facilities in a bold and uncompromising way.

The brief called for a swimming pool and gymnasium to be built at ground-floor level, with other social and civic amenities, including a theatre and lecture hall, above. Although the pool's service spaces could be located within the pillared internal structure of the old factory, Mateo created a new rectangular building to its left to house the pool itself, which, if sited within the old building, would have been incompatible with its structural order and dimensions. There is also a semi-open-air café, a small volume, which Mateo likens to a 'parasitic insect in metal', cleanly juxtaposed to the factory on its right next to the stair tower.

Right: Mateo converted the huge, cast-iron structure of the former factory, preserving the spaciousness of its interior. To the left is the communications/stair tower; to the right the swimming-pool building.

Above: The light steel staircase and platform access from the upper floors to the café.

Right: Slatted panels in
steel and wood on one of
the staircases leading
from the entrance.

227

Mateo tried to maintain a sense of spatial continuity between the pool house and the old building. He used lightweight materials – the showers and locker rooms have diaphanous wood and glass panels – and other surfaces in ceramics and stone give the impression of a carefully crafted but not overworked design. The overall concept of the pool house is based on the repetition of a concrete structure, with elements such as a copper-clad, arched roof (with a cut-out segment letting in light and highlighting its conical shape), galvanized sheet metal and glass, emphatically juxtaposed like various types of skin covering a 'strictly structured skeleton'.

There were two phases of construction – initially the swimming pool and gymnasium and later the second, third and attic floors. These accommodate various social and civic amenities for the local community: a bar-café, seminar rooms and an exhibition space, with a small theatre and lecture hall above. Here also the aim was to respect the spatial characteristics of the old building. This was not done tectonically, but by using bright, contrasting colours in a lightweight construction to personalize each floor.

Light blue, red and yellow predominate – one for each level – but the colours are juxtaposed at intervals along the transverse circulation route on each floor, such as where two walls meet a door. The materials used here, as elsewhere, are 'almost provisional' and, although their 'skins' boldly redefine the old building, they remain consistently distinct from it. Mateo did not break into the old factory's inner spaces more than was necessary. The bar, for instance, is a simple, open volume maintaining the atmosphere of the building as a whole. Partitioning in the administrative areas, which Mateo refers to as 'small things inside a big common space', creates triangular enclosures with the creative, makeshift air of a stage set. Fire doors are huge, striped, sliding constructions, practical and visually arresting.

A new communications/stair tower, housing a ground-floor reception/cloakroom, is connected to the building by a series of angled glass and steel walkways. Finished in stucco, wood and iron panels, its solid grey front becomes lighter and glazed towards the top. At the top a wedged form extends from the side elevation, with an electronic display unit (digitized information with the braille alphabet). At night the whiteness of the main building's structure becomes a clear grid framing the bright new features within, and the slate-grey tower winks enigmatically, its electronic sign being for Mateo an 'allegorical reflection' of the building's new life.

A corridor on the second floor of the old building, towards the connecting bridge to the communications/stair tower. Each floor has its own colour scheme.

John Miller + Partners
The Stevens Building, Royal College of Art
London, UK

The Royal College of Art has occupied a main building next to the Royal Albert Hall on Kensington Gore since 1961, with a number of outlying departments spread over South Kensington. Its aim to centralize its accommodation on one site was encouraged by the Department of Education and Science, in the hope that this would allow for more efficient administration and for closer communication between its departments.

The college already owned property on nearby Queen's Gate and along Jay Mews next to the main block. In 1985 a brief for the latest phase of the Royal College began to take shape, in consultation with John Miller, who was head of Architecture at the college at the time, and whose practice also undertook the design of the Henry Moore Gallery and conversion of the Gulbenkian Hall on the main Kensington Gore site.

The brief evolved was to restore and convert three listed Grade II, five-storey Victorian houses on Queen's Gate and to create a new building on the contiguous site of Jay Mews. These would provide studios, workspaces, ancillary accommodation and a small exhibition space, for the departments of Painting, Graphics, Photography, Film & TV, Illustration and Computer Graphics. The project involved meeting an array of complex space requirements, as well as grappling with planning legislation, to create a versatile new building from a combination of new and old forms.

The existing buildings on Queen's Gate had to be structurally altered to strengthen and upgrade their fabric, and to form a connection with the new strip of building behind them. The latter, made of concrete slabs bonded into the existing structure, assists circulation, but the majority of the newly built accommodation is housed in the new block fronting Jay Mews.

This new building was organized to achieve a scale consistent with the existing mews buildings, whilst also providing four-metre-high painting studio spaces. It is modelled at parapet level with an arcade and steep roof over the top studio spaces. The central bay is projected in sympathy with the more vertical rhythm of the mews, and string courses and parapet soldier courses align with the adjacent buildings. Self-coloured render fits in with the white-washed brickwork predominating in the Mews. Two levels of accommodation (dark rooms and film studios) are situated below ground, with a third floor set beneath the pitched roof and the second floor set back behind a colonnade. There is a two-storey masonry wall up to the parapet, with broad windows divided by the circular columns. The main entrance is on Jay Mews, with rear doors on Queen's Gate serving as emergency exits only, an arrangement which orientates the building towards the main block.

The rotunda lobby is not unlike that of this other building. It leads up a ramp to a stair hall which incorporates a hoist for large paintings; the rectangular area which follows is effectively the hub of the project. The transition between the old and new parts of the building is controlled by this central, top-lit courtyard exhibition space through which the main circulation routes pass at ground- and first-floor levels. Students' work is exhibited in this semi-public space, which brings natural light into the centre of the deep plan, helps to make sense of the other areas, and introduces a much needed communal focus into the project.

The new Stevens Building in Jay Mews, seen from the corner of the Darwin Building on Kensington Gore.

It was a major priority to bring daylight into the heart of the building. Two seminar rooms opening off the first-floor circulation route have north-facing roof-lights; fluorescent lights above the atrium's gridded translucent ceiling add to the natural light here. From this high space, doors lead into the Queen's Gate part of the building. Stairs throughout employ pre-cast terrazzo tread and riser units with Carborundum inserts, the same solution used in the main building.

The architects have varied the heights of the painting studios which, to receive maximum light, occupy the top three floors at the front of the new Jay Mews building, and the top two at the back overlooking the top of the atrium. A system of interlocking spaces with mobile, full-height partitions, and tracks for asymmetric fluorescent luminaires, provides practical components that students can adapt to suit their own purposes. These robust environments do not have the same, lived-in feel of the old painting studios next to the Victoria and Albert Museum, but do possess greatly increased flexibility, efficient services and a high degree of durability, with maple-strip floors that can be sanded and walls that are easily repainted.

The exteriors of the listed Victorian buildings on Queen's Gate had to be preserved, along with the principal internal rooms and three sets of stairs. The stairs are not all necessary within the layout of the building, and their retention, creating three separate circulation systems linked only by small openings, makes for a confusing trip first time around. Main cross circulations are provided at basement, ground- and first-floor levels, above which the new and existing buildings become more discrete and self-contained. The signage system was purpose-designed on ceramic panels by Royal College of Art student Clare Hamilton-Webb.

With its white walls, steel balustrades, maple-strip floors and cool, natural light supported by a mixture of compatible fluorescent lights and metal halogen recessed luminaires, the converted building provides a pleasant environment in which different kinds of practitioners can work. Services run in trunking under the floors, which gives different departments the flexibility to rearrange themselves or add to their electrical equipment at a later stage. Departmental needs, for items like mobile lighting rigs for Photography, Film & TV, were met, and specific areas, such as the double-height photography studios situated on the fourth floor at the back of the pitched roof of the Queen's Gate building, developed as highly serviced facilities. A simple, standard work-bench system was purpose-designed for all studio spaces, with ash-lipped, linoleum-topped tables on chrome legs, a design which was evolved for more technical use in the computer suite, with added adjustable VDU arms and baskets.

With space at a premium, the architects' calm and balanced solution to the brief shows how well they have understood the importance of housing specific activities, but at the same time providing a lively working space. A building like this is not just a set of working areas, but should foster a sense of community, and making the best of its hybrid origins, the central transitional space links new and old, with a bright, uplifting environment which provides a suitably interactive focus for the college.

1 Entrance drum
2 Painting studio
3 Tutor's office
4 Painting office
5 Atrium/exhibition space
6 Film/TV studio
7 Film/TV studio and edit suite
8 Photographic processing room
9 WC
10 Computer studies
11 Illustration studio
12 Exhibition corridor
13 Graphics studio
14 Seminar room
15 Photography head of department
16 Photography studio
17 Photographic darkroom/finishing suite

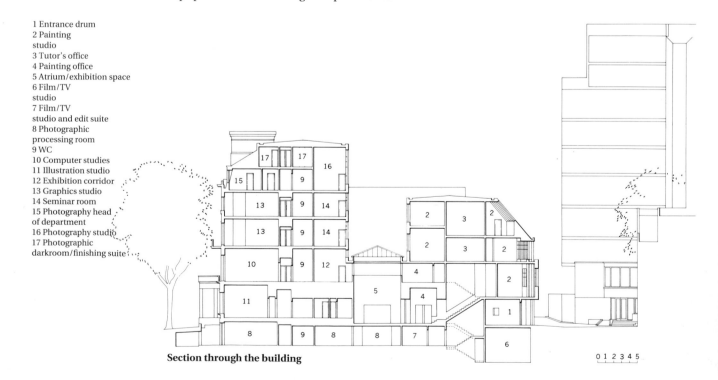

Section through the building

0 1 2 3 4 5

Enric Miralles
Circulo de Lectores
Madrid, Spain

Circulo de Lectores is a long-established book publisher based in Madrid whose editorial headquarters are now part of a unique open-plan space. The building is a converted housing block and now functions as a cultural and publicity centre, hosting a range of book promotions, exhibitions, meetings, literary readings, seminars, and film and video screenings. Enric Miralles, who in 1990 won the competition to design the project with his former partner Carme Pinos, has transformed it into an open, sociable space. The interior has a strongly layered character, with light birch sheet forms introduced at a variety of levels, including the skylights in the ceiling. In his imaginative reading of the client's programme, Miralles has incorporated dynamic structures to create a place with a sense of occasion. The construction budget was around 150 million pesetas.

The 2,700-square-metre space is set behind an open shop front of angled glass panels. These show one of three seated mezzanine areas the architect introduced into the open-plan, ground-floor space. The wing-like structure of the mezzanine curves around from the left side over a book display area and reception, deep into the main entry/exhibition hall. The design has an improvisational feel to it, and apart from the administrative office, every area of the building is multi-purpose and flexible.

Miralles wanted to express a sense of transparency within the interior, and to create an internal landscape that it is exciting to negotiate. He explains that the new structure is supported by the existing building, with 'no new pillars interfering with the plan'. The three mezzanines had to be light, almost skeletal structures as they are hung from the original beams. As with many of his previous projects, the order of his plan for the empty interior takes its cue from the form and topography of the roof panels, which 'describe' the overlapping activities taking place beneath them in curved swathes of space.

He wanted to create a room receiving natural light from above. Asymmetrical

apertures in the ceiling – larger skylights in the main space, narrower slots elsewhere – produce a variety of dappled lighting effects. Miralles also playfully diffuses the impact of light sources by means of a false ceiling with an almost provisional quality, incorporating light, kite-shaped wooden panels which hang from the ceiling like giant bat wings.

The presence of inserted mezzanines and their access stairs means that the building allows for a lot of movement. A narrow slope of fixed, high-backed wooden seats slides its wedge-shaped form into the main space. An exposed balustraded mezzanine above, also with seats, is reached by a light, open-tread staircase visibly hanging off the main beams. Another, circular mezzanine hovers over the central area of the room. Around this structure at ground level there are stout pillars covered in metal-inlaid wood in a two-tone, 'camouflage' pattern. Video monitors are set into these, creating a kind of forest of electronic trees. The central area has no formal boundaries, and even its dividing elements are flexible. A series of runners crossing the underside of the mezzanine support a track on which a linked set of

sliding, wooden-framed exhibition panels can be set up in a variety of spatial configurations. These also serve as doors, dividing the low hallway area below into a series of intimate spaces.

Circulo de Lectores is intended to enhance communication. Its interior elements are all constructed in birch plywood, with a design characterized by what seems like (but is not) random patterning, creating a sense of movement and an absence of formal barriers. Miralles' landscape of overlapping levels and spaces recalls open environments created for communal theatre, such as stage sets by Malevich and Rodchenko in the 1920s, with interconnected areas serving as both stages and auditoria, and so encouraging uninhibited interaction between people.

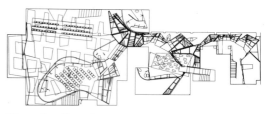

Mezzanine-floor plan

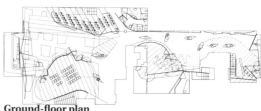

Ground-floor plan

Kiko Mozuna Architects & Associates
Notojima Glass Art Museum
Noto Island, Ishikawa Prefecture, Japan

Right: Each of the curved wall, fixed showcases in exhibition building 2 is fronted by a huge, concave plane of glass which slides towards the showcase next to it to allow access to the exhibits. Japanese lacquer is used to create pedestals for exhibits.

In the seemingly timeless island location of Noto, architect Kiko Mozuna has created a cultural building which fuses a traditional Oriental architectural approach with modern technical skills in an ambitious attempt to harmonize glass, architecture and the environment in a 'city of glass'. Since the Notojima Glass Studio was established in 1982, the island has been known for its innovative glass craftwork. With the coming of the Glass Museum, its role as a creative centre for craft skills in this area has reached new dimensions. The museum collects and displays exceptional examples of historic and contemporary, domestic and foreign glass work, as well as selling the work of the studio.

Mozuna has divided the museum into four parts – two exhibition spaces, a shop/office and open temporary exhibition space. Each corresponds to the position and character of four long-lost gods of ancient Chinese mythology: a green dragon, a white tiger, a red bird and a black turtle. These represent running water to the east, roads to the west, lowlands to the south and hills to the north respectively, the best location being one which combined all these geographical features. The housing of the museum's services required the architect to use reinforced concrete and iron for the structure of each of the four buildings, but in all other respects their composition and zoning was guided by ancient mythology.

Realizing the spaces on the lines Mozuna wanted was a major technical challenge, but he has nonetheless maintained the individual form of each and designed it to fit into the landscape. The buildings resemble a collection of futuristic relics, but Mozuna uses modern technology to ensure that they function as sound interior spaces geared to exhibitions. Exhibition building 1 has been designed like a tunnel, its section gradually decreasing in size as it slopes towards the far end of the building. The second building takes the form of a fan, enclosing a floor area the shape of an incomplete circle. A bridge between the two in sandblasted glass is shaped like a crystal.

Top left: Exhibition building 1 was designed as an all-white tunnel. The circular lines of windows feature hand-etched patterns.

Left: The café on the upper floor of the heavily structured, egg-shaped retail building. Its segmented glass point provides views of the approach road and Notojima's island landscape.

Mozuna took the opportunity to use glass as a major construction material and also employed some of the traditional craft skills practised in the region. His use of Japanese lacquer and wooden panels, for example, helps to create a balance between old and new materials. One hundred and six hand-etched glasses were made for the circular windows on the ceiling of exhibition building 1, together with cloud-shaped doorknobs and glass features on the side of staircases and wash basins. A lighting system using optical glass fibres has been installed in the other exhibition building. The walls of the gallery spaces are painted white to help focus attention on the exhibits, and illuminated with optic-fibre lighting which simulates daylight.

The concept of mythological animals – the sacred guardians of a city – has in the past

been widely applied to oriental city planning in an attempt to guarantee prosperity. Two other elements – a paved garden and neo-oriental details – underpin Mozuna's design. The garden is set out with scattered forms which signify harmony between the environment and architecture. Hence an artificial pond in the middle of one of the exhibition spaces is spatially linked with its backdrop, the Noto Sea. The gate, entrances and passages are designed in modern materials to create a bold synthesis of traditional forms and decorative motifs derived from fractal geometry. This, Mozuna explains, is a neo-oriental approach which gives long-standing Japanese aesthetic concepts a modern interpretation: 'our traditional background in the future context'.

Akiko & Hiroshi Takahashi/Work Station
Sakamoto Ryoma Memorial Hall
Urato, Kochi City, Japan

Right: A spiral staircase housed within a banded glass cylinder provides the main access and is one of the building's key vertical elements.

The Takahashi husband and wife team were the winners of an open design competition held by the local Prefectural government to create a building commemorating Ryoma Sakamoto in a dramatic location on a south-facing hill overlooking the Pacific. Sakamoto was one of the young leaders who took part in the bloodless revolution of 1867 which restored Imperial rule in Japan; he was killed shortly afterwards. Here at Urato, where the ocean stretches as far as the eye can see, people come to watch the huge waves blown in by typhoon winds. The architects took their cue from this dramatic site, exploring structural systems that would both blend in with, and hold their own against, its hilly topography and vast oceanic perspective. Above all, they wanted to provide a changeable sequence of views for visitors moving around the building.

The memorial hall has an innovative structure, and a modern jauntiness, deriving not just from the decorative wave form on its roof, but also from its tilted angle. Supported on two pairs of columns, it resembles a suspension bridge jutting forwards to the sea. The main exhibition space is elevated and open to the surrounding sky, sea and shoreline. On one side it is glazed, with a long staircase zigzagging up its length – a transparent façade which mirrors the ebb and flow of the ocean; the other side is partially encased within a red, sloping truss structure shooting out to sea at a converging angle.

Visitors can enter the main exhibition space by means of a long ramp within the truss form, or they can descend a flight of steps. This means of entering is not unlike going down into the hold of a ship: experiencing an interior which, spatially, reveals itself bit by bit. A reinforced concrete wall below the exhibition floor contains the basement area. This gives the building a third structural system which, along with the suspension structure holding the glazed exhibition hall and truss supporting the approach ramp, give it a strikingly modern character. The construction budget was funded by local contributions and set at an

Above: By night the main glass-box structure of the exhibition hall reveals activities within.

Left: A mezzanine reception area at the front of the exhibition hall from which the huge crashing waves can be watched.

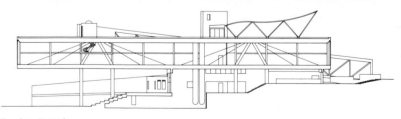

Section (1:400)

240

An exhibition installed within the main display space.

economical level, and the architects battled to keep within it.

The interiors of the exhibition hall and the basement area represent two contrasting styles: one is heavily glazed; a light, neutral box enlivened by its structure and proximity to the elements. In a mezzanine viewing area, soft grey, steel-framed stools and tables have an unassertive presence. Below, in a softer, more embellished meeting room, textural materials such as exposed concrete and wood are used. The library furniture is in Japanese oak.

The two floors are joined by a light spiral staircase in painted steel with linoleum-covered treads and enclosed within a frosted glass cylinder. It is one of the building's most important vertical elements, providing access

to the roof garden. A smaller, bright yellow spiral staircase is contained within the hall's central blue tower. Like a ship, the whole building encourages the visitor to roam around its contrasting spaces. Much of the roof is devoted to a promenade area with seating where people can move about freely.

Hiroshi Takahashi has commented that as the modern environment is gradually transformed by countless images, architecture as a physical presence is bound to recede into the background, 'becoming a mere receptacle'. What matters now, in his view, is a building's technical performance, and its use of natural materials like wood or stone, as well as industrial products. Rather than simulating the natural environment, he feels that it is more desirable to make direct

Left: The main entrance foyer of the building, fitted out with a Japanese tiled floor, glass brick walls and cedar strip ceilings, with routes leading down to the basement library or straight ahead into the exhibition spaces.

Above: One of the two spiral staircases has a yellow swirling structure and leads up to the roof garden. It is made of painted steel and linoleum tile.

or indirect reference to it and, without framing natural vistas too rigidly, he and Akiko give priority in their design work to structures that allow this.

Yannis Tsiomis
Académie Musicale de Villecroze

Villecroze, Salernes, Var, France

Villecroze is a tiny village in a rural area about 20 kilometres north-west of St Tropez in the South of France. Like so many focii of formerly busy farming communities, its identity has gradually faded in recent years as a result of the exodus by the young to the cities. However, Villecroze has been sustained and revitalized by a new project; not a theme park-style trip back to the past, but a practical, creative project which combines musical history with architecture and architectural history with music.

In 1981, in an inspired move, the town hall officials decided to turn the village's Romanesque chapel, a beautiful setting with good acoustics for concerts, into a performance space for musicians from the rest of France and Eastern Europe. As a result of its success, a musical association was formed with a burgeoning programme of activities.

The decision to create a music academy which included an international cultural complex for young musicians from all over the world, was a further, major step towards a complete transformation of the village. The plan was initiated by Anne Grüner Schlumberger, the creator of the musical association, and developed in conjunction with the Municipalité de Villecroze and the Office Public Departemental d'Habitations à Loyer Moderé du Var. Keen to avoid an élitist, seasonal facility, the participants wanted the project to further the life of the village, and its architecture is evolved from the traditional forms of farm buildings.

Yannis Tsiomis, the architect selected to create the 800-square-metre complex, was given a brief to convert a diverse range of existing structures in varying states of dilapidation. Nine duplex apartments in which up to sixteen professional musicians could live and work were new constructions, developed to provide individual phonic and acoustic qualities suitable to the tone and range of different instruments. He also combined the structures of two large existing barns dating from the sixteenth and nineteenth centuries to create a jazz auditorium. An old oil press now houses a hall for chamber music and song, and another outbuilding was used as a large music library. The complex gradually developed into a virtual masterplan extending the village. It includes six units of economically priced housing at the edge of the centre, and a new 300-square-metre public space with a 12,000-square-metre park incorporating an open-air theatre.

The conversion of this miscellaneous group of buildings presented numerous difficulties, calling for a large number of alternative designs. For Tsiomis the project presented two main challenges, to which he endeavoured to find solutions reconciling the modern and the traditional. The client insisted on conserving the walls of the barns, which were in a very dilapidated state. Rather than introduce any great aesthetic innovation externally, these have been renovated with

Cross-section

Above: The Academy complex was created from a number of converted structures, including two 16th- and 19th-century barns. Tsiomis renovated these using local stone and masons, strengthening the thermal inertia of the building. He maintained low-key fenestrations but added a narrow, triple-height glazed entrance which matches the scale of the long approach stair.

Top: An elliptical upper gallery with larch-block floors overlooks the library and provides access to duplex living and working spaces. These are 'small houses within the house', with an atmosphere which combines 'hotel' and 'home'. Tsiomis' balanced design incorporates tall cutaway walls below a lightwell.

sensitivity. New masonry was applied to the later barn in a traditional fashion while the earlier one was substantially reconstructed to revive its original forms and adapt them to its demanding new function. Traditional skills were also employed on the interiors, but the architect took pride in ensuring these were balanced by an equal input of modern, high-performance techniques.

The programme naturally presented a considerable challenge in terms of internal acoustics. Tsiomis did not want their constraints to become the sole determining factor in the design of interior spaces at the Academy, and this led to the creation of new elements including an interior 'street' leading to the private rooms. This has a metal gangway on anti-vibratory piles with an acid-etched glass floor. It has a dual function: the metal frame construction with load-bearing steel posts provides both extraction ducts in the main music hall and supports for the gangway distribution.

Close collaboration and consultation with the musicians allowed Tsiomis to ensure that the interior would be 'neither falsely polyvalent nor neutral'. The duplex apartments are treated as houses within the house, a solution which adapts itself to the acoustic aspect of the brief.

As far as the juxtaposition of new and old is concerned, the architect endeavoured to maintain the old walls and other historic elements, but at the same time did not flinch at introducing new forms which owed nothing to the past. Giving an equal weight to these priorities helped, he says, to resolve 'the false dichotomy between ancient and modern. Integration is a matter not of the eye but of our way of life.'

Biographies

Ahrends Burton and Koralek was formed in 1961 by Peter Ahrends, Richard Burton and Paul Koralek, all of whom were born in 1933 and trained at the Architectural Association, London. Paul Drake (born 1934), Patrick Stubbings (born 1935) and John Hermsen (born 1933) became partners in 1974. AB & K have undertaken a great variety of projects including planning studies, development plans and public buildings, such as work for the DHS and WRHA in 1991 at St Mary's, Isle of Wight, the world's first low-energy hospital; the White Cliff Experience, Dover (1991), and the new British Embassy, Moscow (1988–). Educational projects include Berkeley Library/Arts Building, Trinity College, Dublin; Templeton College, Oxford; and the award-winning residence for Keble College, Oxford and Hooke Park College, Dorset (1982–90). Work is currently being undertaken at Grenoble University, France. Commercial/industrial buildings include the Habitat warehouse, Wallingford; Cummins Engines, Lanarkshire; J Sainsbury, Canterbury; WH Smith, Swindon (the last three won awards); John Lewis, Kingston (1990), and current work to extend the Docklands Light Railway to the east (1987–). The practice's residential work includes three housing schemes in Basildon, one low energy; Nebensahl House, Jerusalem, and Burton House, London.

Allies & Morrison Architects was founded in 1984 by Bob Allies and Graham Morrison. Allies trained at Edinburgh University and worked for architects including Michael Glickman and Michael Brawne. A Rome Scholar in architecture in 1981–2, he lectured at Cambridge University between 1983 and 1987. Morrison trained at Cambridge University and worked for Keijo Petaja, Finland, and in England for architects including YRM. He was elected a national member of the RIBA Council in 1991. Following the practice's early success in the open competition for a new public square at The Mound, Edinburgh, it has been involved with many sites and buildings of historical significance, including the Manor Farm housing development; the Clove Building, Butlers Wharf and 3–4 Ashland Place, all in London, as well as new premises for Scott Howard and Stephen Bull's Bistro and Bar, London. Projects in progress include the refurbishment of London's Centre Point, and London House in the City; the new British Embassy in Dublin; the Liverpool Pierhead civic scheme; Blandford Street (housing/retail); an office building for Whitechapel High Street; Sarum Hall School, London, and Essex University Library extension. In 1993 the practice won a commission to redesign the interior of the Royal Festival Hall.

Roser Amadó and Lluís Domènech are architects. Both were born in Barcelona, in 1944 and 1940 respectively. They studied at ETSAB, specializing in urbanism, and first collaborated in 1970 (with L. Sabater), designing the Sant Feliu de Guixols apartments in Girona, before setting up a joint practice in 1974. Early commissions awarded include the Central Laboratory for the Generalitat de Catalunya, Barcelona; they have since won awards for the College of Architecture at Lerida (1977); a redevelopment plan for the centre of the town (with Joan Busquets and Ramon Puig); a house in Barcelona (1982), and the conversion of the Tàpies Foundation (1986–90). Domènech has taught at ETSAB.

Anderson/Schwartz Architects is a New York-based practice established in 1984 by Ross S. Anderson and Frederic Schwartz, who both graduated from Harvard in 1978 with Masters degrees in architecture. Schwartz was previously director of the New York office of Venturi, Rauch and Scott Brown, and Anderson an associate of MLTW/Turnbull Associates, San Francisco. ASA has been selected for many '40 under 40' architectural media awards, and major projects to date include office interiors for Windham Hill Records, Finlandia Vodka, Apple Computers, Isaac Mizrahi, ITT; and commercial and residential conversions in New York, Wisconsin and California. Current projects include the design of regional government headquarters in South West France (joint venture with Venturi, Scott Brown & Associates), a baseball training camp in Florida and retail planning at Penn Station, New York. The partners have taught at Princeton, Harvard, Yale, Columbia, Pennsylvania and many other universities; their work has been exhibited widely in the USA, and they both won Rome Prizes in 1989.

Ron Arad was born in 1951 in Tel Aviv, and studied at Jerusalem Academy of Art, and the Architectural Association (1974–9). In 1981 he founded One Off Ltd in London with Dennis Groves and Caroline Thorman, designing furniture and products such as the Rover Chair, and the Ariel light. In 1983 he designed One Off's Neal Street showroom, and began exhibiting work at venues in Milan, Tokyo and elsewhere. In 1986 One Off showed new designs including the concrete stereo, and tables and screens designed with Danny Lane who, with Tom Dixon and Jon Mills, held his first exhibition at the showroom. Arad began to take on interior design commissions, such as Bazaar, for Jean Paul Gaultier, London; Equation, Bristol, and a new One Off furniture gallery in Neal Street (all 1986); Dorin Frankfurt, London, and Michelle Ma Belle, Milan (1987). In 1988 he completed a new studio and gallery for One Off in Shelton Street, London, and the following year started to design their next, larger studio, showroom and workshop in Chalk Farm. From this base Arad began work on the interiors of the new Tel Aviv Opera House (with Alison Brooks), and for private residences in London, Milan and Schopfheim. Arad is internationally renowned as a furniture designer, producing collections for Moroso, designs for Vitra, and Zeus, and for his own company One Off (for example the 'Well Tempered', 'Big Easy' and 'At Your Own Risk' chairs), and exhibiting work in major shows such as 'Wohnen von Sinnen', Düsseldorf (1986); 'Nouvelles Tendences', Pompidou Centre, Paris (1987); 'Documenta', Kassel (1987); 'Metropolis', and 'The Chair Exhibition', ICA, London (1988); 'Art and Industry' (one-man show, New York, 1990); Phillips' design installation, Berlin (1991) and 'Design Horizonte', Frankfurt (1991); and at numerous venues throughout Europe.

Bausman-Gill Associates was established in 1982 by architects Karen Bausman and Leslie Gill on their graduation from The Cooper Union, New York. Since 1987 both have been adjunct assistant professors at Parsons School of Design, and from 1990 at Columbia University, GSAPP; collaborating architect Alison Berger is a graduate of Rhode Island School of Design and Columbia. Their work encompasses art objects, interiors and building projects, and has been exhibited at a number of venues. Major design projects include offices for Drenttel Doyle, New York (1987); the Huxford House, Larchmont, New York (1988); Conanicut Island House, Rhode Island; Elektra Entertainment and the award-winning Warner Brothers (both New York, 1992). New York exhibitions include 'Interior Sightings' (John Nichols Gallery, 1985), 'Seasightings', public sculpture at Battery Park, 1985, and 'The London Project' (Artist's Space, 1989). This and 'Bearings' (Princeton University, 1990) were recorded in Princeton publications. In 1992 BGA won an award in 'Emerging Voices', Architectural League of New York.

Jeffrey G. Beers Architects was established in New York in 1986 by Jeffrey Beers, who graduated in architecture from Rhode Island School of Design in 1978, gaining a Fulbright International Fellowship the following year. He worked for I. M. Pei & Partners between 1980 and 1986, and was project architect for the Morton N. Meyerson Symphony Center, Dallas; major complexes in Singapore and Mt. Sinai Hospital, New York City. His own practice work includes corporate interiors (Wildwood, Atlanta, with I. M. Pei, 1989), hotels, nightclubs, retail, cultural (New York Glass Workshop, 1991), residential, and numerous restaurant projects, including China Grill (1987); Symphony Café (1988); 44 (at the Royalton, 1989), and in 1992, Zoë, Brasserie du Theatre, Maxx and Parc 59, all in New York City.

Behnisch & Partners is a Stuttgart-based practice established in 1967 by Günter Behnisch (born 1922 in Dresden; studied at the Technical University of Stuttgart), Winfried Buxel, Manfred Sabatke and Erhard Trankner, who have designed a great variety of projects, many resulting from competitions. The bias is towards large-scale public projects combining new construction technology with craft methods. Numerous commissions, many for schools and sports buildings followed early competition success with the award-winning Olympic Park, Munich (1968–72), including more recently the Solar Institute at the University of Stuttgart (1987); the library of the University of Eichsttt (which won the BDA-Preis Bayern in 1987); administration building for Leybold AG (1987); the German Postal Museum, Frankfurt (1982–90); a kindergarten and station square in Stuttgart (1990); a school and sports hall at Bad Rappenau (1991), and a parliament building in Bonn (1992). Large-scale projects in progress include a solar and water energy centre, Stuttgart; banks in Frankfurt, Munich and Stuttgart; schools, a sports hall, and control tower for the German Flight Safety Bureau.

David Bentheim trained as an environmental and interior designer at the Royal College of Art, London, from 1971 to 1974. Since graduating he has run a number of design-related businesses, including the Hartland Bentheim Design Consultancy and the HB Sign Company, which distributed design products. At the same time Bentheim launched his own interior design practice, first as HB Design and later David Bentheim Interior Design, handling a broad spectrum of interiors and exhibitions in the UK and abroad, including the Cecil Beaton retrospective at the Barbican Gallery, the Harlequin Hotel at Stansted for BAA, and the Minema Café (1992) for the Savoy Group. Practice projects include embassy work for the Foreign and Commonwealth Estates office and a major CTC school, as well as retail, domestic, exhibition and restaurant projects. Bentheim has lectured on design at Cranfield Business School. Ferry Zayadi, who was Head of Design at DBID from 1985 to 1991, and now works in private practice, is an Italian architect who has worked in London since 1973, for architects including Louis de Soissons Partnership.

Berbesson Racine et Associés is an architectural practice headed by Philippe Berbesson (who trained at the École Nationales des Beaux Arts, and des Arts Appliques et Métiers d'Art, Paris) and Marie Racine (École Camondo). In 1992 they moved offices to a boat they had converted at Port Van Gogh on the outskirts of Paris. The firm's work encompasses architecture, interior design and furniture. Major projects include offices for numerous clients including Société Générale, Commerzbank, Young & Rubicam and Landor in France, and Toyota in Nagoya, Japan; showrooms for Apple Computer and Forum Diffusion, both in Paris; restaurants for Jacques Hesse, Issy-les-Moulineaux, and the Urban Sporting Club, Paris; Gallery Urban, Paris; and interior design at Orly Sud airport; retail projects for Carrefour, Chambery; Igin, Paris; Charles Jourdan (Paris, Toulouse, Frankfurt, Geneva and New York); Pryca (throughout Spain) and Euromercato, Naples.

Lennart Bergström Arkitektkontor is a Stockholm-based architectural practice established 35 years ago, and currently headed by Lennart Bergström, Monica Bergström, Calle Bremme, Johannes de Leeuw, Rickard Rotstein, Herbert Schelwiller and Bo Svenssön. Major clients include SAS Airlines (interior design of lounges and ticket offices) and Vingresor travel agency (new hotel concept). Leaders in the development of the combined cell and open-plan office concept, LBA is also known for its buildings for senior citizens and major urban infrastructure projects in Sweden (such as the Vllingby Centre, and Södra Hammarbyhamnen). International projects include hotels in Rhodes (1976–80), Mallorca (1990–91) and Luxembourg (refurbishment, 1986) and The Ark, Hammersmith, London (1991, in collaboration with RALPH ERSKINE and ROCK TOWNSEND), and office/industrial buildings in France.

Architekturbüro Bolles-Wilson was established in Münster, Germany, in 1988 by Peter Wilson (born in 1950 in Melbourne) and Julia Bolles-Wilson (born in 1948 in Münster), who were previously in practice together in London as the Wilson Partnership, between 1980 and 1987. Wilson studied architecture at the University of Melbourne and at the Architectural Association, London (1972–4), where he was Unit Master between 1978 and 1988. Bolles-Wilson trained as an architect at the University of Karlsruhe (1968–76), and carried out postgraduate studies at the AA from 1978–9. Between 1980 and 1985 she taught at Chelsea School of Art. In 1988 Eberhard Kleffner (born in 1947 in Telgte, Germany, and a graduate of the University of Karlsruhe) joined the practice, after teaching at the University of Hannover from 1984 to 1986. Major projects include the new city library, Münster (1987–93); the Blackburn House, London (1987, with Chassay Wright Architects); a kindergarten, Frankfurt (1988–92); and a church centre (1988–92); technology centre (1989–93); warehouse (1989–93) and government office (1991–95), all in Münster; Folly at the Osaka Expo '90; a house in Tokyo (1990–93), and a waterfront and restaurant, Rotterdam (1991–95).

Esteve Bonell (born in Girona, Spain, in 1942) and **Francesc Rius** (born in Barcelona, in 1941) have collaborated on several projects since 1975, in particular on sports complexes such as the Horta Velodrome, for which they won the FAD Prize in 1985, the Brians Penitentiary and the Basketball Pavilion/Sports Palace (1987–91). They both studied at the Barcelona School of Architecture – Rius graduated in 1967, Bonell in 1970 – and are closely connected with the teaching of architecture there as professors and members of the Graduation Board (Bonell since 1972, Rius since 1977). Bonell started his practice in Barcelona in 1975, and in 1977 Josep Maria Gil joined, becoming associated architect. One of Bonell and Rius' recent projects was housing for the Olympic village in Barcelona.

Branson Coates Architecture was formed in 1985 by Nigel Coates and Doug Branson. Nigel Coates was born in 1949 in Malvern, UK and studied at Nottingham University and the Architectural Association (AA), where he has taught since 1976, becoming Unit Master in 1979. In 1983 he founded NATO (Narrative Architecture Today) with eight unit members, publishing a magazine and exhibiting work. Doug Branson graduated from the AA in 1975 and worked for DEGW and in practice as the Branson Helsel Partnership (until 1984). Branson Coates' earliest built projects were a house and shop for Jasper Conran (1985, 1986); and Silver jewellery shop, London (1987), followed in 1988 by two UK retail outlets for Katharine Hamnett and five for Jigsaw. The practice's repertoire of projects in Japan includes the Metropole restaurant, Tokyo (1990), the Bohemia jazz club (1986); Caffe Bongo for Parco, Tokyo (1986); Arca di Noe restaurant, Sapporo (1988); the Hotel Otaru Marittimo (1989); two Katharine Hamnett shops, Tokyo (1990), and the Nishi-Azabu building, Tokyo (1990). 1991 saw the design of the Taxim nightclub in Istanbul, and the Mayflower Golf Club, Tokyo. BCA have designed exhibitions for Dunhill (1988) and the Pompidou Centre, Paris (Situationalist International 1989), and stage sets for Laurie Booth. Current projects include a restaurant and bars for Schipol airport, Amsterdam; modernization and design work for Liberty, Regent Street; and the 20th Century furniture gallery of the Geffrye Museum, London. Coates designs furniture, notably for SCP Ltd (UK), Rockstone (Japan), Bros's, Poltranova, Arredaesse (Italy), V'Soske Joyce (UK, carpets), and Acme (Hawaii, jewellery). In 1992 he curated 'Ecstacity' at the AA, and wrote/presented the film 'Signs of the City' for the British Broadcasting Corporation.

Olivier Brenac and Xavier Gonzalez are architects based in Paris who formed their Atelier d'Architecture in 1978. Brenac (born in 1957 in Castres, France) graduated in architecture in 1973, and later in urbanism (L'École Nationale des Ponts et Chaussées), before working for Badani, Roux-Dorlut and as consultant for CAUE. Gonzalez (born in 1955 in Alicante, Spain) graduated from UP8 in 1981 and worked with Andrée Putman and Tadao Ando from 1985-6. Recent projects include housing in Paris: Tolbiac (1992), and for ZAC Rive Gauche (1992); La Cancava headquarters, Paris (1992); an office building in Budapest (1992); sheltered housing at Noisiel, France (1992); and La Tour sans Fins offices at La Défense, Paris (1991), as well as schools, hospitals and housing developments.

Eduard Bru was born in Spain in 1950, and has practised as an architect since 1975. His major projects include an urban project at the Alhambra, Granada; the Olympic area of the Vall d'Hebron,

Barcelona, and public and private constructions, including the interior design of the Museo del Juguete, Ibi, Spain (1990). He has received the City of Barcelona prize, and has been a FAD awards finalist. Bru's publications include *Arquitectura Espanola Contemporanea* and *Arquitectura Europea* (both published by G. Gili), and from 1980 to 1990 he was a member of the editorial board of *Quaderns* magazine. He sits on the board of the Mies van der Rohe Pavilion Foundation, Barcelona, and from 1988 to 1990 acted as board member for culture for the Architects' Association. Bru has taught in the USA, the UK and Italy.

Luisa Calvi, Marco Merlini and Carlos Moya have worked together on architectural and industrial design projects since 1989 when they set up their studio in Milan. Calvi (born in Milan in 1960) graduated in architecture from the Polytechnic of Milan in 1983, and worked for King-Miranda Associati and Daniela Puppa and Franco Raggi (1981–8). She is assistant professor of industrial design at her former faculty in Milan. Merlini was born in Mantova in 1958, and also worked as a freelance designer (on architectural and graphic design projects) on graduating in design from the Polytechnic of Milan. Moya (born in Catamarca, Argentina, in 1947) graduated in architecture from the Universidad de Cordoba in 1973, and worked in Milan as a freelance architect from 1978 to 1989. He and Calvi have designed lighting for Ve-Art. The trio is corporate identity and product design consultant to IME SpA; interior design projects include fair stands and the Julia Binfield studio, Milan, (1991).

David Chipperfield Architects was founded in 1984, and in 1987 opened a Tokyo office. David Chipperfield was born in London in 1953. He trained at the Architectural Association from 1974 to 1977 and worked for Richard Rogers, NORMAN FOSTER and Douglas Stevens. The practice's award-winning retail interior and residential work (including the Knight house of 1987) has now been augmented by major projects in Japan, including the Matsumoto headquarters, Okayama (1992); the Gotoh Museum, Tokyo (1990), and the TAK Design store, Kyoto (1989–90) and masterplanning studies in Vienna and Frankfurt, as well as a number of shops for Equipment in London, Paris and New York, and Kenzo in London (1990); and furniture for Cassina, Japan. Chipperfield is a founder/director of the 9H Gallery and a trustee of the Architectural Foundation, London. He has been a visiting professor at Harvard, the University of Naples and the Royal College of Art, and is an external examiner at the Polytechnic of Central London and visiting professor at the University of Graz, Austria.

Henri Ciriani (born in Lima, Peru, in 1936) is a Paris-based architect. He studied architecture and town planning at the Universidad Nacional de Ingenieria in Lima, and from 1962 to 1964 was assistant professor at the Universidad. He worked in private practice with various architects before winning a French government scholarship in 1964. From 1969 to 1984 he was professor at the L'École National des Beaux Arts, Paris (U.P.7 and 8), and worked with Michel Corajoud, and Borja Huidobro before setting up his own practice in 1976. In 1983 Ciriani was awarded the National Grand Prix of Architecture. His main built projects are predominantly social housing and facilities in Paris, St Denis (an award-winning child-care centre), Noisy-le-Grand (Noisy II: 300 flats, 1977–80), Evry (Evry II, 1984–5, which won the Palme d'Or National, Palmares de l'Habitat) and Torcy (a child-care centre, 1988–9). In 1991 he completed an office building in Paris for the Finance Ministry, and the Historial de la Grand Guerre in Peronne. Ciriani is professor at the l'École d'Architecture de Paris, and has taught in Peru, Grenoble, Amsterdam and Dublin. Projects in progress include the Research Institute for Ancient Provence/Archaeological Museum in Arles, a social housing project at Bercy, a mixed use complex at Colombes, and housing in The Hague and Nijmegen.

Antonio Citterio and Terry Dwan Architects is a Milan-based practice. Citterio was born in Meda, Italy in 1950. He graduated in architecture from the Polytechnic of Milan in 1980, and worked primarily on industrial and furniture design projects before setting up his own studio in 1981. He works with furniture manufacturers including B & B Italia, Vitra, Kartell and Olivetti. In 1983 he began to work on architectural design projects, collaborating with Gregotti Associati on the renovation of the Pinacoteca di Brera (1983). Terry Dwan, who joined the practice in 1986, was born in Santa Monica, California in 1957 and studied architecture at Yale. Recent projects by the practice include the Esprit headquarters in Milan and shops in Europe; World's Creative Fashion Dome, Kobe (1989, with Toshiyuki Kita); the Polsterfabrik, Neuenburg for Vitra, Germany (1992); shops for Fausto Santini in Paris and Rome (1991–2), and the Corrente building, Tokyo (1992). Two commercial and industrial projects are currently under construction in Milan. Citterio lectures and exhibits throughout Europe. An exhibition of work by the practice was held at Arc en Rêve, Bordeaux, in 1993.

Jo Coenen was born in 1949 in Heerlen, The Netherlands, and graduated from the University of Technology, Eindhoven in 1975. He taught architecture at the School of Architecture in Maastricht, and worked with Aldo Van Eyck and Bosch before establishing Jo Coenen & Co Architekten in 1979. Projects include a library and museum in Heerlen (1986); offices and residences in Delft (1986); a health centre and pharmacy in Eindhoven (1987; 1989); an office building for JCJ Haans, Tilburg (1991); a lecture hall, University of Limberg, Maastricht (1991); Chamber of Commerce and housing association offices, Maastricht (1991), and villas (1990; 1991). Coenen has undertaken masterplanning in The Hague, Maastricht, and Amsterdam, and recently completed the library for the Technical University, Delft. He taught at the School of Architecture, Tilburg, for six years, and in 1987 at the University of Technology, Karlsruhe.

Pepe Cortés was born in Barcelona in 1946, and studied there at the Eina School of Design. In the early 1970s he co-founded the Grupo Abierto de Diseño, and formed his own practice in the late 1970s, designing furniture and interiors. Major projects since 1983 include the roof of the award-winning Azulete restaurant (with Oscar Tusquets and I. Aparicio, 1983), offices for Andecosa, Barcelona Port Authority, Telec, Daniel Hechter (and showroom, with FERNANDO SALAS, 1989), Guillermo Bosch and Tejidos Sivila SA; shops for Focus (with Javier Mariscal), Francisco Valiente (with Eduard Samso, 1986), Trafico de Modas (with Mariscal), Tascon, A/2, Sayes, Salvato, and Calcats Lluch; Big Ben bar-pizzeria-bowling alley (1989), and the Tragaluz restaurant, Barcelona (1990; an FAD award winner). Cortés has designed furniture and products for Amat, Artespana, Akaba, BD, Grupo T, and for Gambrinus restaurant in Barcelona (with Mariscal and Alfredo Arribas), and exhibition stands for SIDI, Telec and Lotusse.

Antonio Cruz and Antonio Ortiz were born in Seville in 1948, graduated from Madrid School of Architecture in 1971, and went into partnership later that year. They have been awarded various prizes, including the Brunel International Award for Railway Design for their design of the Santa Justa railway station, Seville (1991). Other major projects include city archives in Cadiz (1986) and Seville (1987); the Maritime Museum, Cadiz (1989); the Spanish Institute of Culture, Lisbon (1991); numerous housing complexes in Seville, Madrid and Cadiz, and the resettlement of a mining village in Huelva (1992). Work in progress includes a sports complex in Madrid, bus stations at Huelva and government offices in Seville. Formerly professors of design at the Seville School of Architecture, they have also been visiting professors at the École Polytechnique Féderale, Lausanne, ETH/Zurich, and GSD/Harvard and Cornell University in the USA.

Lynn Davis was born in 1947 and studied architecture at Manchester University. She became a registered architect in 1974, establishing her practice, Lynn Davis Architects, in 1980. Her activities encompass commercial, leisure, residential, interior and exhibition projects, including her own Holland Park offices; converted residences in Kent; directors' offices at Thames TV (1988); Althorp Studios, Wandsworth (1988); Ivory Place, an office complex in Holland Park, London (1989), and the Ministry of Sound, London (1991). Lecture venues include the RIBA, the Universities of Cambridge and Liverpool, and Kent Institute of Art and Design. Davis teaches at the Bartlett School of Architecture and has organized and taken part in masterclasses and workshops for the RIBA; she has also broadcast for BBC Radio 4. The practice is currently building a new studio/office block in Hammersmith.

de Architekten Cie is an architectural practice based in Amsterdam, headed by Pi de Bruijn (who joined the firm in 1987), Fritz van Dongen, Jan Dirk Peereboom Valler and Carel Weeber. De Bruijn (born in Losser, The Netherlands, in 1942) trained at Delft, and practised as an architect in Amsterdam, winning a limited competition for the Second Chamber of Parliament building in The Hague in 1980 (completed in 1991). Other projects include the Concertgebouw extension and renovation, Amsterdam; the House of Representatives in The Hague; a city hall extension in Amersfoort; housing, office and mixed-use projects in Amsterdam and Rotterdam; the Central Directie ptt, Groningen; Faculties of Economy and Planning for the University of Amsterdam (1990–); railway stations (Spijkenisse), interior design (Pullman Hotel, The Hague), and urban planning in The Netherlands.

DEGW London Ltd is a London-based architectural and space planning firm first established as the DEGW Partnership in 1973 by Frank Duffy, John Worthington and Luigi Giffone. It is now part of an international group with offices in Glasgow, Madrid, Milan, Paris, Amersfoort, Berlin, Brussels, Manchester and Munich. Notable landmarks in the firm's development during the 1970s include the headquarters for British Nuclear Fuels, Warrington; several interior design/space planning projects for IBM UK, and projects for Christie's, London. Major projects during the 1980s include briefing for the Stockley Park and Broadgate developments; award-winning interior design for Lloyds Bank, Hays Wharf, London; and refurbishment of the 1958 Lloyds Corporation building. Amongst notable activities in the early 1990s are new pathology laboratories for the Great Ormond Street Hospital; and the design of a research and development centre for Olivetti, Bari, Italy. The firm has recently won a major competition to design a large industrial development in Wedding, Berlin. Publications include *Planning Office Space*, by Duffy, Worthington and Managing Director Colin Cave. The firm has undertaken multi-client studies on the impact of information technology on office buildings (ORBIT), the Responsible Workspace, the Intelligent Building in Europe, and recently established the Workplace Forum research programme. Frank Duffy's book *The Changing Workplace* was published in 1991 by ADT/Longman.

Stefano de Martino is a London-based Italian architect who was born in 1955 in St Gallen, Switzerland. He trained at the Bartlett School of Architecture, University College, London (1974–7) and at the Architectural Association (1977–9), and in 1979 became an associate partner of the office of Metropolitan Architecture (OMA), London and Rotterdam, with responsibility for planning and design projects in The Netherlands, including the conversion of Panopticon, Arnhem (1979-80); a new skyscraper/bridge development in Rotterdam (1980-82); Netherlands Dance Theatre, Scheveningen schemes (1980–83); and many major European competitions (1981–3). Between 1983 and 1989 he worked in association with Alex Wall on projects including Globe Video editing studio (1984–7), and house conversion for Zoe Zenghelis (1988–90), both in London, before establishing his own office in 1989. Projects include a marine development plan on the Isle of Wight (1989); Skyros village development, Greece (first prize, 1989); housing (1990–91) and hotel/leisure facilities in London and the Lebanon (1991–2), and interiors for Chiat/Day Advertising Inc, London, with REM KOOLHAAS and DEGW (1990–91). De Martino started teaching at the Architectural Association in 1983, was Unit Master of Diploma Unit 5 from 1988–91, and has exhibited in Italy, the Netherlands, France, Germany, the UK and the USA.

Denton Corker Marshall is an international architectural practice founded in Melbourne in 1972 by John Denton (born 1945), Bill Corker (born 1945) and Barrie Marshall (born 1946), all graduates in architecture from the University of Melbourne (1968), where the partners currently teach. Corker has been president of the Victorian chapter of the RAIA. With offices throughout Australia, and in London, Hong Kong, Tokyo, Singapore, Jakarta and Beijing, the practice's award-winning, multi-disciplinary project list is extensive, including numerous office buildings in Melbourne and Hong Kong; the Como multi-use development, Melbourne (1987); the Power House Museum of Applied Arts and Sciences, Sydney (exhibition design, 1988); Brisbane Expositions pavilions (1988); the Australian Embassy, Tokyo (1990), and the Adelphi Hotel, Melbourne (1993). Current projects include the Australian Embassy, Beijing; Australian War Memorial Exhibition Hall; Monash University, Melbourne campus development; the Peak redevelopment, Hong Kong, and the Governor Phillip Tower/ Museum, Sydney.

Ralph Erskine was born in 1914 in London, and studied architecture at Regent Street Polytechnic, London. After working for Louis de Soisson he moved to Sweden, built his own home near Stockholm and worked as an architect while studying at Stockholm College of Art (1944–5), opening his own office at Drottningholm the following year. Major projects include numerous housing developments, factories, offices, and urban planning predominantly in Sweden and the UK, including the Ski Hotel, Borgafjall, Lapland (1948–50); a paper factory at Fors (1950–3); housing estates in Kiruna (1961–2) and Svappavara (1963); a new town on Resolute Bay, Canada (1973–), and the Byker urban area with housing, schools and shops, Newcastle upon Tyne (1968–82). Since the early 1980s, Erskine has worked in collaboration with various architects, on projects including the Vasa Terminal, Stockholm (1984); an ice skating rink, Märsta (1986); urban renewal in Italy (1985; 1987–8); Måsen, Ejdern & Davan, mixed-use development, Umeå (1986–90), and The Ark, Hammersmith, London (1991, with LENNART BERGSTRÖM ARKITEKTKONTOR and ROCK TOWNSEND). Erskine has received many awards including Officier/Ordre des Arts et des Lettres, France (1986) and Royal Gold Medal (RIBA, 1987).

Sir Norman Foster and Partners, originally known as Foster Associates, was established in 1967 by Norman and Wendy Foster, and is now an internationally renowned architectural practice committed to design based on modern technology, with over sixty awards and citations. Foster was born in Manchester in 1935, and studied at the University of Manchester and at Yale University. In 1963 he founded Team 4 in collaboration with his late wife Wendy and Su and Richard Rogers. Early successes included the Willis Faber & Dumas head office, Ipswich (1971–5, now a listed building), and the Renault Centre, Swindon (1984). Many of the practice's projects have resulted from international competitions, including the Sainsbury Centre for the Visual Arts, University of East Anglia (1978); the Hong Kong and Shanghai Bank (1979–86); the Torres de Collserola communications tower, Barcelona (1988–92), and Bilbao Metro (1988–); Stansted Airport, Essex (1981–91); Century Tower, Tokyo (1987–91); the Carre d'Art gallery/cultural centre, Nîmes (1984–93), and the library for Cranfield Institute of Technology (1989–92). The Sackler Galleries project at the Royal Academy of Arts, London (1985–91) was named RIBA Building of the Year in 1993. Masterplans include King's Cross, London; Nîmes and Cannes, France; Berlin and Duisburg, Germany and Rotterdam, Holland. On a smaller scale, the practice has also designed shops for Esprit (1988) and Katharine Hamnett (1986), furniture for Tecno (1985), street furniture for Decaux, France (1989) and carpets for Vorwerk (1988). Projects in progress include a new headquarters for Commerzbank, Frankfurt; a new airport at Chek Lap Kok, Hong Kong; the Musée de la Prehistoire, Gorges du Verdon, France; one-family houses in Corsica, Germany, Japan and Paris, and new ranges of furniture for Tecno, Milan. Foster has lectured throughout the world and taught architecture in the UK and the USA.

Tony Fretton studied at the Architectural Association, London (1966–72). Between 1978 and 1979 he taught at the Bartlett School of Architecture, University of London, and from 1980–82 and 1988–92 at the Architectural Association. He has been a guest critic at Princeton, SCIARC, Los Angeles, and the Parsons School of Design, New York, and lectured at the RIBA, the Cambridge School of Architecture, and Hull and Edinburgh Schools of Architecture. After working for Arup Associates (1968; 1972–6), Neylan and Ungless (1976–8) and Chapman Taylor Partners Architects (1978–80) he established his own office in London. Projects include the Head over Heels clothing shops, London; Neckinger Mill apartment/studio; Mute Records head office/recording studio (in conjunction with acoustic consultants Recording Architecture); St Peter's School studios/apartments conversion, Vauxhall; the Zelda Cheatle Gallery, London; a house for gallery director Nicholas

Logsdail; both the conversion of (1986), and a new building for the Lisson Gallery, London (1992); residential interiors in London; St John's School studios, London (1992/93), and the Stephen Bartlett product design studio, London (1993). Other activities include performance art with Station House Opera in France and the UK (1981); a film and video installation for the Tyne International Art Triennale, Newcastle upon Tyne (1993); and symposia (Hayward Gallery, ICA, AA, and the Laing, Newcastle upon Tyne).

Spencer Fung Architects was founded in 1990 by Spencer Fung following his award of first prize in a competition for a private housing project in Fukuoka, Japan. Fung studied architecture at Churchill College, Cambridge University and at the Architectural Association, London. In 1987 he won first prize at the fifth RIBA International Student Competition and joined David Chipperfield Architects, working on projects such as the National Rowing Museum, Henley-on-Thames; the Gotoh Museum, Tokyo; the Wilson & Gough Gallery, London; workers' housing and a church in Borneo; the National Bank of Indonesia, Singapore, and the Admiralty Commercial Centre, Hong Kong. The practice's main projects to date include the Isometrix showroom, London (1990); Zoo hairdressers, London (1990); residences in London and Barcelona, and the Designers' Guild headquarters, London (1992). Fung teaches at the University of Bath and North London Polytechnic.

Beth Galí, Màrius Quintana and Antoni Solanas are Spanish architects based in Barcelona who occasionally collaborate on projects. Galí (born 1950, Barcelona) trained in industrial design at Escola EINA there, and as an architect at the ETSAB (1982); she has been Municipal Architect in the Department of Urban Projects, Barcelona City Council (1982–8), Adjunct Architect, Institute for Urban Promotion (1988–), and has won many FAD awards for her product design. Quintana (born Barcelona 1954) trained as an architect at ETSAB (1979), and also worked for Barcelona's Urban Projects Department (1982–8). Since 1989 he has been Professor at ELISAVA. Both he and Galí have directed design collections for Santa i Cole SA. Solanas (born 1946 in Girona) also trained at ETSAB (1971). Since 1981 he has co-directed the Jordi Capell architectural co-operative. Joint projects include housing in Selva de Mar (Galí, Solanas, 1980) and at Port de la Selva (Galí, Quintana, 1990), the Joan Miró Library, Barcelona (all three, 1985), and commercial building, Vilafranca del Penedes (Galí, Quintana, 1989).

Frank Gehry (born in Toronto, 1929) established Frank O. Gehry and Associates in California in 1962. After studying urban planning at Harvard and architecture at the University of Southern California, he worked for practices in the US and in France. Gehry's activities have included furniture design, art happenings and many exhibitions; now expanding his work to Europe, his built projects, many of which have won awards, are mostly in California, including many residences (Schnabel, Winton, and Norton), the Loyola Law School (1981–4); Aerospace Museum (1982–4); Rebecca's Restaurant (1984–6); the Temporary Contemporary gallery space for MOCA, Los Angeles (1983); Chiat/Day/Mojo offices, Venice (1991), and Iowa Laser Laboratory, Iowa City. In 1989 he completed the firm's first European project, the Vitra Museum, Weil, Germany, and has subsequently finished a retail/entertainment complex at EuroDisney near Paris, a retail centre/sculpture in Barcelona, and the American Center in Paris (1993). Currently under construction is the Walt Disney Concert Hall, Los Angeles (awarded in 1989), and in Europe, a headquarters for Vitra in Basel, Switzerland. At the design stage are the Guggenheim Museum, Bilbao; an office building in Prague; social housing in Frankfurt, and offices in Hereford, Germany.

Volker Giencke was born in Austria in 1947 at Wolfsberg, Carinthia. He studied architecture and philosophy in Graz and Vienna, and worked for various practices there, and in Geneva, Munich and Cologne. In 1981 he established Giencke & Co. Major projects include many residences, exhibitions and retail projects in Austria and Germany; the Kamten und Stelemark offices, Graz (1983); a sports hall/Kepler gym in Graz (1987–); the adaptation of the Seckau monastery and gym, Upper Styria (1988–); a Styrian government building (with Fredi Bramberger, 1990–); the Odörfer showroom/

warehouse, Klagenfurt (1989–91); the Austrian pavilion, Expo '92, Seville (1990–2); the Carinthia archives, Klagenfurt (1991–2), and a church in Aigen im Ennstal (1992). In progress are a congress hall/hotel, Klagenfurt; the Austrian Cultural Institute, New York, and student residences in Innsbruck. Giencke has taught architecture at the Technical University of Graz, and is professor at the University of Innsbruck. His awards include the state prize for architecture in Carinthia (1991), and he has exhibited work in Austria, Germany, France, Italy, and most recently in 'Sacred Spaces in Architecture' at the 1992 Venice Biennale.

Peter Glynn-Smith Associates was established in London in 1965 by interior designer Peter Glynn-Smith, who was born near Stoke-on-Trent in 1932. He trained at the Bartlett, University College, London, and then emigrated to California where he worked for Welton Beckett Associates, and for Charles Eames on his IBM Pavilion for the New York World Fair. The practice designs international restaurant, hotel and tourism projects and, recently, interiors for Aberdeen, Heathrow and Gatwick Airports (for which the practice are retained as consultants to BAA). Work includes interiors and furniture for the TI Group, Vosper Thornycroft, The Santini Group (several restaurants in London, and the latest Santini in Milan), the T4 Hilton Hotel at Heathrow and projects for various clients in France.

Gwathmey Siegel & Associates is a New York-based architectural practice established in 1968 by Charles Gwathmey and Robert Siegel who since then have completed over 150 projects, including institutional, university and corporate buildings, housing and residences, and a variety of residential, commercial and corporate interiors. Gwathmey trained at the University of Pennsylvania and Yale University; he has held faculty positions at a number of architectural colleges including Cooper Union, Princeton and Columbia Universities, and visiting professorships at Yale and Harvard. Siegel studied at the Pratt Institute and Harvard University. Both architects have received major awards, and their work has been documented in many exhibitions. Major institutional projects include university buildings at Princeton, Columbia, Harvard, Yeshiva, Cornell, North Carolina and the City University of New York, as well as the American Museum of the Moving Image, New York, new libraries for the New York Public Library, and the renovation of and addition to the Guggenheim Museum, New York; commercial interiors include numerous projects for IBM and Vidal Sassoon, and showrooms for Knoll and Herman Miller. Giorgio Armani, Ogilvy & Mather, McCann Erickson, Sony, AT & T, Damson Oil, Disney Development, the Evans Partnership and Lazard Realty (the International Design Center, Queens, New York) are amongst their clients.

Steven Holl Architects was established in New York City in 1976. Holl (born in 1947, in Bremerton, Washington, USA) is a graduate of the University of Washington, and did postgraduate work at the Architectural Association, London in 1976. His major, award-winning projects include the Berkowitz-Odgis house, Martha's Vineyard, MA (1987); the Hybrid building, Seaside, Florida (1989); the Giada fashion shop, New York (1987); the College of Architecture at the University of Minnesota (1990), and the AGB Library, Berlin (1989). Holl's recent Void Space/Hinged Space housing and retail project at Fukuoka, Japan, received Progressive Architecture and AIA New York City Chapter awards, and his offices for D.E. Shaw, New York, a 1992 AIA National Honor Award. Exhibitions of Holl's work have been held at international venues including MOMA New York, the Walker Art Center, Minneapolis (Architecture Tomorrow, 1991), and there is a forthcoming exhibition in Japan. Holl is professor at Columbia University School of Architecture and Planning, New York, and his book, *Anchoring*, was published by Princeton University Press in 1989.

Hans Hollein was born in 1934 in Vienna, Austria. He studied at the Akademie der Bildenden Kunst, Vienna, as well as at the ITT, Chicago, and the University of California, Berkeley (1960). From 1967–76 he was professor at the Staatliche Kunstakademie Düsseldorf, and since 1976 has been a professor at the Hochschule für Angewandte Kunst, Vienna, and has taught at various colleges in the USA. A prolific product designer as well

as an architect, Hollein's first commission, the renovation of the Retti candleshop, Vienna (1964–5) brought international attention. Notable amongst his more recent commissions are: the Richard Feigen Gallery, New York (1967–9); Seimens headquarters, Munich (1970–75); the Abteiberg Museum, Mönchengladbach (1972–82); Schullin jewellery shops, Vienna (1972–4; 1981–2); Haas-Haus development, Vienna (1985–90), and the Museum of Modern Art, Frankfurt (1987–91). Hollein has also undertaken many urban planning studies in Austria and Germany, and designed products for Franz Wittmann, Cleto Munani, Alessi, Swid Powell, Knoll and Thonet. Projects in progress include Banco Santander, Madrid (1987–); Fukunda Motors Building, Tokyo (1989); The Salzburg Guggenheim Museum (1990–), as well as housing in Germany and Spain. Of his many awards, one of the most recent was first prize in an international competition (1992) to design a museums complex for St Polten, the new capital of Lower Austria.

Michael Hopkins and Partners was established in London in 1976, and is headed by Michael Hopkins CBE (born 1935, Poole; trained at the Architectural Association, London, 1959–62), Patricia Hopkins, John Pringle, Ian Sharratt and William Taylor. Michael Hopkins is a Commissioner with the Royal Fine Art Commission, a member of the RIBA Council and Vice President of the Architectural Association. Principal award-winning projects include the Hopkins family house in Hampstead (1976); the Greene King building, Suffolk (1979); the Schlumberger Research Laboratories, Cambridge (1985); the David Mellor cutlery factory, Hathersage (1988); the Marylebone Cricket Club, London (1987); the Solid State Logic building, Begbroke (1988), and the Bracken House redevelopment, London (1991). Projects on site include Bedfont Lakes masterplan; the new Glyndebourne Opera House and the Inland Revenue Centre, Nottingham. New parliamentary offices for the House of Commons, the Younger Universe redevelopment, Edinburgh, and London Transport projects are amongst those at the design stage.

Franklin D. Israel was born in 1945 in New York City, and trained as an architect at the Universities of Pennsylvania, Yale and Columbia. From 1972 to 1975 he was a Prix de Rome Fellow in Architecture at the American Academy in Rome. He became Adjunct Associate Professor of Architecture at the Graduate School at the University of California in 1977, and established Franklin D. Israel Design Associates in 1983, after working with practices in New York, London and Tehran. Major projects include Limelight Productions, Los Angeles; Virgin Records offices, and an art pavilion in Beverly Hills; Propaganda Films, Hollywood; Tisch/Avnet Productions, Los Angeles, and residences in Malibu, Los Angeles and New York. The firm is currently designing housing in The Hague, The Netherlands, and a masterplan for part of northern Tokyo. Israel has lectured at numerous colleges in the USA and abroad, and exhibited work in London, Paris, Rome and the USA (most recently, in 'Six Mementos for the Next Millenium', 1989, Walker Art Center and touring). A monograph, *Cities Within*, was published by Rizzoli in 1993.

Toyo Ito was born in Nagano, Japan, in 1941, and graduated in architecture from Tokyo University in 1965. After working for Kiyonori Kikutake (1965–9) he established Urban Robot in Tokyo which became Toyo Ito & Associates in 1979, the year he won a Japan Airlines design commission. Ito has designed numerous residences in Japan, and since the mid-1980s larger scale architectural projects, receiving awards for his house in Kasama (1981); the Silver Hut, Tokyo (1984); the Nomad restaurant, Tokyo (1985/6); the guesthouse for the Sapporo brewery, Hokkaido (1989), and the Yatsushiro Municipal Museum (1991). Other major projects include the Tower of Winds, Yokohama (1986); I- and T- Buildings, Asakusabashi and Nakameguro (1989–90); the Opera House, Frankfurt (lighting, 1991); the U-Gallery, Yugawara (1991); the F-Building, Tokyo (1991); the 'Egg of Winds' image/information gate at Okawabata Rivercity 21 residential complex (1991); JAL office interiors, New York (1992); the Hotel P, Hokkaido (1992), and an amusement complex in Nagayama (1992). Ito is a visiting lecturer at the University of Tokyo and Japan Women's University. Exhibitions include the Pao dwelling project, Tokyo (1985/6) and 'Transfiguration', Europalia '89, Belgium. A monograph on Ito was published by Editions du

Moniteur in 1991, and his work featured in 'Architecture in a Simulated City' (1992, INAX).

Jestico + Whiles is an architectural practice formed in London in 1977: the principals are Tom Jestico, John Whiles, Robert Collingwood and Tony Ingram. Industrial projects at Epsom (1979) and Waltham Cross (1982) employ lightweight structures and manufacturing-derived technologies; Bruges Place (1985), Hawgood Street (1986) and Carlow Street (1990), all in London, combined workspace, industrial use and housing, and the practice has also designed many low-energy workspaces, for Friends of the Earth (1981 and 1986); the Policy Studies Institute (1986); the British Council offices in Prague (1990), and Stukeley Street, London (1991). Current work includes a cultural centre in Madrid, an embassy building in Latvia and an urban transport interchange.

Carlos Jiménez was born in 1959 in Costa Rica, and moved to the USA in 1974, where he studied architecture at the University of Houston, graduating in 1981. In 1983 he established his own practice, building his own studio in Houston. Projects complete to date include housing, mostly in Houston, and cultural buildings such as the Houston Fine Art Press (1989) and the Lynn Goode Gallery, Houston (1991). He is currently designing an office building and art school for Houston Museum of Fine Arts. Jiménez is a visiting lecturer at the Southern California Institute of Architecture and the University of Houston. His designs have been exhibited widely within the USA, in Moscow and Helsinki, and documented in a monograph published by G. Gili (1991).

Ben Kelly Design was established in London in 1977 by designer Ben Kelly (born in 1949), who studied environmental/interior design at the Royal College of Art, graduating in 1974. Elena Massucco (born in 1958) joined the practice in 1987, and Chris Cawte (born in 1962) in 1991; key designers who have worked for BKD include Sandra Douglas (born in 1958) and Peter Mance (born in 1963); all four are graduates of Kingston Polytechnic's interior design course. Kelly's early individual projects included the Howie Shop (1977); work for Malcolm McLaren/The Sex Pistols; and Lynne Franks' first office (1981–6). BKD's major projects include the pioneering Hacienda nightclub, Manchester (1982); Smile hairdressers (1983); a shop and office for Quincy (1987–88); Dry bar, Manchester (1989); Factory Communications' headquarters, Manchester (1990); 4AD offices, London (1991); Ten bar and DLC hairdressers, Glasgow (1991); Lynne Franks PR's Harrow Road offices, London (1991); Production video company offices (1992), and TV commercial sets (1992). Kelly has taught interior/3D design at Kingston Polytechnic for 13 years, and acts as external assessor at Glasgow School of Art. *Plans & Elevations*, a book on the practice, was published in 1990, and BKD featured in 'Sublime: The Sol Mix', an exhibition on Manchester music and design, as part of the 'Door Window Staircase' exhibition, Kelvingrove, Glasgow (1992).

King Kong Production was set up in Milan in 1985 by Stefano Giovannoni (born La Spezia, Italy, 1954) and Guido Venturini (born Alfonsino, Italy, 1957) who graduated from the Faculty of Architecture in Florence, going on to teach and research there, and more recently at the Domus Academy, Milan. Founder members of the Bolidist movement, the duo's preoccupations lie with avant-garde design of all kinds. They have designed objects for companies including Alessi, Arredaesse and Flos; installations for the Sawaya & Moroni showroom; the interior of Bar Maddalena, Prato (1990/91) and exhibitions ('Capitales Européennes', Pompidou Centre, Paris, 1991; 'Nuovo Bel Design', Milan, 1992); participated in competitions held in Japan, the USA and Italy, and exhibited at the Paris, Venice, São Paolo and Barcelona Biennales (1982; 1985; 1985; 1987); in 'The Domestic Project', Milan Triennale, (1986); 'Atelier Nouveau', Seibu, Tokyo (1986); 'Imagined Cities', Milan Triennale (1987); and 'Signs of the Habitat', Grand Palais, Paris (1988).

Rem Koolhaas was born in Rotterdam in 1944, and studied at the Architectural Association in London from 1968–72, and at Cornell University and the Institute of Architecture and Urban Studies, New York. In 1975 he founded Office for Metropolitan Architecture (OMA) with Elia and Zoe Zenghelis and Madelon Vriesendorp. Major projects include the Netherlands Dance Theatre, The Hague (1987);

Byzantium complex, Amsterdam (1985–91); Kunsthal art centre, Rotterdam (1987–92); Museum Park, Rotterdam (1988–92); award-winning Nexus housing, Fukuoka, Japan (1989–91); the Congrexpo, a cultural hall in Lille, France (1991–), and the major Euralille urban project, Lille, France (1988–), with Jean Nouvel, Christian de Portzamparc and Kazuo Shinohara. Exhibitions include 'Deconstructivism' (MOMA, New York, 1988); 'The First Decade', Boymans Museum, Rotterdam (1989), 'Energieen' (Stedelijk, Amsterdam 1990), and 'La Congestion' (MOMA, New York, 1993).

Shiro Kuramata (1934–1991) was born in Tokyo, trained in woodwork at Tokyo High School of Technical Art and graduated from the Kuwasawa Design Institute in 1956. In 1965 he established his own practice and from the 1970s became widely renowned for his interior and furniture design projects for Issey Miyake, Esprit and Tokio Kumagai, among them many bars (Lucchino, Comblé and Oblomova at Hotel Il Palazzo, Fukuoka) and shops (Yoshiki Hishinuma, SPIRAL, Japan). His furniture (the 'How High the Moon' chair of 1986 is the most famous) for clients including Idée, Vitra and Memphis, has been exhibited widely and is represented in museum collections throughout the world. In 1990 he was made a Chevalier des Arts et des Lettres.

José Antonio Martinez Lapeña and Elías Torres Tur established their architectural practice in Barcelona in 1968 after studying at the Escuela Tecnica (ESTAB) there. Lapeña (born in 1941 in Tarragona) now teaches at the Escuela Tecnica del Valles in Barcelona (ESTAV); Torres (born in 1944 in Ibiza) has taught at ESTAB and has also been visiting professor at Harvard and UCLA. Major projects include housing in Barcelona and Ibiza; the award-winning Villa Cecilia gardens, Barcelona; the monastery of Sant Pere de Rodes, Girona (1980–90); Barcelona Activa headquarters (1987–8); the Mora d'Ebre Hospital, Tarragona (1982–88), for which they won a FAD Award in 1988; Folly No. 7 at Expo '90, Osaka, Japan; Olympic Village apartments, Barcelona (1989–91), and the Ronda Promenade (1988–91) and Banco de Gestíon e Inversíon Financiera (1990).

Christian Liaigre is a French designer born in 1943 at Niort, Deux-Sevres. He studied at the École des Arts Décoratifs, Paris, then worked as Design Director of the fabric house Nobilis Fontan, and designed furniture for Hugonet and Mirak (USA). In 1987 he established his own firm, designing furniture and interiors for banks in Paris and Brussels, the peers' chamber in the French Senate, and the library in the Lloyds building, London. Large interior commissions have included the French embassies in Warsaw and New Delhi; Hotel Montalembert, Paris (1990); offices and a residence for Kenzo; shops for Cerruti and Manuel Canovas, and the Hotel Guanahani on St Bart's in the Caribbean. Liaigre has recently renovated designer Robert Mallet-Stevens' former apartment in Paris; current projects include offices for Credit Mutuel, Paris; a private museum of Lalique glassware in Kamakura, and a group of residences in Osaka, Japan. He has designed furniture for Louis Vuitton, and has a showroom at rue de Varenne, Paris.

Alberto Lievore & Asociados is the practice of Argentinian architect and furniture designer Alberto Lievore, who has lived in Barcelona since 1977. He trained as an architect at the University of Buenos Aires, Argentina, while also working as a designer of institutional furniture and equipment. His furniture and lighting for Perobell (for whom he designed a showroom in 1983 with Alberto Arola), Simeyco, Andreu, Divano and Kron has received national and international awards. Interior design projects include exhibition stands, showrooms, and corporate image work, for clients such as SIDI, the Spanish Red Cross, Buffeti, IMPI, Ercros. Caja Murcia and Institute de la Juventud. Lievore often collaborates with architect Eduardo Campoamor.

John Lum (born 1961 in Long Beach, California) is an Associate of the San Francisco-based architectural and planning firm Reid & Tarics Associates. He studied architectural engineering at California Polytechnic State University, gaining further degrees from the École des Beaux Arts, Fontainebleau, France, and in Florence via the California State international programme. Before joining RTA, he designed sets, display systems and boutiques for Enrico Coveri, a Florence-based fashion house. Lum's major projects to date include two elementary schools: Jean Parker in Chinatown, San Francisco and the award-winning Peggy Heller, Atwater; a showroom for AT&T and an office for GAPA Community HIV Services. His design for the Urban Eyes optometry office won three major US awards in 1992. Lum's current project for RTA is the O'Connor Hospital masterplan/medical building in San Jose.

MacCormac Jamieson Prichard is a London-based architectural practice founded in 1972 by Richard MacCormac (born 1938), Peter Jamieson (born 1939) and David Prichard (born 1948). MacCormac and Jamieson both trained at the University of Cambridge and at University College, London (1965). From 1991–3 MacCormac was President of the Royal Institute of British Architects. Prichard trained at the Bartlett School of Architecture, University College, London (1969). The work of the practice encompasses offices, university and public buildings, public and private housing, commercial projects such as the redevelopment of Spitalfields Market, London, as well as masterplans and urban design for sites such as Paternoster Square and London's Docklands, and new towns in the UK. Award-winning projects include the Sainsbury Building, Worcester College, Oxford (1980); Niccol theatre/ community centre, Cirencester (1983); New Court, Fitzwilliam College, Cambridge (1985); county council offices in Havant (1986), and Blue Boar Court, Trinity College, Cambridge (1990). In 1992 the practice won a competition to design buildings for Balliol College, Oxford. MacCormac has taught, lectured and published widely; Jamieson teaches at the University of Cambridge; Prichard teaches at Brighton Polytechnic and is RIBA External Examiner at the Bartlett.

José Luis Mateo was born in Barcelona in 1949 and studied architecture at ETSAB, graduating in 1974. Recent projects include law courts at Badalona (1987–91); a sports arena for the Universidad Autonoma, Barcelona (1987–90); Catex complex conversion, Barcelona (1985–92), and housing at Calle Pallar, Barcelona (1986–9) and in The Netherlands. Mateo has won the city of Barcelona award (1986), and in 1990 commissions for Salou and Barcelona's Periferia. He is currently working on a major multi-use complex in the Diagonal, Barcelona (1988–) and urban projects in Rheims and The Hague. Mateo, whose work has been exhibited in France, Germany and Switzerland, is Professor of Architecture at ETSAB, and visiting professor for colleges in Paris, Oslo, Karlsruhe, Berlin and Santa Monica. From 1981 to 1990 he edited *Quaderns* magazine.

Rick Mather (born in 1937 in Portland, Oregon, USA) studied architecture at the University of Oregon and urban design at the Architectural Association (AA), before starting his own practice in London designing institutional, residential and commercial projects. These include the masterplan and renovation of the AA (1978–83); award-winning buildings at the University of East Anglia, Norwich (UEA 1982–3); the remodelling of the Waddington Galleries (1988); three Zen restaurants in London (1985–6), Hong Kong (1988) and Montreal (1990), and La Lumière office development, London (1991). Work in progress includes the masterplan for the expansion of UEA (new low-energy residences and a drama centre) and a residential complex at Keble College, Oxford. The work of the practice has been exhibited in the UK, the USA and France.

John Miller + Partners is a long-established architectural practice based in London, formerly known as Colquhoun + Miller (from 1961–1989). Founder John Miller was educated at the Architectural Association between 1951 and 1956, and his academic appointments include Professor of Environmental Design, Royal College of Art, London, 1975–85. The other partners are Richard Brearley, who joined in 1975, a graduate of the University of Nottingham (1964–7) and Su Rogers, a graduate of the London School of Economics and Yale School of Architecture (1961–3), and partner, successively, in Team 4 Architects (1963–7), Richard & Su Rogers Architects (1967–70) and Piano + Rogers (1970–72), and Director of the Royal College of Art Project Office. Projects encompass educational and community work; cultural buildings and housing, including the conversion of the Royal College of Art's Gulbenkian Hall/galleries (1989) and new faculty building design (1991); the Whitechapel Art Gallery extension/conversion (1985); the Nomura Gallery and bookshop, Tate Gallery (1991); exhibitions at the Hayward Gallery; Alcoy/La Riba housing/commercial buildings, Valencia (1992), and housing developments in Spitalfields (1992) and Milton Keynes. Two major health and university buildings in East Anglia go on site in 1993.

Enric Miralles was born in Barcelona in 1955 and trained as an architect at ETSAB in 1978. He worked with Helio Pinon and Alberto Viaplana from between 1973 and 1984, and in 1983 established a studio with architect Carme Pinos. They have won several awards and competitions including the headquarters of Artespana, Barcelona; a new cemetery at Igualada (1985); the Centro Social, Frankfurt (1991); an FAD prize for the La Llauna School interiors, Badalona, Paleo Icaria, Olympic Village (1989–92), and Tiro con Arco Olympic archery range (1992). Miralles has been professor at ETSAB since 1985, and visiting professor at universities in the USA, Italy, the UK, Germany and Austria. He is currently chair of the design department at Frankfurt's Stadeschule, and in 1991 won the ITALSTEAD for Europe Prize at the Venice Architecture Biennale. The work of the practice has been exhibited in New York, Stuttgart and Paris. Miralles established a solo practice in 1990, completing the Circulo de Lectores centre, Madrid, in 1992. Current projects include sports centres at Huesca and in Alicante; an extension of the Ferrocarril station, Takaoka, and the Unazuki pavilion, both in Japan.

Eric Owen Moss (born in 1943) established his architectural practice in 1976, and is now based in Culver City. He studied architecture at the University of California's Berkeley College of Environmental Design and at Harvard Graduate School. Major award-winning projects include the Petal House (1984) and the Fun House (1980); numerous industrial conversions in Los Angeles and Culver City, such as 8522 National (1988); the Lindblade Tower (1989); the Paramount Laundry (1989); Gary Group (1990); Scott Mednick Associates (1990). Projects in progress include Samitaur I and II, Los Angeles; the Wedgwood Holly complex, Culver City, and S.P.A.R City, Los Angeles/Culver City. Moss is Professor of Design at the Southern California Institute of Architecture, and has lectured internationally. His work has been exhibited widely in the USA and in Europe.

Kiko Mozuna was born in 1941 in Kushiro City, Hokkaido, and graduated from the University of Kobe in 1965. His current practice, initially called Monta Mozuna, was founded in 1976. Major projects include many residences in Hokkaido and elsewhere in Japan; award-winning museums, a school, a hotel and a fisherman's wharf development in Kushiro City (1982/89); O Art Museum, Tokyo (1987); Museum of Informal Art, Nagano (1989); Shimokawa City Tower, Hokkaido (1991), and Notojima Glass Art Museum, Noto Islands, Ishikawa (1991). Projects under construction include the Nishiwaki Museum of Science; Tamana Museum of History; Oguni Ski Lodge; Ohya Duomo concert hall, Hyogo, and the L Co headquarters, Tokyo. Mozuna's work has been exhibited internationally, and publications include *Folio XIV: Kojiki of Architecture* (Architectural Association, London, 1991), *Sonar* (Toto Co, Japan, 1992) and *Cités et Mythologies* (Seido, Japan, 1987).

Walter Nägeli was born in 1951 in Germany, and trained as an architect at ETH, Zurich. After working for various practices around the world, in 1979 he began work with JAMES STIRLING, MICHAEL WILFORD AND ASSOCIATES, and from 1984–92 was chief architect of the practice's Berlin office. He was project architect for the Wissenschaftszentrum, Berlin (1979–87), and designed the B. Braun complex at Melsungen, Germany with STIRLING AND WILFORD (1986–92). From 1990 he has run his own practice in Berlin with Renzo Vallebuona, working with various clients in Germany. Nägeli has taught at Harvard Graduate School, Cambridge University, the Polytechnic of North London and the Architectural Association (with Zaha Hadid).

Torsten Neeland (born in Hamburg in 1963) studied industrial design at the Hochschule für Bildende Künste Hamburg between 1984 and 1989. He has designed products for ANTA (lighting and candlesticks) and Anthologie Quartett; furniture for Reim Interline, and display systems for Estée Lauder, Vorwerk, and West, as well as the interiors of the Uta Raasch fashion boutiques in Düsseldorf and Hamburg; Ocky's, Hamburg, apartments in Hamburg (for Naefke, 1990–), and the Mandel + Wermter advertising agency (1992). Exhibition venues have included Möbel Perdu, Hamburg; Zeus, Milan; Nolte European Design, New York, and Düsseldorf Museum of Arts. Current projects include a shoe shop in Hamburg, new lighting for ANTA and furniture for Candide.

Boris Podrecca was born in 1940 in Belgrade, Yugoslavia, and studied sculpture at the Hochschule für Angewandte Kunst, Vienna. He graduated in architecture from the Technische Universität, and the Akademie der Bildenden Kunst in Vienna. He has since taught architecture at the Technische Universitäts in Munich (1975–9) and Vienna (1979–83), at the Hochschule in Vienna, and has been visiting professor at Harvard (1987) and colleges in Lausanne, Paris, Pennsylvania, Venice and London. Since 1988 he has been professor and head of architecture/environmental design at the Technische Universität, Stuttgart. Major works include numerous residences, exhibitions, offices, hotel, retail and cultural buildings, urban planning and restoration projects in Austria, Italy, Germany and Slovenia. Podrecca has also designed furniture for Wittmann, Alari-Stefanelli and Matteo Grassi, and exhibited work at venues in Austria, France, Italy, the USA and the UK. In 1986 he was made a Chevalier des Arts et Lettres, and in 1992 he won the Jose Plecnik prize, Ljubljana, for the renovation of Tartini Square, Piran, Slovenia.

Rock Townsend was formed in London in 1971 by architects David Rock and John Townsend, and the practice now has offices in London and five other UK cities. Widely known for their work in urban design, leisure and tourism, market analysis and inner city renewal (under the name of CIVIX, a related company), they function as developers as well as designers, and frequently work in association with other practices including Winskell Architects in Newcastle, LENNART BERGSTRÖM ARKITEKTKONTOR AB, Stockholm (their most recent single project partnership is The Ark in London, with architect RALPH ERSKINE), and Ballini Pitt, Luxembourg. Activities include urban planning at Hereford, Ware and Leamington Spa; the Crowndale Centre conversion, Camden; originating the Barley Mow and 5 Dryden Street small business workspace developments, London; and numerous speculative and corporate office, and 'design and construct' projects in London, and around the UK. In 1980 Townsend founded the Housing Services Agency to assist single homeless persons in London.

Fernando Salas is an architect based in Barcelona. Born in 1950 in Sta. Cruz de Mudela, Spain, he worked for architects Oriol Bohigas, José María Martorell and David Mackay (MBM), before setting up his own firm in 1975. His work encompasses office, retail and showroom interiors and furniture, for clients including Roberto Verino (the FAD award-winning showroom, Barcelona, 1991; and shops in Orense, Madrid and Paris in 1992); Deni Cler (Barcelona shop, 1992); Daniel Hechter; Toreros Management (office, Barcelona, 1992), and CGZ (shops in Madrid and Mallorca, 1990), Puente Aereo (1985–7), and Battery Street (1988). He has collaborated on projects with Javier Mariscal (Bar Terraza, Barcelona, 1990, with Alfredo Arribas), for whom he designed a studio in 1989. From 1984 to 1985 he taught at the Elisava design school in Barcelona.

Afra and Tobia Scarpa began working together in 1958 after graduating from the University of Architecture in Venice. Afra was born in 1937 in Monteverna, Italy; her husband Tobia, the son of noted Italian architect Carlo Scarpa, was born in Venice in 1935, and spent some time working in the glass industry before their collaboration began, working first in glass with Venini at Murano. Their work embraces diverse fields of creativity, from award-winning furniture, lighting, products, to interior design and architecture in Italy, France and Japan (residences; commercial buildings for companies such as Benetton, from 1966 onwards; shops for Unifors, and the recent Punto SIP telephone offices in Treviso). Furniture clients include Cassina, B & B Italia, Molteni, Unifors, Casas and Meritalia, and they have also designed lighting for Flos; key works are included in the permanent collections of museums around the world.

Kazuyo Sejima was born in 1956 in Ibaraki Prefecture, Japan. She graduated in architecture from the Japan Women's University in 1981, and joined TOYO ITO & ASSOCIATES. In 1987 she established Kazuyo Sejima Architect & Associates. Her major projects to date include the Platform houses (I–III, 1988; 1990); exhibition design for 'Transfigurations' at Europalia '89, Brussels (1989); Castelbajac Sport shop (1991), and Saishunkan Seiyaku Women's Dormitory, Kumamoto City (1991). She is currently designing N-House and Pachinko Parlor. Sejima has won a number of awards, including Young Architect of the Year in 1992, given by the Japan Institute of Architects, and has exhibited work at in Japan since 1988.

Smith-Miller + Hawkinson Architects was established in New York in 1982 by architects Henry Smith-Miller and Laurie Hawkinson. Smith-Miller trained at the Universities of Princeton, Yale and Pennsylvania. From 1966 to 1968 he was a Fulbright Scholar in Architecture, based in Rome, and went on to work for Richard Meier. He has taught at many colleges, including SCIARC, Santa Monica; Harvard, and the Universities of Washington and Virginia. Hawkinson studied fine art at the University of California, Berkeley, and architecture at the Cooper Union, New York. She has curated many exhibitions for the Institute of Architecture and Urban Studies, New York, created installations, and has been vice-president of the Board of Directors of the Wooster Group in New York since 1985. Major projects include many residences in New York and California, and offices in New York; New Line Cinema East and West headquarters (1986; 1991); masterplan for North Carolina Museum of Art (1988); The New Museum/Museum of Contemporary Hispanic Art, New York (1990); award-winning Continental Airlines facilities design (1990); Kovel Building, Telluride (1991). Projects in progress include various residences; the Hetrick Martin Institute Youth Centre and Harvey Milk School, New York; an amphitheatre and outdoor cinema at North Carolina Museum of Art, and the entrance court, amphitheatre and studios at New Jersey Institute of Technology.

Philippe Starck (born in Paris in 1949) is a prolific designer of products, furniture and interiors. His main interior projects include apartments at the Elysée Palace for President Mitterrand (1982); Café Costes, Paris (1984); Manin, Tokyo (1986); La Cigale Theatre, Paris (1987); the Royalton and Paramount Hotels, New York (1988 and 1990); Nani Nani office building, Tokyo (1989); La Flamme d'Or for Asahi, Tokyo (1989); Teatriz restaurant, Madrid (1990); Hugo Boss showroom, Paris (1991); Coppola hair salon, Milan (1991); galleries at MOMA Groningen, The Netherlands (with Alessandro Mendini and Frank Stella 1990–1), and buildings for 'Starck Street', Paris. From 1985 to 1992 he designed and art-directed for the French furniture company XO; his own inspired output of new collections of furniture (for international clients such as Vitra, Disform, Driade, Flos, Kartell) and product design (currently for over 30 companies including Alessi, L'Oreal, Owo, Jean-Claude Decaux, Beneteau, Vuitton and FSB) continues unabated. His latest interior design projects include Le Baron Vert (office building, Osaka); residences in Los Angeles, Madrid and Anvers, Belgium; and Laguiole, Paris (a knife shop). Starck is a Chevalier des Arts et des Lettres.

James Stirling, Michael Wilford and Associates was established in 1971 by James Stirling (born in 1926 in Glasgow; studied architecture at the University of Liverpool, and town planning in London; died 1992) and Michael Wilford (born 1938, Surbiton; studied at the Northern Polytechnic School of Architecture). Stirling worked in private practice with James Gowan from 1956 until 1963, when he went solo, and Wilford (who had joined the practice in 1960) became first senior assistant, and, later, associate partner (1965–71) before they joined forces in practice together. Both partners have taught internationally; in 1977 Stirling became Professor at Düsseldorf Kunstakademie. Two projects had brought Stirling early acclaim: Leicester University's Engineering Building (1959–63, Stirling and Gowan), and the Cambridge History Faculty Library (1964–7, Stirling). In 1977 the practice won a major limited competition for the Staatsgalerie, Stuttgart, Germany (1977–84). This led to many more cultural buildings, including the Sackler Museum, Harvard University (1979–84); the Wissenschaftszentrum, Berlin (1979–87); the Clore Gallery extension at the Tate Gallery, London (1980–6); the Tate Gallery, Liverpool (1984–8), and the Performing Arts Center, Cornell University (1983–8). Projects in production include a music school and theatre academy, Stuttgart (1987–); Brera Museum, Milan (1987–); Science Library, University of California at Irvine, Los Angeles (1988–); 5–7 Carlton Gardens, London (1988–); a stadium development, Seville (1988–); Temasek Polytechnic, Singapore (1991–); Pier 8 plan/ Performing Arts Centre, Salford (1991–), and a passenger interchange/bus station, Bilbao (1992–). Their most recently completed major project, the B Braun headquarters, Melsungen, Germany, carried out in association with WALTER NÄGELI, was completed in May 1992, one month before James Stirling's death in June. Stirling's many awards included RIBA Gold Medal for Architecture (1980) and the Pritzker Prize, USA (1981).

Studio Granda is a Reykjavik-based architectural practice founded in 1987 by Steve Christer (born Blackfyne, UK, 1960) and Margret Hardardottir (born Reykjavik, 1959). Christer studied architecture at the University of Newcastle upon Tyne; Hardardottir at Edinburgh University, and they both graduated from the Architectural Association, London, in 1984. The Radhus/City Hall in Reykjavik is their first major built project, the result of a 1987 competition, completed in 1992. In 1989 they won the Aktion Poliphile competition to design a two-part private residence (known as Houses of Delia and Saturn) in Wiesbaden, Germany, also completed in 1992. Other projects include residences in Iceland, landscaping in Reykjavik and competitions for public buildings in the city. The partners have exhibited in Iceland, Germany, Norway, Switzerland, Austria and the UK.

STUDIOS Architecture is an international design practice founded in 1985 with offices in London, Paris, San Francisco and Washington DC, and headed by Erik Sueberkrop, Phil Olson, Darryl Roberson and Gene Rae. Sueberkrop was born in Hamburg and was educated at the University of Cincinnati, USA; he led the practice's design for the Knoll showroom, Frankfurt (1992). STUDIOS has designed award-winning corporate interiors in the USA, Europe and Asia, and their work has been widely exhibited. Current projects include conferencing facilities for Société Générale, Paris; Silicon Graphics' European headquarters at Cortaillod, Switzerland; 3Com manufacturing headquarters in Dublin; interiors for the Asian Pacific Trade Centre in Osaka, and the Petronas headquarters in Kuala Lumpur.

Yannis Tsiomis was born in 1944 in Athens, and studied architecture at the École Polytechnique there. He moved to Paris in 1967 and worked for Candilis while studying at the École Nationale Supérieure des Beaux Arts, graduating in 1969. In 1983 he received a doctorate from EHESS for his study of Neoclassical architecture, and in 1988 became Professor of History and Theory of Architecture at the École d'Architecture de Paris La Villette, UPA 6. He is currently involved with a number of research projects for DEA, the Ministry of Education and the European Community. He teaches in London, Athens, Milan, and Brazil, and has written extensively on architectural history and theory. Based in Paris, the Atelier d'Architecture et d'Urbanisme Yannis Tsiomis was established in 1984, and has completed a variety of projects in France, including the Robert Denos Theatre, Ris-Orangis (1975–6); the Theatre Gerard Philipe, Bonneuil-sur-Marne (1987–9); Académie Musicale de Villecroze, Var (1987–9); the design (1989–90) and extension of Galerie Karsten Greve, Paris; a private music performance space, Paris (1991); the Espace d'Art Contemporain (1990–91), a gallery/atelier and offices (1992–) for Renn Productions, Paris, and the Technopole, Mulhouse (1992–). Tsiomis has also designed housing and a school in Frankfurt; a studio and residences in Paris; is completing villas in Greece, and, on a larger scale, has undertaken urban projects at Saint-Denis, Mulhouse and Villecroze.

Shigeru Uchida was born in Yokohama, Japan, in 1943 and graduated from the Kuwazawa Design School, Tokyo, in 1966. In 1981 he founded Studio 80 with Ikuyo Mitsuhashi and Toru Nishioka. Interior design clients include Issey Miyake, Yohji Yamamoto and Asahi Beer (La Ranarita/Guest Room, Tokyo 1991). In 1989 Uchida was art director of the Hotel Il Palazzo, and designed the interiors with Ikuyo Mitsuhashi. Uchida is equally well known for his furniture and product design: he organized the KAGU Tokyo Designers' Week (1988–91) and has exhibited internationally, more recently in the 'Creativity of Form' at Europalia (1989), 'SAD: Home Sweet Home', Paris (1990), 'Furniture as Remembrance' at Pastoe, Milan (1992) and 'Horizontal + Vertical' at Sagacho, Tokyo (1992).

Wickham & Associates was established in London in 1971 by Julyan Wickham (born in 1942), who studied at the Architectural Association (1961–6), and worked for Edward Cullinan Architects. He has taught at many colleges in the UK and the Netherlands, and is currently external examiner at Glasgow School of Art. Partner Tess Wickham (born in 1945) studied at the London School of Economics and worked as a designer for Pearce Marchbank and with Wickham, becoming a partner in 1981. Commissions have included urban studies and projects, such as St Mary Abbotts housing/ health buildings (1988); new buildings, including a department for a psychiatric hospital in Boekel, The Netherlands (1982); Horselydown Square, London (housing/offices/shops, 1985–91); Hotel Pefcos, Rhodes (1988); office buildings at Gainsford Street, Mill Street, Herbal Hill and Brook Green, London (1989); publishing warehouses in Bury St Edmunds (1989–90); conversions such as recording studios/flats/office for Led Zeppelin (1974–5), and offices for Music Sales Ltd (1989); the interior design of houses in the UK; and restaurant/bars in London, including Dingwalls, Camden (club facilities, 1973); the Zanzibar Club, Covent Garden (1975); Corney & Barrow (1983) and Le Champenois (1985), both in the City; Kensington Place (1988; extension, 1992), and Harvey Nichols' Fifth Floor food hall/bar/restaurant (1992). Projects in progress include housing in Scotland and England, offices in London and Bury St Edmunds, and a clinic for the Dutch national health service.

Jean-Michel Wilmotte was born in 1948, and studied at the École Camondo before establishing Governor, his practice, in Paris in 1975 to design interiors, furniture and lighting. In 1986 offices in Nîmes and Tokyo were opened. Wilmotte's work includes architecture and urban landscaping/ street furniture, and major projects include the renovation of Nîmes' town hall and museum (1987–90); the design of a new opera house (1988); galleries and a bookshop at the Grand Louvre (1990); the Technal showroom, Toulouse (1990); Grenier à Sel showrooms, Avignon; Espace Kronenbourg, Paris (1990); the Bunkamura Cultural Centre, Tokyo (1990); the Hotel Le Phare in Honmuku, Japan (1991–92); the Hôtel du Cheval Blanc, Nîmes (1991–2); the Assemblée Nationale (1991–2), and BASF-France offices, Levallois-Perret (1992). Wilmotte is currently working on the Musée des Beaux-Arts, Lyon, airports at Roissy and Nîmes-Garon (with ADP); first-floor galleries in the Richelieu wing of the Grand Louvre, and the Institut International de la Mode, Marseilles.

Work Station was founded in Yokohama in 1988 by Akiko Takahashi (born 1958, in Shizuoka Prefecture) and Hiroshi Takahashi (born in 1953 in Tokyo). Both trained as architects at the Tokyo Institute of Technology, and worked at the Institute and for practices including Kazuo Shinohara Studio. Major works to date include the 5 Spans House (1991) and the Sakamoto Ryoma Memorial Hall, Kochi (1991). Their 1991 proposal for the Nasunogahara Harmony Hall received an honorable mention from Shinkenchiku. Their activities have included the IKD Project, and they have won awards from Kochi Urban View and the Japan Institute of Architects.

Workshop was established in 1978 by Koh Kitayama (born 1950, in Kagawa, Japan), Michio Kinoshita (born 1951, in Hyogo, Japan) and Akio Yachida (born 1951, in Niigata, Japan), all graduates in architecture from Yokohama National University. Major works include the Anagura bar (1986) and Doma restaurant/bar (1986), both in Tokyo; the San-va-Shi bar, Nagoya (1987); the Naebe Prive housing complex/hotel, Niigata (1988); the Tokyo Kaisen fish market/restaurant, Tokyo (1989); residences in Tokyo (1990; 1991); T-Lattice and S-Lattice office buildings, Tokyo (1991), and the BEAM cultural centre, Tokyo (1992). Work has been exhibited at the AXIS and Hillside Terrace galleries, Tokyo; in 'Emerging Japanese Architects of the 1990s' (Columbia University and international tour), and 'Invisible Language' (Parsons, New York, 1991; and the Architectural Association, London, 1992).

Credits

Isaac Mizrahi & Company
104 Wooster Street, New York, NY 10012, USA
Architects: Anderson/Schwartz Architects. Project team: Ross Anderson (partner in charge); M. J. Sagan (project manager); Joanne M. Robinson; Caroline Schiele; Frederic Schwartz; Samuel Tomos; Janice Kitchen; Eric Robbins. Client: Isaac Mizrahi/Isaac Mizrahi and Company. Main contractor: Kahn-Snyder Company. Sub-contractors: Klesco Builders; Solo Metals; Steven Truslow. Engineering consultant: CJJ Inc. Sound consultant: Snow H. Production. Lighting: Jan Kroeze. Furniture: designed by Anderson/ Schwartz, manufactured by Solo Metalworks Ltd and Steven Truslow.

One Off Ltd
62 Chalk Farm Road, London NW1, UK
Designer: Ron Arad Associates. Design team: Ron Arad; Alison Brooks; Alex Meitlis. One Off project team: Ron Arad; Caroline Thorman; Shaun Crown; Rachel Reynolds; Ian Whittaker; Matthew Stanwix; Jules Goss; Duncan McVean; Jacinda Lynch. Ron Arad Associates project team: Ron Arad; Alison Brooks; Charles Walker; Monique van Den Hurk. Engineer: Niel Thomas/Atelier One. Contractors: L. D. Engineering Ltd (steel superstructure); Atelier One (roof membranes); A.S.A.P. Construction Ltd (building work). Bridge fabrication: Midson Engineering Ltd; One Off. Electrical work: Jim Holland. Flooring: Tom Linham; Duncan McVean. Decorating: Capital Pro Painters. Furniture: Ron Arad/One Off, manufactured by One Off; Moroso; Vitra.

Warner Bros. Records
75 Rockefeller Center, New York, NY 10019, USA
Architects: Bausman-Gill Associates. Project team: David Wilbourne (project architect); Karen Bausman (partner in charge); Adi Shamir (designer); Alison Berger (designer); John Blackmon; Denise DeCoster; John Ginocchio; Alicia Imperiale; Rob Luntz; Kevin McClurkan; Ann O'Dell; Jackie Pilliciotti; Bryce Sanders; Gary Shoemaker; Mabel Wilson; James Hicks; Nandini Bagchee. Client: Warner Bros. Records, New York. Main contractors: Mison Inc. (architectural metalwork); Bauerschmidt & Sons (architectural woodwork). Structural engineer: Edwards and Hjorth. Electrical/mechanical engineer: Hartmann and Concessi. Audio/visual consultant: Audio Video Crafts. Stair fabricator: Ernst Stair. Electrical: Inner City Electrical. Ceiling and suspension systems: National Acoustics. Lighting: Artemide. Furniture consultant: Manes Space. Reception desk: Bauer Schmidt and Sons. Conference tables: Crucible; Kern and Rockenfield. Painting contractor: Hudson-Schatz Painting Co. Plaster panels: Stucco Lustro Veneziano. Flooring: Port Morris Tile and Terrazzo Corp. (slate); D. Magnan and Co. Inc. (terrazzo); Atlas Carpet Mills; Saxony Carpet (cork); Einstein-Moomjy (rug); Contract Distributors; Jack Lenor Larsen (Tonga sisal tile). Screen wall: Karen Bausman; Alison Berger. Architectural metal and glass: Mison Inc.

Plenary Complex of the German Federal Parliament
Bonn, Germany
Architect: Behnisch & Partners. Partners: Günter Behnisch; Winfried Buxel; Manfred Sabatke; Erhard Trankner. Project team: Gerard Staib (partner in charge); Hubert Eilers; Matthias Burkart; Eberhard Pritzer; Alexander von Salmuth; Ernst-Ulrich Tillmanns (project architect); Steffi Georg; Bernd Linder; Falk Petry; Jurgen Steffens; Arnold Ehrhardt; Alexander von Padberg (project group); Ulrich Liebert; Heinz Schroder; Bernd Troske (on-site supervision). Client: German Federal

Parliament, represented by the German Federal Building Administration. Structural design: Schlaich, Bergermann and Partners. Heating, ventilation and sanitary installations: Ingenieurplanung S. H. Keppler. Electricity: Ingenieurgesellschaft Zimmermann + Schrage. Electro and room acoustics: Graner & Partner. Lighting: Lichtdesign Ingenieurgesellschaft mbH; Lichtplanung Bartenbach. Façade consultant: Berthold Mack. Artworks: Sam Francis; Nicola de Maria; Mark di Suvero; Joseph Beuys; Hermann Glockner. Landscaping: Behnisch & Partners with Hans Luz + Partner.

Agence Berbesson Racine et Associés
Port Van Gogh, 2 Quai Aulagnier, 92600 Asnières, France
Architects: Berbesson Racine et Associés. Project team: Philippe Berbesson and Marie Racine. Main contractors: Cantier Van Praet (ship building); ADAC (fitting out). Lighting: Louis Poulsen (bracket lamp); IPSO (halogen recessed lighting); Artemide (desk lamps); Berbesson Racine (hanging lamps); Ticino (electrical fittings). Furniture: Charles Eames for Forum Diffusion; Marcatre; Berbesson Racine. Flooring: Briatte.

Tour sans Fins
Arche de la Défense, Paris, France
Architects: Olivier Brenac and Xavier Gonzalez. Client: S.C.I. Tour sans Fins. Electrical consultant: F.B.I. Joinery: Taravella. Glass partitions: A.F.B. Bret. Furniture: Vitra (Charles Eames); Cassina (Le Corbusier); de Sede (Andrée Putman, Jean Nouvel and Jean-Michel Wilmotte). Mural: Gatimalau.

Julia Binfield
Via Voghera 9/A, Milan 20144, Italy
Architects: Luisa Calvi, Marco Merlini and Carlos Moya. Client: Julia Binfield Graphic Design and Illustration. Main contractor: Alessandro Passi. Sub-contractors: Santo Vicentini (steel fabrications); Finessi and Gambini (furniture). Ceiling lights: Paolo Rizzato ('Costanza' for Luceplan). Wall lights: Sirrah ('Edison 36'). Floor lights: Isamu Noguchi ('Akari'). Meeting- room furniture: Arne Jacobsen for Fritz Hansen. Office furniture: Ernesto Rogers for Olivetti Synthesis.

Matsumoto Corporation
1-40 Ezucho, Okayama, Japan
Architects: David Chipperfield Architects. Project team: Renato Benedetti; Jan Coghlam; Jamie Fobent; Haruo Morishima; Rik Nys; Jonathan Sergison. Associate architects: Matsumoto Corporation Inc. Project team: Hiroshi Asano; Heihachiro Kishida; Akimasa Hatamoto. Client: Matsumoto Corporation Inc. Producer: Hamano Institute. Lighting: Matsumoto. Lighting supplier: Matsushita. Furniture and fittings: Cassina; Okamura; Taiyokanamono Co. Ltd.

J.C.J. Haans
Mina Krusemanweg, 5032 ME Tilburg, The Netherlands
Architect: Jo Coenen & Co.; Gilberte Claes (interior design). Client: J.C.J. Haans Trading Company. Main contractor: Aannemingsmaatschappij Heerkens Van Bavel bv. Aluminium and glass façade: Trube and Kings. Fitted furniture: IBV Interieurs. Furniture supplier: Marian Coenen Interior Design Shop. Consultant: Ad van der Pas.

The Second Chamber of Parliament
Binnenhof 1a, 2513AA The Hague, The Netherlands
Architect: Pi de Bruijn/de Architekten Cie. Client: Second Chamber of the States General. Main contractors: Government Buildings Agency; Project Management Directorate. Principal: Aanneming Maatschappij; J. P. van Eesteren B. V., Rotterdam. Lighting design: Rijjksgebouwendienst; P. B. de Bruijn. Electrical and security installation: Van Rietschoten en Houwens. Civil engineers: Adviesbureau D3BN. Acoustics: Peutz & Associes; DGMR Raadgevwende Ingenieurs B.V. Brazilian stone supplier: Zeidler & Wimmel.

Chiat/Day Advertising Inc.
Berkshire House, 168/178 High Holborn, London, UK
Architect: Stefano de Martino, with Nick Boyarsky, Nicola Murphy, Simon Steel Hart. Project team: Rem Koolhaas, DEGW London Ltd. Client: Chiat/Day Advertising Inc. Main contractor: Quickwood Ltd. Quantity surveyor: Andrew Turner & Co. Structural engineers: Carter Clack Partnership. Service engineers: Peter Hazard Design Associates. Furniture: Stefano de Martino; made by Jeremy Hughes (joinery); Jeremy and Louise Hughes (upholstery); Terry Flowers (fibreglass); David Racz (metalwork). Suppliers: Architectural Trading Co. (chairs); Erco, Hitech (light fittings); Elementer (ironmongery); Jandor (steel-framed doors); Jaymart (choir matting flooring).

The Australian Embassy
Minato-ku, Tokyo, Japan
Architect: Denton Corker Marshall Pty Ltd. Client: Overseas Property Group, Australian Government Department of Administrative Services. Site superintendent/project director: Bob Beecroft. Contractor: Takenaka Corporation/Hazama Corporation Joint Venture. Project management (prte contract): Denton Corker Marshall Pty Ltd. Architectural graphics: Emery Vincent Associates. Structural engineers: Ove Arup & Partners. Services engineer: Rankine & Hill Pty Ltd. Suppliers: Pilkington (Australia) Ltd (glass); The Martin Group (stone); Hancock Bros. (timber). Tokyo support: Ashihara International & Associates (architecture); Takumi, Orimoto (structure); Anuzuka Engineering Consultants (services). Quantity surveyors: Rider Hunt Melbourne; Kyowa Quantity Surveyors Co. Ltd. Landscape design: Denton Corker Marshall.

The Ark
Talgarth Road, Hammersmith, London, UK
Architects: Ralph Erskine, in collaboration with Lennart Bergström Arkitektkontor and Rock Townsend. Project team for Ralph Erskine: Ralph Erskine (partner in charge); Vernon Gracie (project architect); Dina El Midani. Project team for Lennart Bergström: Bo Stevensson (partner in charge); Lars Wilson (project architect); Brian Adma; Rolf Ariestig; Ana Bethancour; Mario Castillo-Belmar; Mats Ericsson; Sema Eser; Lars Estlander; Birgitta Hogstedt; Magnus Jording; Jan Liedstrom; Paul Morrison; Anders Nystrom; Colin Pillay; Jan Erik Sikkeland; Jacob Wilson; Jorgen Wohlert. Project team for Rock Townsend: Alistair Hay (partner in charge); Gordon Swapp, Mark Asipowicz (project architects); David Britch; Keith Fairburn; Kathryn Grosseman; Ian Hopton; Tom Nyhuss; Simon Reid; Tania Stirling; Gary Taylor; Ken Taylor; Helen Thomas; David Westburgh; Mike Worwood; Colin Winter; Jalel Yeganeh; Laurence York-Moore. Client: Talgarth Estates B.V. Project and construction managers: Åke Larsen Ltd. Structural engineers: Scandiaconsult AB (superstructure); Andrews Kent and Stone (foundations and basement). Electrical engineers: Dale and Goldfinger; Gösta Sjölander AB. Mechanical engineers: Scandiaconsult AB; Dale and Goldfinger. Lighting: Lighting Design Partnership. Acoustics: Scandiaconsult AB; Arup Acoustics. Landscaping: Jakobsen Landscape. Suppliers: Joinex (woodwork in bar-café); Svenska Tyger (pub sofa fabric); Fredericia Stolefabrik, Karl Anderson & Soner (pub chairs); Nordisk Galleriet/Flexform (summit room sofa, armchairs); Joinex (summit room table and cupboard); Proform (summit room floor lamps).

Designers' Guild
Olaf Street, London W11, UK
Architect: Spencer Fung Architects. Project team: Spencer Fung; Nick Peri; Kamran Subhan. Lighting consultants: Isometrix. Furniture and fittings in office areas: designed by Spencer Fung Architects, or existing. Structural engineers: Chan Associates. Environmental engineers: Atelier Ten. Quantity surveyors: Boyden & Co. Client: Designers Guild Ltd. Main contractor: Heath Construction. Sub-contractors: Paxman Joineries Ltd, Piper Products Ltd, Ardern Hodges Ltd (joinery); IMA Fabrications (general metalwork); T. Nevill & Co. (metalwork for reception counter, fabric frames/rods, café tables); Centre Ltd (servery counter). Terrazzo: Pallam Precast. Conference room and cellular office furniture: 'Piceno' designed by James Irvine for Cappellini. Flooring: Forbo-Nairn Ltd (linoleum); Three Shires Ltd (sisal). Partitions: Claydon Aluminium Ltd. Textiles: Designers' Guild.

Chiat/Day/Mojo
Main Street, Venice, California, USA
Architect: Frank O. Gehry & Associates, Inc. Client: Chiat/Day/Mojo. Collaborating artists (binoculars/giant light bulbs): Claes Oldenburg; Coosje van Bruggen. Project team: Frank O. Gehry (principal/design); David Denton (principalmanagement); C. Gregory Walsh (project designer); Craig Webb (project architect); Alan Ali; Gerhard Aujernhammer; Perry Blake; Thomas Duley; Anne Greenwald; Robert Hale; Victoria Jenkins; Alex Meconi; Clive Wilkinson. Associate architect: Leidenfrost/Horowitz & Associates.

Odörfer
Fallegasse 1, Sudring, A-9020 Klagenfurt, Austria
Architect: Volker Giencke. Collaborating architectural team: Eeva-Liisa Pelkonen; Uta Giencke. Client: Odörfer Rohrenhof. Collaborators: Christo Grigorow (engineer); Christian Bartenbach (lighting engineer); Friedrich Panzer (glass painter). Main contractors: Urbas (metalwork); Ast & Co. (building enterprise). Lighting supplier: SMS-Lichtsysteme. Glass roof: Klemt-Feinbau. Glasswork: Temmel Glas. Steel furniture: Metallbau Treiber. Wooden furniture: Felix Pleschek. Automatic doors: Wrulich. Marble and granite floors: Colazzo. Tiles: Krainer. Terrazzo: Duralit. Rubber floor: Heschl. Carpet: Alfred Hohenberger. Canvas: Hubert Raudaschl.

D.E. Shaw & Company
120 West 45th Street, New York, NY 10036, USA
Architect: Steven Holl Architects. Project team: Steven Holl (principal); Thomas Jenkinson (project architect); Scott Enge; Todd Fouser; Hideaki Ariizumi; Adam Yarinsky; Annette Goderbauer. Engineer: Robert Derector Associates. Technological consultant: Scott Fenton. Construction manager: Clark Construction. Doors: Metaline (metal); Progressive (custom); Atlas (security). Paintwork: Benjamin Moore. Lighting: SPI, Hand Fabrication; F.J. Grey Glass; Lightolier. Furniture: Progressive; Montis and Herman Miller.

Limelight Productions
6806 Lexington Avenue, Los Angeles, California 90038, USA
Architect: Franklin D. Israel Design Associates, Inc. Client: Limelight Productions. Main contractor: The Dunn Company. Executive desk: Terra Design. Furniture: Franklin D.Israel (design); Mike & Daniel Dunn (cabinetwork). Lighting design: Saul Goldin. Suppliers of LUMA: American Acrylic Corporation.

20-22 Stukeley Street
London WC2, UK
Architect: Jestico + Whiles. Project team: Tony Ingram (partner); Tony Ling (project architect); Eoin Keating. Collaborators: Price + Myers (structural engineer); Gregory Associates (quantity surveyors); HGS (M.&E. consultants); Watts & Partners (surveyors). Client: Burswood BV. Main contractor: R. Mansell Ltd. Lighting: Patrick Roberts Lighting. Reception furniture and fittings: Rod Smith. Flooring: Naturestone (slate); Domus Tiles; Phoenix Flooring Ltd. Glasswork: Nazeing Glass. Architectural metalwork: General Welding and Metalwork. Sub-contractors: Stannah Lifts (lift contractors); T.W. Ide (lift enclosure and entrance glazing); Alan Hone (door, glazing and steel contractor); Seniac Metal Casements (external windows); Solaglass (fire screens); K.C. Construction (brickwork and blockwork); Rone Roofing (asphalt roofing and paving).

Lynne Franks PR
327-329 Harrow Road, London W9, UK
Designer: Ben Kelly Design. Project team: Ben Kelly; Elena Massucco; Chris Cawte. Client: Lynne Franks PR. Structural engineer: Dewhurst McFarlane. Main contractor: Rutledge Contracts Ltd. M.&.E consultant: Pearce and Associates. Quantity surveyor: Ostrowski Associates. Lighting: Tamlite. Entrance floor: Empire Stone. Red linoleum floor: Forbo Kromenie. Stainless steel countertops: GEC Anderson. Metalwork: Metheralls, General Welding and Metalwork Co. Ltd. Glass blocks: Luxcrete. Partition glazing: Solaglas. Canteen and conference chairs: Arne Jacobsen. Reception sofas: Tecno. Coffee tables: Isamu Noguchi. Conference table base: Tom Dixon. Glass-topped table: 'Nomos' by Norman Foster for Tecno.

Scott Mednick Associates
Culver City, California, USA
Architect: Eric Owen Moss. Project team: Eric Owen Moss (principal); Greg Baker; Dana Swinsky Cantelmo (project architects); Todd Conversano; Lucas Rios; Jenifer Rakow; Scott Nakao; Sumathi Ponnambalam; Jose Pimental; Elissa F. Scrafano. Client: Frederick Norton Smith (owner); Scott Mednick Associates (tenant). General contractor: A.J. Contracting of California. Structural engineer: Kurily, Szymanski & Tcherkow. Mechanical engineer: AEG Systems. Electrical engineers: Silver, Roth & Associates. Steel fabricator: Teters Construction. Lighting: Saul Goldin & Associates. Furniture and furnishings: Eric Moss Architects.

Saishunkan Seiyaku Women's Dormitory
Kumamoto City, Kumamoto Prefecture, Japan
Architect: Kazuyo Sejima Architect & Associates. Client: Saishunkan Seiyakusho Co., Ltd. Structural engineers: Matsui Gengo and O.R.S. Air-conditioning: System Design Laboratory. Electrical consultant: Shimada Equipment Design Office. Lighting: Yamagiwa; Daiko. Furniture: Inoue Industries; Idée (tables and chairs); Actus (chairs). Textiles: Nuno Co. Ltd. Flooring: ADVAN Co. Ltd. Glasswork: Asahi Glass Co. Ltd.

New Line Cinema
East Coast headquarters, 333 7th Avenue, New York, USA
Architects: Smith-Miller + Hawkinson Architects. Project team: Henry Smith-Miller, Laurie Hawkinson (principals in charge); Jorge Aizenman (project architect); Eric Cobb; Charles Renfro; Jane Wason; Fritz Read; John Conaty; Kit Yan; Belen Moneo; Yolande Daniels. Client: New Line Cinema Corporation. Main contractor: NSC Construction. Structural engineer: Severud-Szegezdy. Mechanical engineer: Carstel. Lighting: Claude Engle and Associates; Lightolier. Audio-visuals: Harry Joseph and Associates. Furniture and fittings: Knoll International; AI; Pallazzetti.

New Line Cinema
West Coast headquarters, 114 North Robertson Boulevard, Los Angeles, CA, USA
Architects: Smith-Miller + Hawkinson Architects. Project team: Henry Smith-Miller; Laurie Hawkinson (principals in charge); Charles Renfro; Robert Rothblatt (project architects); Margi Northard; Jane Wason; John Conaty; Kit Yan; Nicole Koenigsberger; Randy Goya. Client: New Line Cinema Corporation. Main contractor: Archetype Construction Inc. Structural engineers: Steven Mesey and Associates. Mechanical engineers: Carstel. Lighting: Lightolier. Furniture and fittings: Knoll International; AI; Pallazzetti.

B Braun Melsungen AG
Melsungen, Germany
Architects: James Stirling, Michael Wilford and Associates, in association with Walter Nägeli. Project team: Ludger Brands; Robert Haas; Regula Kloti; Brenden MacRiabhaigh; Bernd Reinecke; Hella Rolfes; Jacques Throin; Renzo Vallebuona; Siegfried Wernik; Georg Braun; Annegret Burg; Desmond Byrne; Conni Conradi; Martin Focks; Ferdinand Heide; Lothar Hennig; Renate Keller; Thjomas Kellermann; Joachim Kleine-Allekotte; Sabine Krause; Ralf Lenz; Jorg Liebmann; Gudrun Ludwig; Sean Mahon; Bernd Niebuhr; Paul Panter; Dieter Pfannenstiel; Maria Rossi; Norberto Schornberg; Mirjam Schwabe; Julia Tophof. Students: Alois Albert; Mathias Frank; Michael Kassuba; Matthias Konsgen; Wolfgang Latzel; Rudolf Neumann; Ulrike Passe; Klaus Schafer; Mario Waltero; Hans-Peter Weiss; Gretchen Werner; Gabdriele Witt. Client: Braun Melsungen AG. Tenders and site supervision: Walter Hotzel; Büro am Lutzowplatz. Landscape: Gunnar Martinsson; Karl Bauer; A. Zilch Garten und Landschaftsbau. Load-bearing structure: Polonyi and Fink GmbH. Overall planning of technical equipment: Rud. Otto Meyer. Engineers: Büro Kittelberger. Electrical consultants: AEG (heavy current); Ulrike Brandi (lighting); Siemens (light current). Traffic engineering: Gischow and Partner. Storage technology: OWL Logiisitk System; Buchs/Aarau. Acoustics: BeSB GmbH. Fire advice: Hosser; HAB & Partner. Civil contractors: Gerdum & Breuer GmbH & Co. KG; Hermanns-Karl Holzapfel GmbH & Co. KG; Philipp Holszman; Frolich Bauunternehmung AG; Hochtief AG; Dickert. Steelwork sub-contractors: Victor Buyck Stahlbau GmbH; Stahlbau Lampster. Façade Building A: HKR – Systembau GmbH. Roofs, metal façade: G.H. Montage GmbH. Roofs: Deutsche Asphalt GmbH. Suspended ceilings and dry walls: HFF, Hozexport-Import. Double floors: Mero-Werke GmbH & Co.; Goldbach GmbH. Linoleum: Forbo Teppich Werke GmbH. Carpets: DLW AG. Sun-protection technology: Warema Renkhoff GmbH & Co. KG. Office cabinets: Waiko Systembüro; Bode Innenausbau. RWA light cupolas: Greschalux GmbH & Co. Fire prevention wooden doors: Webu GmbH. Fire prevention steel doors: MTS GmbH & Co. Betriebs. Painting and floor laying work: Konrad Steffen; Franz Kohler GmbH. Tiling: Glassner. Metalwork: August Truss. Screed or claywork: Emanuel Ziehe GmbH; Fuhmann Estriche. Metal and glass façade. Building F: Versbach. Magnesiaclay: Duralit KG. Blacksmith

work: Richter and Co. GmbH; L. Holienhorst Metalverabreitung GmbH. Wooden and polar windows, Building A: POLAR – Fenster. Wooden windows: Bommhardt. Infrastructure and roadworks: Kirchner & Co. KG. Earthwork, roadworks and paving: Franke OHG. Paintwork: Elert GmbH & Co. KG.

Reykjavik City Hall
Tjarnagata 11, Reykjavik, Iceland
Architect: Studio Granda. Project team: Steve Christer; Jóhann Einarsson; Margrét Hardardóttir; Haraldur Helgason; Steiner Sigurdsson. Client: the City of Reykjavik. Main contractor: Ístak. Contractors: Álstoo (curtain walling); Fedhaus Fassaden and Fenster (windows). Consultants: Línuhönnun (concrete/waterproofing); Booth Muirie (roof cladding). Structural and mechanical engineer: Almenna Verkfraedistofan. Electrical engineer: Rafhönnun. Site supervision: Mat. Plasterwork: Rádverk. Stonework: Steinsmidja S. Helgason. Stone and tilework: Ragnar Hansen. Steelwork: Málmsmidjan; Vélsmidja Einars Gudbrandsson; Vélsmidjan Orri. Paintwork: Elvar Ingason; Jém H. Ólafsson. Paint: Harpa; Málning. Wooden flooring: Parketgólf. Wooden doors: Selkó. Lighting: Erco; Bega. Fixed furnishings and handrails: Bíró Steinar; Trésmidjan Borg; Kjörvidur, Trésmidjan Borg; Trésmidjaverkstaedi Reykjavíkur. Veneered doors and wall panelling: Beyki. Café and staff restaurant tables: Sess. Office desks and shelving, office and meeting chairs: GKS; Küsch & Co. Café and staff restaurant chairs: Cidue. Waiting area seating: Modern Design Furniture. Audience seating: Castelli. Food service counters: Frostverk. Kitchen: HG Heildverslun; Zanussi. Specialist glass: Glertaekni. Glass: Glerborg. Curtain walling: Schüco. Sandstone: Cumbria Stone Quarries. Solar blinds and projector screens: Technical Blinds. Ironmongery: FSB; BKS; Dorma. Clock: Smith of Derby. Tiles: Vouge.

Knoll International
Schaumainkai 69, Frankfurt am Main 70, Germany
Architects: STUDIOS Architecture. Project team: Erik Sueberkrop (principal); Peter VanDine (studio director); Arthur Collin (project manager). Associate architect: NHT & Partner. Client: Knoll International. Main contractor: Philipp Holzmann. Mechanical contractor: Kretz & Wahkl GmbH & Co. KG. Electrical contractor: Wero. Lighting: Lighting Design Partnership. Metalwork: Limited Productions, Inc. Joinery: 3R Messesbau GmbH. Carpet: Ruckstuhl. Ironmongery: Technolumen.

BASF-France
Avenue Georges Pompidou 49, Levallois-Perret, Paris, France.
Interior architect: Jean-Michel Wilmotte. Project team: Christain Oudart; Marc Vareille; Marc Dutoit. Building architect: Ceria et Coupel. Client: BASF-France. Developer: France Construction. General contractor: Bouygues. Engineers: Serete. Lighting: I Guzzini. Furniture: Jean-Michel Wilmotte. Office furniture and signage: G. A. Potteau.

S-Lattice
2-31-20 Sendagaya, Shibuya-ku, Tokyo, Japan
Architect: WORKSHOP. Client: St Vermeer. Structural engineer: Kozoh Keikaku, Plus One. Construction: Fujita Corporation. Engineer: Chiku Engineering Consultants. Lighting: WORKSHOP.

Stephen Bull's Bistro & Bar
71 St John's Street, London EC1, UK
Architect: Allies and Morrison Architects. Project team: Bob Allies; Graham Morrison; Robert Maxwell; Paul Summerlin; Lucy Britton; Pauline Stockmans. Client: Stephen Bull. Main contractor: Howard and Constable. Structural engineer: Price and Myers. Service engineer: M. J. Bone. Electrical services: Max Fordham and Partners. Quantity Surveyor: Boyden and Co. Lighting: ERCO Lighting Ltd. Furniture: Punt Moblesi de Padova (chairs); Howard and Constable (tables, bar, sideboards); Bim Burton; Co-existence (table tops). Timber floor: Campbell Marson. Stone floor: Stone Age. Papier mâché pots and wall hangings: Sarah Williams. Staircase: East London Copperworks. Mechanical services: Economic Heating. Joinery and metalwork: Marshall Howard. Gate: Gittins and Mellor. Coat rails: SS Fabrications. Kitchen: Crane.

Zoë
90 Prince Street, New York, 10012, USA
Architects: Jeffrey G. Beers Architects. Collaborators: Michael F. Parlamis (engineer); John Kneapler (graphics). Client: Thalia and Stefano Loffredo. Main contractor: Frank Parlamis Inc. Sub-contractors: Stefano Loffredo (stone and tile work); Nancy Kearing (painting). Lighting: Jeffrey G. Beers Architects; CSL Lighting; Cosmo Lighting; Di Bianco Lighting; Times Square Lighting. Furniture: Shelby Williams customized by Jeffrey G. Beers Architects (dining chairs); ICF (bar stools). Stone and tile suppliers: Carminart Tiles. Fabric: Unika Vaev. Glasswork: S.A. Bendheim Glass.

Minema Café
43 Knightsbridge, London SW1, UK
Designer: David Bentheim Interior Design. Project team: David Bentheim; Ferry Zayadi; Robert White; Andy Jackson. Client: Savoy Hotel. Main contractor: Newmann Shopfitting. Structural engineer: Barton Wells. Mechanical and electrical engineers: Gilby Warren. Lighting: Reggiani; Concord. Flooring and table tops: Stonit. Metalwork: Riley's. Glasswork: Preedy Glass. Furniture in atrium: Enzo Mari (chairs); Juan Ortinez (bar stools). Catering equipment: Kestral. Sculpture and signage: Newmann Signs. Graphics: The Foundation.

El Tragaluz
Passatge de la Concepcio 5, Barcelona, Spain
Architect: Pepe Cortés. Collaborators: Jesus Jimenez (engineer); Javier Mariscal (graphic designer); Isabel Esteva (muralist). Client: Rosa Mama Esteve. Main contractor: Prodelta. Sub-contractors: Balleste (steel fabricator: skylight); Luis Bru (mosaics). Bar, Restaurant and Tragarapid lighting: Pepe Cortés ('Piscis' bar and restaurant lamps produced by Mobles 114). Bar and Tragarapid stools: Oscar Tusquets, produced by Carlos Jane. Tragaluz chairs: Fatima Villasela. Bar chairs: Nancy Robins.

The Ministry of Sound
103 Gaunt Street, London SE1, UK
Architect: Lynn Davis Architects. Client: The Ministry of Sound. Collaborators: Lack Conacher (engineer); Keith Slaughter (acoustic specialist). Main contractor: Mantisson. Sub-contractors: C. J. Bartley (electrical); Kingdom Coverings (urinals, troughs); John Hart (plumbing); BML Services (steelwork). Lighting: ENTEC. Dance floor: V. A. Hutchinson. Soundproofing material: Pencoed ('Rockwool'); 'Ticoflex'; Richard Lees Ltd (ribdeck).

Bar Maddalena
Piazza S. Agostino 2, Prato, Florence, Italy
Designers: King Kong Production. Project team: Stefano Giovannoni; Guido Venturini. Client: Cavicchi Brothers. Main contractor: D'Anteo (furniture and bar). Sub-contractors: Iagulli (sculpture); Electech (blue lighting). Lighting: Guzzini; Electech. Flooring: Fumagalli.

Santini
Corso Venezia 3, Milan 20121, Italy
Designer: Peter Glynn-Smith Associates. Client: Santini Group FER, Italy. Main contractor: Frizerga. Engineer: Dr Giovanni Merighi. Lighting: P.G.S.A.; Light Products. Furniture: Flexform (chairs); Matteo Grassi (bar stools). Curtains: Rubelli (restaurant); Percheron (private dining rooms). Rug: V'Soske Joyce. Mini sculptures: Celia Barker-Mill. Specialist lacquer work: Francis Hamel-Cooke, London. Specialist furniture and fittings: P.G.S.A., made by Frizerga. Exterior courtyard furniture: Martin Ryan.

Hôtel Montalembert
3 rue Montalembert, 75007 Paris, France
Designer: Christian Liaigre. Client: Grace Leo Andrieu. Furniture, fittings and lighting: Christian Liaigre. Stair banisters and wall sconces: Eric Schmitt. Hall artwork: Bruno Taconet.

Bar Rothko
Consell de Cent 255, 08011 Barcelona, Spain
Architect: Alberto Lievore & Asociados. Collaborating architect: Eduardo Campoamor. Collaborating designers: Jeanette Altherr; Irene Coll. Client: Nicolas Pulido. Main contractor: Emiliano Sierra. Sub-contractors: Peries S.A. (electrical); CUB (plaster works and painting). Lamp: Iserma. Lighting suppliers: Erco. Furniture and fittings: Alberto Lievore & Associados. Manufacturers: Simeyco Sal (Rothko chair and bar stools); Divano S.A. ('Alban' armchair); Andreu World S.A. ('Rothko' tables).

Now And Zen
4a Upper St Martin's Street, London WC2, UK
Architect: Rick Mather Architects. Project team: Rick Mather; Ian Hay; Michael Delaney; Tim Dodd; Glyn Emrys; Rebekah Staveley. Collaborators: Peter Henderson Associates (quantity surveyor); Dewhurst MacFarlane (structural engineer); Pell Frishmann (alterations); Fulcrum Engineering (services). Client: Bliadwood Ltd. Main contractor: Pat Carter Shopfitting and Specialist Contracts. Graphic designer: Howard Waller. Slate floor tiles: Kirstone Green Slate Quarries Ltd. Carpet: Adam Carpets. Light fittings: SKK Lighting; Light S.A.; AC/DC Lighting Ltd (neons). Toughened, laminated and plate glass: Firman Ltd. Curved glass: Interglass Ltd. Glass bowls: Jeff Bell. Furniture: Marland Contract Furniture. Kitchen and bar equipment: Advanced Engineering.

Nexus-III
Shirakwa-higashiiru, Nawate-dori, Higashiyama-ku, Kyoto, Tokyo, Japan
Designers: Afra and Tobia Scarpa. Collaborator: Yoshiteru Uesato (Seisetsusha). Client: Omori Kosen Corn. Main contractor: Hakusuisha Corp. Sub-contractor: Ogawa Electrical Engineering. Project co-ordinator: ARC International. Lighting: Flos. Furniture: Afra and Tobia Scarpa for Meritalia SpA. Flooring: Osaka Processing Inc.

Paramount Hotel
235 West 46th Street, New York, USA
Designer: Philippe Starck. Development group: Morgans Hotel Group. Project team: Michael Overington (director of development); Anda Andrei (director of design); Lisa Atkin (creative director). Architects: Haigh Space Architects; Leitenberger/Bronfman Associates. Collaborator: Frederique Valette. Client: Ian Schrager, Morgans Hotel Group. Mechanical engineer: Ambrosino DePinto and Schmieder. Structural engineer: Stanley H. Goldstein PC. Construction managers: Clark Construction Corp.; Morgans Hotel Group. Lighting: Jules Fisher and Paul Marantz. Furniture: Marco Zanuso; Franco Albini; Jean Michele Frank; Antonio Gaudí; Carlos Riart; Jasper Morrison; Marc Newson. Children's playroom: Gary Panter. Colour consultants: Donald Kaufman/Kaufman Colour. Graphics: Tracy Turner. F. F. & E.: Pamela Durante; Helka Puc.

La Ranarita/Guest Room
Azumabashi, Tokyo, Japan
Designers: Shigeru Uchida, Studio 80. Client: Asahi Breweries Ltd. Main contractor: Ohbayashi Corporation. Sub-contractor: Matsuya Co. Ltd (La Ranarita); Takashimaya Co. Ltd (Guest Room). Lighting: Harumi Fujimoto; Ushio Spax Inc. Furniture: Chairs.

Hôtel du Cheval Blanc
1 Boulevard des Arènes, Nîmes, France
Architect: Jean-Michel Wilmotte. Project team: Jean-Michel Wilmotte; Sabine Boyer-Gibaud; Claire Sentis; Claude Thomas; Pascal Petit. Client: SENIM. Engineer: OTH. Furniture: Jean-Michel Wilmotte.

John Lewis
Wood Street, Kingston upon Thames, Surrey, UK
Architects: Ahrends Burton and Koralek. Partner in charge: Paul Koralek. Partners: Paul Drake; Patrick Stubbing; Assistant architects: Nazar Alikhan; John Attwood; Robert Axton; Manual Bouza; Carl Callaghan; Athol Corbett; Hugh Davies; Robert Davys; Kate Edwards; Claire Gerard; Darius Gilmont; Jane Howson; Mike Jones; Mark Kelly; David Leuthold; Anna McLean; Liz Marley; John Martin; Terry McCarthyr; Catherine McDougall; Brian O'Reilly; Jenny Papaioannou; Mungo Park; Andrew Parker; Norman Partridge; Richard Paxton; Lucy Pedlar; Douglas Schwab; Jilli Vickerson; Hugh Waine; Woon Juen Yee; Mei Yu. Client: John Lewis Partnership. Main contractor: Mowlem Building. Project management: Clarson Goff Associates. Structural and drainage engineers: Ove Arup and Partners. Electrical and H&V Design: John Lewis Partnership. Shopfitting design: John Lewis Partnership. Coffee shop design: Pennington Robson. Lighting consultant: Friedrich Wagner, Lighting Design, Vienna. Quantity surveyor: Davis Langdon and Everest. Steelwork: Tubeworkers. Roof glazing: Heywood Glazing Systems. Internal door ironmongery: Elementer Industrial Design. Windows and entrances: Solaglas Architectural Systems. Roof glazing and copings: Heywood Glazing Systems. Lowered ceilings and light fittings: Industrolite. Archaeological preservation: Punford South Limited. Electrical services: WES Electrical Services Ltd. Mechanical services: Crown House Engineering. Lifts, escalators: Otis Elevator Co. Ltd. Fire protection: Wormald Fire Systems. Internal balustrading and handrailing (atrium): Starkie Gardner. Rubber flooring: Trim Flooring Co.

Jigsaw
31 Brompton Road, London SW3, UK
Architects: Branson Coates Architecture Ltd. Project architect: Gerrard O'Carrol . Client: Jigsaw Limited. Main contractor and shopfitter: Claremont Construction Ltd. Structural engineer: Dewhurst McFarland and Partners. Quantity surveyor: Bernard Williams Associates. Copper Column: designed by Branson Coates and manufactured by Protosheet Engineering Ltd. Special glasswork: designed by Nigel Coates, made by Simon Moore at Glassworks London Ltd. Mannequins: Nigel Coates. Lighting: Omniate Ltd. Mural: Stewart Helm. Carpet: designed by Branson Coates and made by V'Soske Joyce (UK) Ltd. Console wall table: designed by Nigel Coates and made by Bim Burton at Workshop 119. 'Tongue' chair: designed by Nigel Coates, manufactured by SCP Ltd.

Fausto Santini
4ter rue de Cherche-Midi, Paris, France
Architects: Antonio Citterio and Terry Dwan Architects. Project team: Antonio Citterio, Terry Dwan, Patricia Viel, Antonio Virga. Client: Fausto Santini s.r.l. Main contractor: Lachant Frères. Sub-contractors: Cantu' Ottone (furniture and lamps); Flaminio Marin and Co. (flooring); Corbella (Paris limestone display); Espace-Volume – JB Las Martre (plasterwork); L.P. Électricité (electrics).

David Mellor
Butlers Wharf, London SE1, UK
Architect: Michael Hopkins and Partners. Project team: Michael Hopkins; John Pringle; Bill Dunster; Ernest Fasanya; Lucy Lavers; Iveno Kezic. Client: David Mellor Design Ltd. Main contractors: Sir Robert McAlpine Management Contracting Ltd; David Mellor Design Ltd. Concrete contractor: Silver Construction Ltd. Structural engineer: Büro Happold. Quantity surveyor: Pritchard Williams and Hunt.

SPIRAL
AXIS Building, B1, 5-17-1 Roppongi, Minato-ku, Tokyo, Japan
Designer: Shiro Kuramata. Client: Nichinan Co. Ltd. Furniture and fittings: Shiro Kuramata.

Urban Eyes
2301 Market Street, San Francisco, California, USA
Architect: John Lum/Reid & Tarics Associates. Millwork and custom casework: Mordaunt Woodworking. Custom steel chairs: Innovative Constructions. Lighting: Koch and Lowy; Peerless; Belfer. Furniture and finishes: John G.H. Lum. Wood flooring: Tarkett.

Uta Raasch
ABC Strasse 9-11, 2000 Hamburg 36, Germany
Designer: Torsten Neeland. Project team: Torsten Neeland; Hartmut Kaiser; Anke Osthues. Client: Uta Raasch/Cissule. Furniture and fittings: Torsten Neeland. Coat-hangers: Anthologie Quartett. Carpenter: Gunter Zimmermann. Metalworker: Kristen Metalbau. Glasswork: Schroder.

Mazda Lietz
Waidhofen, Ybbs, Austria
Architect: Boris Podrecca. Project team: Boris Podrecca; Gotthard Eibock; Neville Selimic; Alain Tisserand; Gerhard Schaller; Sasa Uran. Client: Lietz GesmbH. Main contractor: Ing. Rainer Halbach. Lighting: Froschauer OHG. Furniture and fittings: MS Metallbau Seyriehner. Furniture: Fa Leopold Brandi; Fa Winter. Walls: Ing. Wolfgang Deseyve. Partitions: Metallkonstruktionen Wippel GmbH. Flooring: Liemer GesmbH (terrazzo); Fa Hege. Walls: Taborsky VertriebsgesmbH. Ceiling: Fa Dietmar Linninger. Glass partitions: Peter Lisec GesmbH.

Roberto Verino
Gran Via de les Corts Catalanes, 653 1010 Barcelona, Spain
Architect: Fernando Salas. Project team: Fernando Salas Sierra; Miriam Izquierdo Jaumot; Ester Balana Vilanova. Client: Roberto Verino. Main contractor: Prodelta. Consultant: Justo Roman. JRP, S.L. Lighting: 'Tolomeo' lamps by Michele de Lucchi and Giancarlo Fassina for Artemide. Furniture and fittings: designed by Fernando Salas; supplied by Vincon; Idea Mueble.

Fifth Floor, Harvey Nichols
101–125 Knightsbridge, London SW1, UK
Architect: Wickham & Associates. Design team: Helen Abadie; Alex Michaelis; Nic Sampson; David Taylor; Fai Tsang; Julyan Wickham; Tess Wickham; Desmond Lavery. Production team: Richard Davies; Max Edwards; Susan Hillberg; Ying Ying Hui; Danielle Mantelin; Joyce Owens; Thierry Ploum; Sanya Polescuk; Jamie Campbell; Richard Wilding; Philip Toms; Tim Pitman; Aidan Stretch. Collaborating engineers: Max Fordham and Partners; Whitby & Bird. Client: Harvey Nichols & Co. Ltd. Main contractor: Laing Management Interiors. Sub-contractors: Spectrum (main roof lights, metal screen walls, metal fittings with associated joinery and electrical work); Logic Design & Fabrication (metalwork to furniture, revolving door and grocery shelving); Becher Joinery (bar joinery, wine shop fittings, restaurant furnishings); Rod Smith (flower stand and other metalwork); DMK Designs, Paul White (joinery and fittings); Intermura Furniture (upholstery); Hansens (kitchen equipment); Cole Carpentry (furnishings and food hall fittings). Lighting: designed by Wickham & Associates in conjunction with Max Fordham and Partners. Furniture and fittings: designed by Wickham & Associates. Quantity surveyor: E.C. Harris & Partners.

Fundació Antoni Tàpies
C/Aragon 255, Barcelona, Spain
Architects: Roser Amadó and Lluís Domènech. Collaborators: Anton Alsina, Ramón Domènech. Client: Fundacion Antoni Tàpies and the Ministerio de Cultura, Spain. Main contractor: Sapic S.A. Structural engineer: Agustin Obiol. General installations: J.G. Asociados. Lighting: Piero Castiglioni. Acoustics: Higini Arau; L.C. Físicas. Metal structure: Estudios y Montajes Vilalta S.A. Paintwork: Pidersa. Carpenter: Francisco Llorens S.A. Natural stone: Mármoles del Vallés. Electrical engineer: Elinsa. Air-conditioning: Fluidsa.

Kita Griesheim-Süd
Kiefernstrasse 24a, Griesheim-Süd, Frankfurt am Main, Germany
Architect: Architekturbüro Bolles-Wilson and Partner. Project team: Peter Wilson; Julia Bolles-Wilson; Eberhard Kleffner. Client: the City of Frankfurt – Building Department. Furniture: School Department of the City of Frankfurt.

Badalona Sports Palace
Alfonso XII s/n, Badalona, Barcelona, Spain
Architects: Esteve Bonell and Francesc Rius. Project team: Esteve Bonell; Francesc Rius; (Architects) Robert Brufau; Agusti Obiols; Luis Moya; Enrique Rego; Pere Pius; Moises Aguilar; M. Christine Aubry; Nicole Bongard; Jaume Calsapeu; Felix Khun; Thomas Lussi; Josep Llobet; Desirée Mas; Alan Mee. Client: COOB'92 (organizing committee for the Barcelona Olympics). Main contractor: Dumez - Copysa. Installations: IDOM. Metal structure: Vitoria Urssa. Court wood floor: Tariparq. Metalwork: Ajimar. Brickwork: Almar. Façade stone: Inmar. Outside floor: Escofet.

Museo del Juguete
Ibi, Alicante, Spain
Architect: Eduard Bru. Project team: Eduard Bru; Neus Lacomba. Exhibition construction: Expográfic/ Marcella Chinchilla; Pere Garcia (director).

Historial de la Grande Guerre
Place du Château, Peronne-Somme, France
Architect: Henri Ciriani. Project team: Henri Ciriani; J. C. Laisne (building); J. Nicolas (furniture, signage). Client: Départment de la Somme. Main contractor: Leon Grosse. Museological design: Répérages S.A.R.L. Lighting specialist: Licht Design. Audio-visual: C.E.M. Signage: Studio Mutterer. Design of central exhibition hall: Henri Ciriani with L. Guyon and J. Nicolas. Structural engineer: Marc Mimram. Scobat (BET); Inex. (heating, ventilation); Segef (sanitary). Landscape design: M. Courajoud.

Santa Justa Railway Station
Seville, Spain
Architects: Antonio Cruz/Antonio Ortiz Arquitectos. Project team: Carlos Castro; Jose R. Galadi; Luis Guitierrez; Anne Catherine Javet; Miguel Maese; Juan Carlos Mulero; Peter Putz; Blanca Sanchez; Miguel Velasco; Pieter Weijnen; Michael Zegers. Client: RENFE. Site supervision: Bureau of Construction for Overland Transport. Supervising engineer: Rafael Molla. Construction company: FOCSA. Construction supervisor: Ignacio Ruiz Larrea. Furniture and fittings: Addison Design Consultants.

Stansted Airport Terminal
Stansted, Essex, UK
Architects: Foster Associates. Lead designer (transit system and infrastructure: BAA Consultancy. Client: Stansted Airport Ltd. Main contractors: Laing Management Ltd; BAA Consultancy. Quantity surveyors: BAA Consultancy, with Beard Dove; Currie & Brown. Structural engineering: Ove Arup & Partners (terminal and BR station); Environmental services engineering and movement systems engineering: BAA Consultancy. Lighting (public areas): Claude and Danielle Engle. Acoustics: ISVR Consultancy. Environmental wind engineering: University of Bristol. Fire engineering/ drainage: Ove Arup & Partners. Graphic design: Pentagram. Large scale graphics: Bull Signs. Carpet design: Ron Nixon. Carpets: Brintons Ltd. Landscaping: Adrien Lisney & Partners. Ecology: Penny Anderson. Screens: Giuseppe Boscherini. Satellite 1 fit-out: Carlton Building Services Ltd. Architectural metalwork: Custom Metal Fabrications Ltd. Lighting: Erco Lighting Ltd (terminal and BR station public areas, directional signs); Osram GEC Ltd (satellite and BR station). Metalwork: Euramco Engineering Ltd. Electrical services – terminal: Matthew Hall Mechanical & Electrical. BR station fit-out: McLaughlin & Harvey plc. Elevators: Otis Elevators plc. Desks: Parnall Contracts. Architectural metalwork, glazed screens: W & G Sissons Ltd. Concourse glazing – satellite 1: Stoakes Systems Ltd. Granite floors (terminal, BR station and satellite 1). Public seating: Tecno (UK) Ltd. Terminal steelwork: Tubeworkers Ltd.

The Sackler Galleries, Royal Academy of Arts
Piccadilly, London W1, UK
Architect: Sir Norman Foster and Partners. Project team: Norman Foster; Spencer de Grey; Tim Quick; John Small; John Silver; Michael Elkan; Julia Barfield. Client: Royal Academy of Arts. Structural engineer: YRM Anthony Hund Associates. Services engineer: James R. Briggs. Lighting consultant: George Sexton Associates. Historic building consultant: Julian Harrap Architects. Quantity surveyor: Davis Langdon and Everest. Construction management: Bovis Construction. Structural steel and miscellaneous metalwork: Custom Metal; Fabalwork. Roofing: Coverite Palace Gates. Historic fabric cleaning: Szerelmey Cox. Stone paving: Zanetti & Bailey. Joinery: Finecraft; Vogue. Timber floors: Campbell Marsden. Decorations: W.S. Harvey. Mechanical and electrical installation: Benhams. Lift installation: Otis. Glazed wall cladding: GIG. Signs: Bull Signs. Furniture: Osiris. Demolition and builder's work: Gsex, UK.

Lisson Gallery
52-54 Bell Street, London NW1, UK
Architect: Tony Fretton. Project team: Tony Fretton; Michael Casey; Karen Teideman; Pia Petterson. Client: Lisson Gallery. Main contractor: E.C. Sames and Co. Structural engineers: Price and Myers. Services engineer: Max Fordham and Partners. Quantity surveyor: Philip Pank Partnership. Mechanical/electrical sub-contractor: Stats; Lee Beesley (electrical). Steel frame erectors: Steve Palm. Architectural metalwork: Rod Smith. Pavement lights: HW Cooper & Co. Flooring: J. Brown Flooring (linoleum). Woodwork: Woodline Products. Glazing: Glass Rule Ltd. Door handles: Elementer. Security: Rouse Security System.

Joan Miró Library
C/Vilamari 61, 08015 Barcelona, Spain
Architects: Beth Galí; Màrius Quintana; Antoni Solanas. Project team: Marcos Roger; Alfonso de Luna; Hubert van der Linder; Alessandra Dini; Joaquim San Joan; Maura Monente; Jordi Jansa; Mechthild Stuhlmacher. Client: the City of Barcelona. Main contractor: Gines y Navarro Construcciones S.A. Surveyor: Joaquim Lara. Structural consultant: Augusti Obiol. Structural engineer: Tecnor. Installations: Mila-Ventura. Air-conditioning: Josep Maria Milian; Clima Confort. Electrical engineer: Camunsa. Lighting: Mr Garcia; Punto Luz; C/Pau Claris. Furniture: Gama. Audio-visuals: Konik. Carpentry: Llorenc.

The Guggenheim Museum
1071 Fifth Avenue, New York 10128, USA
Architects: Gwathmey Siegel & Associates. Principals: Charles Gwathmey, Robert Siegel Associate in charge: Jacob Alspector. Project architects: Pierre Cantacuzene; Gregory Karn; Earl Swisher. Project team: Paul Aferiat; Pat Cheung; Nancy Clayton; Marc Dubois; Steven Forman; David Fratianne; Gerry Gendreau; Siamak Hariri; Anthony Iovino; Dirk Kramer; Matthew Krahe; Dan Madlansacay; Jeffrey Murphy; Roy Pertchik; Jorgan Raab; Joe Ruocco; Gary Schoemaker; Robert E. Siegel; Christine Straw; Irene Torroella; Alexandra Villegas; Peter Wiederspan; Ross Winter; Stephen Yablon. Client: The Solomon R. Guggenheim Foundation. Main contractors: George A. Fuller Co.; Lehrer McGovern Bovis. Structural Engineer: Severud Associates. Mechanical engineers: John L. Altieri. Lighting consultants: Light and Space Assoc. Ltd. Theatre consultant: Peter George Associates. Restoration consultant: Building Conservation Assoc. Inc. Landscape consultant: The office of Pat DeBellis. Graphics consultant: Vignelli Associates. Curtain wall consultant: Heitman & Associates, Inc.

Museum für Moderne Kunst
Domstrasse 10 D-6000, Frankfurt am Main, Germany
Architect: Hans Hollein. Project team: Franz Madl (project manager); Shinichi Eto; Walter Kirpicsenko; Bernd Kretz; Mirislaw Machnacz; Rainer Pirker; Hans Streitner; Taro Abe; Haiko Achilles; Sina Baniahmad; Thomas Herzog-Punzenberger; Toshiko Kawaguchi; Noburu Kimura; Stefan Maisch; Erich Pedevilla; Madeleine Jenewein; Dorrit Korger; Dorit Pachler; Elisabeth Rahbari. Client: City of Frankfurt – Cultural Department. Project management: Dezernaut Bau – Hochbauamt. Structural engineer: Gert Rosenboom. Heating, ventilation, air-conditioning and plumbing engineer: Fricket-Ruch-Kluck. Elevator engineer: Werner Wiesbaden. Daylighting: Institut für Tageslicht. Construction Management and Supervision: Frankfurter Aufbau AG.

Yatsushiro Municipal Museum
Kumamoto Prefecture, Japan
Architects: Toyo Ito & Associates. Client: Yatsushiro City. Construction: Takenaka Corporation/Wakuta Construction/Yonemoto Construction. Structural engineers: Kimura Structural Engineers. Mechanical services: Uichi Inoue Research Installation. Electrical works: Ohtaki E & M Consultants. Exterior: Nancy Finley. Furniture: Teruaki Ohashi Atelier; Toyo Ito and Associates. Exhibition fixtures: Teruaki Ohashi Atelier. Lighting planner: Yamagiwa Labo. Graphic design: Sun-Ad Company Ltd.

Lynn Goode Gallery
2719 Colquitt Street, Houston, Texas, USA
Architect: Carlos Jiménez Architectural Design Studio. Collaborating engineer: Jon Monteith. Client: Lynn Goode. Main contractor: Joe Larrow/E.J. Bran. Lighting: Energy Lighting Systems. Furniture: Carlos Jiménez; Carlton Cook Company. Flooring: National Terrazzo Tile and Marble Inc.; Schenck and Company Flooring. Elevator: Inclinator of America.

Monastery of Sant Pere de Rodes
Port de la Selva, Alt Emporda, Catalunya, Spain
Architects: José Antonio Martinez Lapeña and Elías Torres Tur. Project team: José Lapeña; Elias Torres; Albert Ferrer Mayol; Ana Moreno Duran; Xavier Bonet Lluch. Client: The Government of Catalunya. Main contractor: Construcciones Guardiola S.L. Display cases: Joan Falguerona. Furniture, fittings and additional display units: Lapeña and Torres.

Fitzwilliam College Chapel
Huntingdon Road, Cambridge, UK
Architect: MacCormac Jamieson Prichard. Project team: Richard MacCormac; Peter Jamieson; Dorian Wiszniewski; Andrew Taylor; Pankaj Patel; Peter Greenwood; Oliver Smith. Collaborator: Ove Arup and Partners. Client: Fitzwilliam College. Main contractor: Johnson and Bailey Ltd. Sub-contractors: Taylor Maxwell; E.J. Anderson; Histon Concrete. Structural and services engineers: Tudor Salusbury; Ove Arup and Partners. Quantity surveyor: Dearle and Henderson. Joinery contractor: Johnson and Bailey Limited. Modelmaker: Thorp Modelmakers Ltd. Organ builders: P.D. Collins. Lighting: Aqua Electrical Ltd. Furniture: Stoneyford Design Ltd. Ironmongery: Thomas Laidlaw (East Anglia) Ltd. Steelwork: Crofton Engineering Ltd.

Can Felipa Cultural Centre
Poble Nou, C Pallars 277, 08005 Barcelona, Spain
Architect: José Luis Mateo. Project team: Antonio Montes; Vicente Guallart; Jaune Avellaneda, Antonio Montes; Robert Brufau; Eduardo Hernando; Josep Juvilla; Jordi Lleal; Francesc Roldos; Maurice Carbo; Angels Ulla; Albert Artigas; Ferran Cardenas; Gracia Borrell. Client: Ajuntament de Barcelona. Main contractor: Dragados y Construcciones. Lighting: Mefi S.A. Furniture and fittings: Directe. Steelwork: Secura; J. Balaguer. Flooring: El Corte Ingles S.A. Glasswork: Morgua S.A. Painting: José A. Muniesa. Woodwork: Carpinteria Triangulo S.A.

The Stevens Building, Royal College of Art,
Kensington Gore, London SW7, UK
Architect: John Miller + Partners. Project team: John Miller; Su Rogers; Richard Brearley (partners in charge); Patrick Theis (assistant in charge); Tina Bird; Tim Boyd; John Carpenter; Norman Chang; Louise Cotter; Hester Gray; Neil Harkess; Simon Lanyon-Hogg; Alex Michaelis; Pankaj Pandya; Bryn Riches; Chris Roche; Dean Smith; Graham Smith; Mark Titman. Collaborators: Ove Arup and Partners (structural and mechanical engineers); Davis Langdon and Everest (quantity surveyors). Client: Jocelyn Stevens, Rector, Royal College of Art. Main contractor: Myton Ltd. Sub-contractors: Haden Young Ltd; Phoenix Electrical Company Ltd; Express Lift Company Ltd. Lighting: L. B. Lighting Ltd; Phillips Ltd. VDU Equipment: Strand Lighting; A. S. Green Ltd. Flooring: Diespeker (Terrazzo) Ltd; Lamacrest; Hewetson. Movable screens: Uniwall Ltd. Ceramic signage: Clare Hamilton-Webb.

Circulo de Lectores
C/O'Donell 14, Madrid, Spain
Architect: Enric Miralles. Project team: Enric Miralles; Francesc Pla; Josep Sallo; Josep Mias; Joan Navarro; Albert Salazar. Main contractor/lighting: Albert Ribera Aparevador (Sallo S.A.). Client: Circulo de Lectores. Fixed chairs: designed by Enric Miralles. Movable chairs: designed by Arne Jacobsen and made by Selex Inovator. Paintwork: Juan Antonio Luengo. Glazing: Magisa.

Notojima Glass Art Museum
125-10 Koda, Noto Island, Kashima-Gun, Ishikawa Prefecture, Japan
Architects: Kiko Mozuna Architects & Associates. Client: Municipality of Ishikawa Prefecture. Collaborating engineer: Murakami Institute of Engineering Ltd; Sakurai System Co. Ltd. Main contractor: Kajima Corporation. Sub-contractors: Arisawa Co. Ltd; Sakamuro Denki Ltd; Daiichi Kogyo Co. Ltd; Sanei-Setsubi Co. Ltd. Lighting: Asahi Glass Co. Ltd. Furniture and fittings: Mizukami Kensetsu Ltd; Shikko Ltd. Flooring: Mizukami Kensetsu. Metal ceilings: Takano Sasshu Kogyo Co. Ltd. Halfmoon-shaped objects on tower: Wakasa Tekko Ltd. Aluminium convex caps on museum shop: Tsuneishi Ship Buildings Co. Ltd.

Sakamoto Ryoma Memorial Hall
830 Shiroyana, Urato, Kochi City, Kochi 780, Japan
Architects: Akiko and Hiroshi Takahashi/Work Station. Client: Kochi Prefecture. Collaborating structural engineer: Toshihiko Kimura. Main contractor: Taisei Co. Ltd. Sub-contractor: Daio Construction Co. Ltd. Lighting consultant: Kanyo Engineering Inc. Display consultant: Nomura Display Co. Ltd. Lighting fixtures: Yamagiwa Trading Co. Ltd; Matsushita Electric Works Ltd. Furniture: Knoll International (lobby); Workstation (library and resting area). Flooring: Kawara-Naganokawara Co. Ltd. Carpet: Suminoe Co. Ltd.

Académie Musicale de Villecroze
(Anne Schlumberger Music Centre), Villecroze, Var 83690, France
Architect: Yannis Tsiomis. Project team: Yannis Tsiomis; Patrick Bertrand (project architect); Michael Fenker, with Y. Andreadis; K. Lamy; Y. Haskaris; J. Scheffler; E. Violeau; Z. Castoriadis. Client: Fondation Schlumberger. Main contractor: Enterprise Andreutti. Metalwork: Van Mullem. Joinery: Duclos-Merly; J.P. Brun. Plumbing, heating, ventilation and sanitary installations: Vitalis & Laugier. Electrical and heating engineer: L'Ours Électrique. Structural engineer: A. Maschas/BACON Ingénierie. Thermal consultant: Isocrate. Paintwork and glazing: Vita Germain. Plasterwork: Gross Charles. Ironwork: Andreutti. Iron furniture: Société Diagonal Indigo. Stone furniture: Maurel les Aires. Acoustics: J. Leguy. Raised floors: Briatte. Wooden staircases: Technobois. Glasswork: Charles Costa. Stonework: Gulleron.

Addresses of Architects, Designers & Suppliers

AC/DC Lighting Ltd, Unit 18, Churchill Way, Lomeshaye Industrial Estate, Nelson, Lancs. BB9 6RT, UK. **Actus**, BYGS Building 1 2F, 2-19-1 Shinjuku, Shinkuku-ku, Tokyo, Japan. **ADAC**, 127 rue Marceau, 93100 Montreuil, France. **Adam Carpets**, Greenhill Works, Birmingham Road, Kidderminster D410 2SH, UK. **Addison Espana S.A.**, Calle Velazquez 100-30D, 28006 Madrid, Spain. **Advanced Engineering**, Enterprise House, Farrington Field Estate, Farrington Gurney, Bristol BS18 5NN, UK. **ADVAN** Co. Ltd, 2-19-13 Jingumae, Shibuya-ku, Tokyo, Japan. **Ahrends Burton and Koralek**, 7 Chalcot Road, London NW1 8LH, UK. **Allies and Morrison Architects**, 54 Newman Street, London W1P 3PG, UK. **Roser Amadó i Cercós Lluis Domènech i Girbau Arquitectes**, Aribau 152. 2n2a, 08036 Barcelona, Spain. **American Acrylic Corporation**, 400 Sheffield Avenue, West Babylon, New York, NY 11704, USA. **Anderson/Schwartz Architects**, 40 Hudson Street, New York, NY 10013, USA. **Andreu World S.A.**, Cno de los Mojones KM 2.5, 46970 Alaguas, Valencia, Spain. **Georges Andreutti**, Quartier les Défends, 83930 Villecroze, France. **Anthologie Quartett**, Schloss Huennefeld, Bad Essen 1 D4515, Germany. **Aqua Electrical Ltd**, Aqua House, Rose and Crown Road, Swavesey, Camb. CB4 5RB, UK. **Ron Arad Associates**, 62 Chalk Farm Road, London NW1 8AN, UK. **Archetype**, 4052 Del Rey Avenue, Venice, California, USA. **Ardern Hodges Ltd**, 17 Barnsbury Terrace, Barnsbury Square, London N1 1JN, UK. **Artemide**, Via Brughiera 6, 20010 Pregnana Milanese, Italy. **Artemide UK**, 17-19 Neal Street, London WC2H 9PU, UK. **Ove Arup & Partners**, 79-81 Franklin Street, Melbourne, Victoria, Australia. **Asahi Glass Co. Ltd**, 2-1-2 Marunouchi, Chiyoda-ku, Tokyo, Japan. **Ast & Co.**, Villacher- Strasse 57, A-9020 Klagenfurt, Austria. **Atelier International**, 30-20 Thompson Street, L.I.C., New York, NY 11101, USA. **Atrium**, 22-24 St Giles High Street, London, UK.

J. Balaguer S.A., Vineta 23-13, Hospitalet Dell, Barcelona, Spain. **Celia Barker-Mill**, 2 grand rue Amiral SaP, 30170 St Hippolyte, Gard, France. **Christian Bartenbach**, Rinner-Strasse 14, A-6071 Aldrans, Innsbruck, Austria. **Bauerschmidt & Sons**, 119-20 Merrick Blvd, St Albans, New York, NY 11434, USA. **Bausman-Gill Associates**, Room 611, 611 Broadway, New York, NY 10012, USA. **Becher Joinery**, Church Wharf, Corney Row, Chiswick, London W4, UK. **Beermann Parkett GmbH & Co.**, Bechumer Strasse 9, 4410 Warendorf, Germany. **Jeffrey G. Beers Architects**, Suite 6a, 141 East 55th Street, New York, NY 10022, USA. **Behnisch & Partners, Freie Architekten BDA**, Büro Sillenbuch, Gorch-Fock-Strasse 30, 7000 Stuttgart 75, Germany. **Belfer**, 1703 Valley Road, Ocean, NJ 07712, USA. **Jeff Bell**, Unit 11, 2 Somerset Road, London N17 9EJ, UK. **David Bentheim Interior Design**, 3 Rossetti Studios, 72 Flood Street, London, UK. **Lennart Bergström Arkitektkontor**, Rosenlundsgaten 29, 116 69 Stockholm, Sweden. **Beyki**, Tanfarhofda 11, is 112 Reykjavik, Iceland. **BKS**, Postfach 100210, Heidestrasse 71, D-5620 Velbert 1, Germany. **BML Services**, 45 St Dunstans Drive, Gravesend, Kent ME1O 2AA, UK. **Bode Innenvausbau**, Industriestrasse 17, 3504 Kaufungen, Germany. **Architekturbüro Bolles-Wilson and Partner**, Alter Steinweg 17, 4400 Münster, Germany. **Esteve Bonell & Francesc Rius**, C. Corcega 288 1.2a, 08008 Barcelona, Spain. **Fa Leopold Brandi**, Seebachgasse 5, 3340 Waidhofen, Ybbs, Austria. **Branson Coates Architecture**, 23 Old Street, London EC1V 9HL, UK. **Olivier Brenac & Xavier Gonzalez**, Atelier d'Architecture, 59 rue de Turenne, 75003 Paris, France. **Brent Metalwork**, Alperton Lane, Wembley, Middx HAO 1SJ, UK. Briatte, ZA Villemer RN 17, Le Thillay, 95500 Gonesse, France. **Brintons Ltd**, 21-23 Queensdale Place, London W11 4SQ, UK. **J. Brown Flooring**, Unit 6/7, Orient Industrial Park, Simmons Road, London E10 7NB, UK. **Eduard Bru**, Balmes 110 1.2a, 08008 Barcelona, Spain. **Luis Bru**, Entic Grandados No. 64, Barcelona 08008, Spain. **J. P. Brun**, Ebenisterie de la Clape, Hameau de la Clape, 83300 Drauignan, France. **Bull Signs**, Bayhorne Lane, Walthamstow, London E17 6DQ, UK. **Bim Burton**, Bartlett, The Woodwork Shop, 22 Gordon Street, London NW1, UK. **Jim Burton**, JB Carpentry Services, Beech Works, 75a Beechwood Road, Luton, UK.

Luisa Calvi, Marco Merlini, Carlos Moya, Via Vigevano 31, 20144 Milan, Italy. **Campbell Marsden**, Unit 34, Wimbledon Business Centre, Riverside Road, London SW17 OBA, UK. **Cantu' Ottone**, Via Domea 10, 20063 Cantu, Italy. **Cappellini S.p.A.**, Via Marconi 35, 22060 Arosio, Italy. **Carlton Building Services Ltd**, 16-18 Balham Grove, London SW12 8AY, UK. **Carlton Cook Company**, 1715 West 26th Street, Houston, Texas 77008, USA. **Carminart Tiles**, 61 North Saw Mill River Road, Elmsford, New York, NY 10523, USA. **Carpinteria Triangulo S.A.**, Triangulo 10, Monticade I Reixach, Barcelona, Spain. **Pat Carter Shopfitting & Specialist Contracts**, 13 Granard Avenue, London SW15 6HH, UK. **Cassina**, Via Luigi Busnelli 1, Meda 20036, Milan, Italy. **Cassina Japan Co. Ltd**, 2-9-6 Higashi, Shibuya-ku, Tokyo 150, Japan. **Castelli S.p.A.**, Via Torregiani 1, Bologna 40128, Italy. **Centre Ltd**, 24 New Road, Rubery, Birmingham B45 9HU, UK. **Ceria Coupel**, 6 esplanade de la Manufacture, Issy-les-Moulineaux 92130, France. **Chairs**, AXIS Bldg. 413, 5-17-1 Roppongi, Minato-ku, Tokyo 106, Japan. **David Chipperfield Architects**, 1A Cobham Mews, Agar Grove, London NW1 9SB, UK. **Cidue S.p.A.**, Via San Lorenzo 32, Carre Vincenza 36010, Italy. **Henri Ciriani**, 93 rue de Montreuil, 75011 Paris, France. **Antonio Citterio and Terry Dwan Architects**, Via Lovanio 8, 20121 Milan, Italy. **Brian Clarke**, 80 Peel Street, London W8, UK. **Jo Coenen & Co.**, Bouillonstraat 14, 6211 LH Maastricht, The Netherlands. **Marian Coenen Interior Design Shop**, Van Heeswijkstraat 1, 5071 CT Udenhout, The Netherlands. **Coexistence**, 288 Upper Street, London N1 2TZ, UK. **Colazzo**, Seebach 37, A-9125 Kuhnsdorf, Austria. **Cole Carpentry**, 125/6 Bolingbroke Grove, London SW11 1DA, UK. **Concord Lighting**, 174 High Holborn, London WC1V 7AA, UK. **Contract Distributors**, 505 Park Avenue, New York, NY 10022, USA. **Pepe Cortés Asociados S.L.**, Santa Teresa 6, 08012 Barcelona, Spain. **Cosmo Lighting**, Light Solutions East, 110 Greene Street, New York, NY 10012, USA. **Établissement Charles Costa**, 77 rue de la Plaine, 75020 Paris, France. **Crans (UK) Ltd**, 6 The Crescent, Woldingham, Surrey CR3 7DB, UK. **Crofton Engineering Ltd**, Cambridge Road, Linton, Cambridge CB1 6NN, UK. **Crucible**, 366 West 15th Street, New York, USA. **Antonio Cruz/Antonio Ortiz Arquitectos**, Santas Patronas 36, 41001 Seville, Spain. **CSL Lighting**, 928 Broadway, Suite 1010, New York, NY 10010, USA. **CUB**, Princesa 58, Pral. 2a, 08003 Barcelona, Spain. **Cumbria Stone Quarries**, Silver Street, Crosby, Ravensworth, Penrith CA10 3JA, UK. **Custom Metal Fabrications Ltd**, Horton Road, West Drayton, Middx UB7 8JE, UK.

Daiko, Suzae Building, 1-15-8 Kaigan, Minato-ku, Tokyo, Japan. **Lynn Davis Architects**, 13 Harnet Street, Sandwich, Kent CT13 9ES, UK. **de Architekten Cie**, Keizersgracht 113, 1015 CJ Amsterdam, The Netherlands. **DEGW London Ltd**, Porters North, 8 Crinan Street, London N1 9SQ, UK. **Stefano de Martino**, 38 St John Street, London EC1M 4AY, UK. **Denton Corker Marshall Pty Ltd**, 49 Exhibition Street, Melbourne 3000, Victoria, Australia and 14 Devonshire Street, London W1N 1FS, UK. **Wolfgang Deseyve**, Plenkerstrasse 37, 3340 Waidhofen, Ybbs, Austria. **DGMR B.V.**, Sonsbeekweg 32, 6914 BBD Arnhem, The Netherlands. **Di Bianco Lighting**, 8018 Third Avenue, Brooklyn, New York, NY 11209, USA. **Directe**, Pau Claris 149, Principal -2a, 08009 Barcelona, Spain. **Divano S.A.**, En Proyecto 2, 46470 Albal, Valencia, Spain. **Tom Dixon**, 12 Dolland Street, London SE11 5LN, UK. **DLW AG**, Verkaufsbüro Frankfurt, 6000 Frankfurt/M 1, Germany. **DMK Designs**, 1-5 Chance Street, London E1 6JT, UK. **Domus Tiles**, 33 Parkgate Road, London SW11 4NP, UK. **C. Doring**, Holzgraben 15, 6000 Frankfurt/M 1, Germany. **Dragados y Construcciones**, Via Laietana 33, 7.1., 08003, Barcelona, Spain. **Sarl Duclos-Merly**, ZA de la Baume, 83690 Salernes, France. **Duralit**, A-8641 St Marein im Murztal, Austria.

Ecart International S.A., 111 rue St Antoine, 75004 Paris, France. **Electech**, Via Nazionale 90, Fontechiara (AR), Italy. **Elementer Industrial Design Ltd**, Progress House, Whittle-Parkway, Slough, Berks. SC1 6DG, UK. **Elert GmbH & Co. KG**, Postfach 129, .pa ä6440 Bebra, Germany. **Empire Stone Ltd**, Narborough, Leicester LE9 5GR, UK. **Claude Engle and Associates**, 10,000 Popomac Avenue, N.W., Washington DC 20007, USA. **Entec**, 517 Yeading Lane, Northolt, Middx UB5 6LM, UK. **Erco Lighting Ltd**, 38 Dover Street, London W1X 3RB, UK. **Ralph Erskine Architect Planner AB**, Box 156, Gustav III väg.4, 17802 Drottingholm, Sweden. **ESA**, Mainzer Landstrasse 683, 6000 Frankfurt/M 80, Germany. **Espace Volume – JB Las Martre**, 7 rue des Frères Chapelle, 92170 Vanves, France. **Euramco Engineering Ltd**, High Street, Meldreth, Camb., UK. **Expográfic**, Avenida Madrid 150-152, 08190 Valldoreix, Barcelona, Spain.

Joan Falguerona S.L., Carrietera D'Olot S/N, 17850 Besulei, Girona, Spain. **F.B.I.**, 188 boulevard Gabriel Peri, 93110 Rosny- sous-Bois, France. **Fedhaus Fassaden and Fenster**, 4407 Emsdetten, Grevener Dam 239 249, Germany. **Martin Feicht GmbH & Co. KG**, Karl- Schmid-Strasse 16, 8000 Munich 82, Germany. **Finecraft Vogue**, Arundel Road, Uxbridge, Middx UB8 2RX, UK. **Finessi and Gambini**, Via F. Bandiera, 20052 Monza, Milan, Italy. **Firman Ltd**, 84 Straight Road, Romford RM3 84B, UK. **Jules Fisher and Paul Marantz Inc.**, 126 Fifth Avenue, New York, USA. **Flexform S.p.A.**, Via Einaudi 23/25, 20036 Meda, Milan, Italy. **Flos S.p.A.**, Via Moretto 58, 25121 Brescia, Italy. **Terry Flowers**, 8 High Street, Upnor, Rochester, Kent, UK. **Forbo-Nairn Ltd**, Contracts Products Division, Leet Court, 14 King Street, Watford, Herts. WD1 8B2, UK. **Forbo Teppich Werke GmbH**, Steubenstrasse 27, 4790 Paderbom, Germany. **Max Fordham and Partners**, 43 Gloucester Crescent, London NW1 7PE, UK. **Forum Diffusion**, 55 rue Pierre Demours, 75017 Paris, France. **Sir Norman Foster and Partners**, Riverside Three, 22 Hester Road, London SW11 4AN, UK. **The Foundation**, 8 French Place, London E1, UK. **Froschauer OHG**, Hausnummer 56, 3321 Ardagger Markt, Austria. **Frostverk**, Smidsbud 12is 210, Gardabae, Iceland. **FSB**, Nieheimer Strasse 38, D-3492 Braker, Germany. **Fuji House Industry Co. Ltd**, 1532 Otsu Osone, Nangoku-City, Kochi 783, Japan. **Harumi Fujimoto, M.G.S. Co. Ltd**, Tanizawa Bldg, 3-2-11 Nishi-Azabu, Minato-ku, Tokyo 151, Japan. **George A. Fuller Co.**, 919 Third Avenue, New York, NY 10022, USA. **Fumagalli**, Via Rosselli 14, Bergamo, Italy. **Spencer Fung Architects**, 43 Pall Mall Deposit, 124-128 Barlby Road, London W10 6BL, UK.

Beth Galí, Rambla Caputxins 74, pral. Barcelona 08002, Spain. **Gama S.A.**, Avenida de Sarrià, 11-13 Barcelona, Spain. **Gatimalau**, 50 rue Saint Sabin, 75011 Paris, France. **GEC Anderson Ltd**, 89 Herkomer Road, Bushey, Watford WDZ 3LS, UK. **Frank O. Gehry & Associates**, Inc., 1520-B Cloverfield Boulevard, Santa Monica, CA 90404, USA. **Volker Giencke**, Mozartgasse 6, A-8010 Graz, Austria. **GIG**, A-1010 Vienna, Weihburggasse 9/111, Austria. **Gines y Navarro Construcciones S.A.**, C/Aragon 310, Barcelona, Spain. **Gittins and Mellor Ltd**, Cooper Street, Wolverhampton, West Midlands, UK. **Glass Rule Ltd**, Drumaline Ridge, Worcester Park, Surrey RT4 7JT, UK. **Glerborg**, Dalshravni 5, is 220 Hafnarfjoravr, Iceland. Glertaekni, Bildshofda 18, 12 112 Reyjkavik, Iceland. **Peter Glynn-Smith Associates**, 32 Duncan Terrace, London N1 8BS, UK. **Goldbach GmbH**, Hunsruckstrasse 40, 6230 Frankfurt/M 80, Germany. **Saul Goldin & Associates**, 1818 S. Robertson Boulevard, Los Angeles, California, USA. **F. J. Gray Glass Co.**, 139-24 Queens Blvd, Jarnaica, Queens, New York, USA. **A.S. Green & Co. (Lancs.) Ltd**, Winchester Road, Haydock Lane Industrial Estate, Merseyside WA11 9QX, UK. **Entreprise Charles Gross**, Le Mas de l'Amourie, Seillans 83440, France.**Vicente Guallart**, Nou de la Rambla 24, 08001 Barcelona, Spain.**Guzzini**, Via Statale SS77, Recanati, Italy. **Gwathmey Siegel & Associates Architects**, 475 Tenth Avenue, New York, NY 10018, USA.

Haigh Space Architects, 63 Pemberwick Road, Greenwich, Connecticut, USA. **Hakasuisha Corp.**, 1-15-27 Higashi-Shinsaibashi, Chuo-ku, Osaka, Japan. **Matthew Hall**, P.O. Box 28, 17 Portman Road, Ipswich IP1 2BX, UK. **Francis Hamel-Cooke**, Flat 3, 23 College Cross, London N1, UK. **Hand Fabrication, Clark Construction**, 117 Hudson Street, New York, NY 10013, USA. **Fritz Hansen**, DK-3450 Allerod, Denmark. **Ragnar Hansen**, Haaleitisbravt 57, is 108 Reykjavik, Iceland. **Hansens**, 306-306a Fulham Road, Chelsea, London SW10 9ER, UK. **Julian Harrup Architects**, 95 Kingsland Road, London E2 8AG, UK. **Hazama Corporation**, 5-8 Kita-Aoyama 2-chome, Minato-ku, Tokyo, Japan. **Heath Construction (St Albans) Ltd**, 58 Coombes Road, London Colney, Herts. AL2 1ND, UK. **Fa Hege**, C. Baumgartner Strasse 10, 4650 Lambach, Austria. **HG Heildverslun**, Fakafeni 9, is 108 Reykjavik, Iceland. **Heschl**, Unterer Heidenweg 27, 9500 Villach, Austria. **Hewetson Floors Ltd**, Nicholas House, River Front, Enfield EN1 3TW, Middx, UK. **Alfred Hohenberger**, St Veiter-Strasse 22-24, A-9020, Austria. **Steven Holl Architects**, 435 Hudson Street, 4th Floor, New York, NY 10014, USA. **Hans Hollein Architekt**, Argentinierstrasse 36, 1040 Vienna 4, Austria. **Philip Holzmann GmbH**, Haupmiederlassung Frankfurt, 6078 Neu-Isenburg, An der Gehepitz, Germany. **Alan Hone**, Burnham House, 267-269 Farnham Road, Slough SL2 1HA, UK. **Michael Hopkins and Partners**, 27 Broadley Terrace, London NW1 6LG, UK. **Howard and Constable Contracts Ltd**, Canalside Studios, 2-4 Orsman Road, London N1 5QJ, UK. **Hudson-Schatz Painting Co.**, 429 W. 53rd Street, New York, NY 10019, USA. **Jeremy and Louisa Hughes**, 6 Lowry Crescent, Mitcham, Surrey CR4 3QS, UK. **Huma Glas B.V.**, Nikkelstraat 24, 2984 AM Ridderkerk, The Netherlands. **Hús and Lagnir**, Rettarhalsi 2, is 110, Reykjavik, Iceland. **V.A. Hutchinson**, 8 Madeira Avenue, Bognor Regis, West Sussex PO22 8DX, UK.

Iagulli, Via Grazia Deledda 5, Prato (Fl), Italy. **IBV Interieurs**, Jules Verneweg 27-29, 5015 BE Tilburg, The Netherlands. **ICF**, 305 East 63rd Street, New York, NY 10021, USA. **T. W. Ide**, Glasshouse Fields, London E1 92A, UK. **Idea Mueble S.A.**, Via Augusta 185, 08021 Barcelona, Spain. **Idee**, 5-4-44 Minami Aoyama, Minato-ku, Tokyo, Japan. **IMA Fabrications**, 221 Hatfield Road, St Albans, UK. **Elvar Ingason**, Vnnarbravt 12, is 170 Seltjarnarnes, Iceland. **El Corte Ingles S.A.**, Freuderberg, Aosias March 38, Barcelona, Spain. **Inoue Industries**, 3-31-15 Matsunoki, Suginami-ku, Tokyo. **Inovative Constructions**, 3623 Adeline Street, Emeryville, CA 94608, USA. **Interglass Ltd**, Greenfield Industrial Estate, Tindale Crescent, Bishops Auckland, County Durham DL14 9TF, UK. **Intermura Furniture**, Ellingfort Road, Hackney, London E8 3PA, UK. **IPSO**, 10 bis rue de la Ferme, 92250 La Garenne Colombes, France. **James Irvine**, c/o Cappellini S.p.A, Via Marconi 35, 22060 Arosio, Italy. **Iserma**, Sancho de Avila 105-111, 08018 Barcelona, Spain. **Isometrix**, 2 Frederick Mews, Kinnerton Street, London SW1X 8EQ, UK. **Franklin D. Israel Design Associates Inc.**, 254 South Robertson Blvd, Suite 205, Beverly Hills, CA 90211, USA. **Ístak**, Skulatun 4, 105 Reykjavik, Iceland. **Toyo Ito & Associates, Architects**, Fujiya Bldg, 19-4 1-chome, Shibuya, Shibuya-ku, Tokyo 150, Japan. **Iwanaga-Gumi**, Minami-Kumamoto 4-4-10, Kumamoto City, Japan. **Ixors**, 1-2-23-408 Moto-Asabu, Minato- ku, Tokyo, Japan.

Arne Jacobsen, c/o Coexistence Ltd, 288 Upper Street, London N1 2AS, UK. **Jandor Metal Doors Ltd**, Manor Farm Road, Wembley, Middx HAO 1WJ, UK. **Carlos Jane**, Apartado 243-08400, Grandollers-CTRA N-152, Barcelona, Spain. **Jaymart Flooring**, Woodlands Trading Estate, Eden Vale Road, Westbury, Wilts. BA13 3QS, UK. **Jestico + Whiles Architects**, 14 Stephenson Way, London NW1 2HD, UK. **Carlos Jiménez Architectural Design Studio**, 1116 Willard Street, Houston, Texas 77006, USA. **Johnson & Bailey Ltd**, 511 Coldhams Lane, Cambridge CB1 3LN, UK. **Joinex AB**, S-931 88 Sikelleftea, Sweden. **Harry Joseph and Associates**, 110 West 94th Street, New York, NY 10025, USA.

Kahn-Snyder Company, 253 Church Street, New York, NY 10013, USA. **Kajima Corporation**, 1-3-4 Mandai, Niigata Prefecture, Japan. **Kankyo Engineering Inc.**, Daiichi-Kiki Building, 2-23-31 Meguro, Meguro-ku, Tokyo 153, Japan. **Kaufman Color**, 89 Jane Street, New York, USA. **Kawara-Naganokawara Co. Ltd**, 4-3 Syonosiba-cho, Aki-City, Kochi 784, Japan. **Nancy Kearing**, 80 Forsyth Street, New York, NY 10002, USA. **Ben Kelly Design**, 10 Stoney Street, London SE1 9AD, UK. **Kern and Rockenfield**, 345 Devoe Street, Williamsburg, Brooklyn, New York, NY 11211, USA. **Kingdom Coverings**, 20 Bridge Street, Thrapston, Kettering, Northants. NN14 4LR, UK. **King Kong Production**, Via Gulli 4, 20147 Milan, Italy. **Kjorvidur**, Tronuhrauni 5, 15-220 Hafnarfjordvr, Iceland. **Klemt-Feinbau**, Ludwig-Merck-Strasse 6, D-8

Munich, Germany. **Knoll International**, Hirakawa-cho Building, 2-6-1 Hirakawa-cho, Chiyoda-ku, Tokyo 102, Japan. **Knoll International**, 105 Wooster Street, New York, NY 10012, USA. **Koch and Lowy**, P.O. Box 304, 487 West Main Street, Avon, MA 02322-0304, USA. **Franz Kohler GmbH**, Deichwiese 15, 6432 Heringen-Widderschausen, Germany. **Konic**, c/Varsovia 72, Barcelona, Spain. **Rem Koolhaas**, Boompjes 55, 3011XB Rotterdam, The Netherlands. **Krainer**, Draubodenweg 23, A-9500 Villach, Austria. **Kristen Metalbau**, Wallgraben 49, 2100 Hamburg 90, Germany. **Jan Kroeze**, 225 Lafayette Street, Room 1001, New York, NY 10012, USA. **Kuchen und Ideen re-ell GmbH**, Berliner Strasse 29, 6000 Frankfurt/M 1, Germany. **Kusch and Co.**, Postfach 1151, D-5789 Hallenberg, Germany.

Lachant Frères, 140 rue deMulhouse St Quentin, Paris, France. **Thomas Laidlaw (East Anglia) Ltd**, 30 Clifton Road, Cambridge CB1 4ZH, UK. **Laing Management Interiors**, Management House, Alma Street, Luton, Beds. LU1 2PL, UK. **José Antonio Martinez Lapeña and Elías Torres Tur**, Roca i Batlle 14, 08023 Barcelona, Spain. **L.B. Lighting Ltd**, The Metro Centre, St Albans Road, St Albans, Herts. AL4 9AT, UK. **Richard Lees Ltd**, Weston Underwood, Derby DE6 4PH, UK. **Lehrer McGovern Bovis**, 387 Park Avenue South, New York, NY 10016, USA. **Leitenberger/Bronfman Associates**, 37 King Street, Chappagua, New York, NY 10574, USA. **Leonhard Bürogestaltung GmbH**, Bockenheimer Landstrasse 98-100, 6000 Frankfurt/M 1, Germany. **Leptien 3 GmbH**, Stephanstrasse 1-3, 6000 Frankfurt/M 1, Germany. **Christian Liaigre**, 61 rue de Varennes, 75007 Paris, France and 122 rue de Grenelle, 75007 Paris, France (showroom). **Lichtdesign & Lichtplanung Bartenbach**, Rinnerstrasse 14, A 6071 Aldrans, Innsbruck, Austria. **Lichttechnische Planung GmbH**, Ludwig-Hinnerth Strasse 9, A-3021 Pressabaum, Vienna, Austria. **Liemer GesmbH**, St Peter Hauptstrasse 31, 8042 Graz, Austria. **Alberto Lievore & Asociados**, Placa de Berenguer el Gran 1 atico, 08002 Barcelona, Spain. **Light and Space Assoc. Ltd**, 288A Vanderbilt Avenue, Brooklyn, New York, NY 11200, USA. **Lighting Design Partnership**, 45 Timber Bush, Leith, Edinburgh, Scotland, UK. **Lighting Systems**, 1212 Westheimer, Houston, Texas 77006, USA. **Lightolier**, 100 Lighting Way, Secaucus, New Jersey 07094, USA. **Light Projects**, 23 Jacob Street, London SE1 2BG, UK. **Limited Productions Inc.**, 1290 Bodega Avenue, Petaluma, CA 94952, USA. **Fa Dietmar Linninger**, Pyburg 29, 4482 Ennsdorf, Austria. **Peter Lisec GesmbH**, Bahnhofstrasse 34, 3363 Hausmening- Amstetten, Austria. **Logic Design and Fabrication**, 38 Graham Street, London N1 8JX, UK. **Luceplan S.p.A.**, Via E. T. Moneta 44/46, 20161 Milan, Italy. **Juan Antonio Luengo**, Los Clerigos 11 äi2, P El Espinar, Spain.

MacCormac Jamieson Prichard, 9 Heneage Street, Spitalfields, London E1 5LJ, UK. **Magisa**, Ctra. de Girona a Ripoll, Cornella de Terri, 17844 Girona, Spain. **D. Magnan & Co. Inc.**, 32 Cortlandt Street, Mount Vernon, NY 10550, USA. **Manes Space**, 30 West 21st Street, New York, NY 10010, USA. **R. Mansell Ltd**, City Road, London E1, UK. **Mantisson**, Greswolde House, 197a Station Road, Knowle, Solihull, West Midlands B93 OPU, UK. **Flaminio Marin and Co.**, Via Varanini 29/A, Milan, Italy. **Javier Mariscal**, Pellaires 30-38, 08019 Barcelona, Spain. **Marland Contract**, 47 Hawthorne Avenue, Timperley Altrincham, Ches. WA15 6TN, UK. **Marshall Howard Ltd**, Andre Street, Hackney, London W8 2AA, UK. **Campbell Marson**, Unit 34, Wimbledon Business Centre, Riverside Road, London SW17 OBA, UK. **José Luis Mateo**, Balmes 110, pral 1a, 08008 Barcelona, Spain. **Rick Mather Architects**, 123 Camden High Street, London NW1 7JR, UK. **Matsushita Electric Works Ltd**, 1048 Oaza Kadoma, Kadoma City, Osaka 571, Japan. **Matteo Grassi**, 22066 Mariano, Via S. Caterina da Sienna 26, Italy. **Etablissement Maurel**, Les Aires, 83630 AUPS, France. **McLaughlin & Harvey PLC**, Jeffreys Road, Brimsdown, Enfield EN3 7UB, Middx, UK. **Mefi S.A.**, Berenguer de Palou, 83-85, 08027 Barcelona, Spain. **Mellows PPG Ltd**, Ridgacre Road, West Bromwich, West Midlands B71 1BB, UK. **Giovanni Merighi**, 19/1 Viale Sabotino, Milan 20135, Italy. **Meritalia S.p.A.**, Via Como 76/78, 22066 Marriano Comense, Como, Italy. **Mero-Werke GmbH & Co.**, Siegerter Strasse 50, 5230 Frankfurt/M 80, Germany. **3R Messebau GmbH**, Neurothstrasse 2, 6370 Oberursel, Germany. **Metal & Glass Design Ltd**, 21/22 Poland Street, London W1V 3DD, UK. **Mettallbau Treiber**, Dreihackengasse 20-23, A-8020 Graz, Austria. **John Miller + Partners**, The Elephant House Brewery, 35 Hawley Crescent, London NW1 8NP, UK. **Enric Miralles Arq.**, 52 Avinyo St., 08002 Barcelona, Spain. **Miroiterie Bret**, 32 rue Gay Lussac, 94430 Chennevieres, France. **Mison Inc.**, 131 Varick Street, New York, NY 10013, USA. **Mizukami Kensetsu Ltd**, 960 Kobuminami Kanazawa City, Ishikawa, Japan. **Mobles 114**, Enric Granados 114, 08008 Barcelona, Spain. **Modern Age Furniture**, 795 Broadway, New York, NY 10003, USA. **Montis**, Steenstraat 2, NL-5107 NE Dongen, The Netherlands. **Einstein Moomjy**, 150 East 58th Street, New York, NY 10155, USA. **Simon Moore**, Glassworks, 12 Victoria Terrace, London N4, UK. **Mordaunt Woodworking**, 1805 Second Street, Berkeley, CA 94710, USA. **Moroso S.p.A.**, Via Nazionale 60, Cavalicco de Tavagnacco, 33010, Italy. **Jasper Morrison, c/o SCP Ltd**, 135-139 Curtain Road, London EC2A 3BX, UK. **Eric Owen Moss Architect**, 8557 Higuera Street, Culver City, CA 90232, USA. **John Mowlem & Co.**, Foundation House, Eastown Road, Bracknell RG12 2UZ, UK. **Kiko Mozuna Architects & Associates**, 6-5- 29 Ookura Setagaya-ku, Tokyo 157, Japan. **José A. Muniesa**, Berlin 82-84 1020, 08028 Barcelona, Spain. **Murguia S.A.**, Crta del Medio 50, 08940 Cornella, Barcelona, Spain. **Myton Ltd**, Bridge House, Westmount Centre, Delamere Road, Hayes, Middx UB4 OHD, UK.

Nägeli Vallebuona, Maybachufer 5, D-1000 Berlin 44, Germany. **National Terrazzo Tile and Marble Inc.**, 5728 Hood Street, Houston, Texas 77023, USA. **Naturestone**, 1A Kings Ride Park, Ascot, Berks. SL5 8AR, UK. **Torsten Neeland**, Brahmsallée 19, 2000 Hamburg 13, Germany. **T. Nevill & Co.**, 2/6 Gourley Place, Tottenham, London N15 5NS, UK. **Newman Shopfitters Ltd**, Lagonda Road, Billingham, Cleveland TS23 4JA, UK. **Marc Newson**, 94 rue Saint Denis, 75001 Paris, France. **Isamu Noguchi, c/o Shed Srl**, Viale Umbria 42, 20135 Milan, Italy. **Nomoto Mokkojo Co. Ltd**, 4-1-1 Soto-Kanda, Chiyoda-ku, Tokyo 101, Japan. **Nomura Display Co. Ltd**, 4-6-4 Shibaura, Minato-ku, Tokyo 108, Japan. **Notojima Glass Workshop**, 112-113 Notojima-cho, Kashima-gun, Ishikawa, Japan. **NSC Construction**, 165 Duane Street, New York, USA. **Nuno Co. Ltd**, AXIS Bldg, 5-17-1 Roppongi, Minato-ku, Tokyo, Japan.

Ogawa Electrical Engineering, 5-23-5 Hoshida, Katano-shi, Osaka, Japan. **Teruaki Ohashi Atelier**, House 4 Ohbayashi, 2-3 Kanda- Tsukasacho, Chiyoda-ku, Tokyo 101, Japan. **Okamura Corporation**, 2- 14-2 Nagata-cho, Chiyoda-ku, Tokyo 100, Japan. **Jom H. Olafsson**, Haaleitisbravt 153, is 102, Reykjavik, Iceland. **Claes Oldenburg/ Coosje Van Bruggen**, 556 Broome Street, New York, NY 10013, USA. **Olivetti Synthesis S.p.A.**, Via Corusio 2, 20123 Milan, Italy. **Osaka Processing Inc.**, 1-12-12 Yamada-Higashi, Suita, Osaka 565, Japan. **Osiris**, Sail Loft, Dreadnought Wharf, Thames Street, Greenwich, London SE10 9BY, UK. **Osram GEC Ltd**, P.O. Box 17, East Lane, Wembley, Middx HA9 7PG, UK.

Pallam Precast, 187 West End Lane, London NW6, UK. **Palazzetti Inc.**, 515 Madison Avenue, New York, NY 10016, USA. **Friedrich Panzer**, Prenning, A-8121 Deutschleistritz, Austria. **Parketgólf**, Skutvvogi 11, is 200 Kopavogvr, Iceland. **Frank Parlamis Inc.**, 328 Atlantic Avenue, Brooklyn, New York, NY 11201, USA. **Parnall Contracts**, Lodge Causeway, Fishponds, Bristol BS16 3JU, UK. **Parquets Briatte**, ZA Villemer RN7 – BP, 20 95500, Le Thillay, France. **Paxman Joineries Ltd**, Shoeburyness, Essex, UK. **Peerless**, P.O. Box 304, Berkeley, CA 94702-0556, USA. **Pennington Robson**, Tea Warehouse, 10 Lant Street, London SE1 1QR, UK. **Peutz & Associates B.V.**, Paletsingel 2, 2718 NT Zoetermeer, The Netherlands. **Philips Lighting Ltd**, City House, 420-430 London Road, Croydon CR9 3QR, UK. **Phoenix Flooring Ltd**, Arisdale Avenue, South Ockenden, Essex RM15 5TR, UK. **Piper Products Ltd**, 55 Mabledon Avenue, Ashford, Kent, UK. **Felix Pleschek**, Karl-Huber-Gasse 15, A-8041 Graz, Austria. **Boris Podrecca**, Edelhofgasse 10, Vienna A-1180, Austria. **Pohlschroder**, Hannoverschestrasse 22, 4600 Dortmund 1, Germany. **Port Morris Tile and Terrazzo Corp.**, 1285 Oak Point Avenue, Bronx, New York, NY 10474, USA. **G. A. Potteau**, 16 quai des Celestins, 75006 Paris, France. **Louis Poulsen**, 9 rue Coypel, 75013 Paris, France. **Prodelta**, Diagonal 539, 2-1, 08029 Barcelona, Spain. **Progressive**, 22 Southern Blvd, Nesconset, NY 11767, USA. **Project Construction**, Alessandro Passi, Via Alpi 1, 24050 Spirano, Bergamo, Italy. **Punto Luz**, c/Pau Claris 146, Barcelona, Spain.

Màrius Quintana, c/o Beth Galí, Rambla Caputxins 74 i pral, Barcelona 08002, Spain.

David Racz, c/o The Architectural Association, School of Architecture, 34-36 Bedford Square, London WC1B 3ES, UK. **Hubert Raudaschl**, Ried 155, A-5360 St Wolfgang, Austria. **Reggiani Ltd**, 12 Chester Road, Borehamwood, London, UK. **Republic Merchants Inc.**, 3rd Floor, 71 Chien Kan North Road, Section Taipec, Taiwan. **Patrick Roberts Lighting**, Edenbridge, Kent, UK. **Nancy Robins**, Pan Claris 181, 08037 Barcelona, Spain. **Rock Townsend**, 35 Alfred Place, London WC1 7DP, UK. **Rockwool**, Pencoed, Mid Glamorgan, CF35 6NY Wales. **Rutledge Contracts Ltd**, Hatherley Mews, London E17 4QP, UK. **Martin Ryan**, The Coach House, Gate Burton, Gainsborough, Lincs, UK.

Fernando Salas Studio, Palo Alto Pellaires 30-38, Pobel Nou, 08019 Barcelona, Spain. **Sallo S.A.**, Pla de Montfullà, Bescano 17162 s/n, Girona, Spain. **E.G. Sames & Co. Ltd**, 417 New Cross Road, London SE14 6TA, UK. **America Sanchez**, Aribau 245 Entlo 3a, 08006 Barcelona, Spain. **Sapic S.A.**, C/Evaristo Arnus 56, 08014 Barcelona, Spain. **Saxony Carpet**, 979 Third Avenue, New York, NY 10022, USA. **Schenck & Company Flooring**, 910 Winston Street, Houston, Texas 77009, USA. **Eric Schmitt**, 123 rue de Grenelle, 75007 Paris, France. **Schroder Spezialglastechnik**, Sven GeiB, Buchenweg 20, 2086 Ellerau, Germany. **Scott Howard Systems Furniture**, Business Design Centre, Suite 111, Upper Street, London N1 OQH, UK. **SCP Ltd**, 135-139 Curtain Road, London EC2A 3BX, UK. **Secura SAL**, Mestre Millet 14, Gava, Barcelona, Spain. **Kazuyo Sejima Architect & Associates**, 2-4-4 601, Ebisu-minami, Shibuya-ku, Tokyo, Japan. **Sellex**, Paseo Duque de Mandas, Torre de Atotxa, 1. planta, local 53, 20012 San Sebastian, Spain. **Sess**, Faxafeni 9, is 108 Reykjavik, Iceland. **MS Metalbau Seyriehner**, Ybbsitzerstrasse 29, 3340 Waidhofen, Ybbs, Austria. **George Sexton Associates**, 1841 Colombia Road, NW Suite 210, Washington DC 20009, USA. **Shikko Ltd**, WA42-2 Yoshitake-cho, Komatsu City, Ishikawa, Japan. **Emiliano Sierra**, Placa Sant Joan 3, Sant Joan d'Espi, Barcelona, Spain. **Sikkens**, Via Ponte alle Mosse 25, Florence, Italy. **Silfa**, Via Provinciale 67, Borgo a Buggiano (PT), Italy. **Simeyco Sal**, Carretera a Goizueta, 20120 Hernani, Spain. **Sirrah S.p.A.**, Via Molino Rosso 8, 40026 Imola, Bologna, Italy. **W & G Sissons Ltd**, Calver Mill, Calver, Sheffield S30 1XA, UK. **SKK Lighting**, 34 Lexington Street, London W1, UK. **SKK S.A.**, Abeel Straat 81, 1800 Vilvoorde, Belgium. **Slate Quarries Ltd**, Skelwith Bridge, Ambleside, Cumbria LA22 9NN, UK. **Rod Smith**, 62-68 Rosebery Avenue, London EC1R 4DR, UK. **Smith-Miller + Hawkinson Architects**, 305 Canal Street, New York, NY 10013, USA. **Smith of Derby, Modland Clock Works**, 27 Queen Street, Derby DE1 3DU, UK. **SMS Lichtsysteme**, Walter Weyrer-Strasse 15, A-6020 Innsbruck, Austria. **Snow H. Productions, Inc.**, 111 School Street, Yonkers, NY 01701, USA. **Société Diagonal Indigo**, 52 rue des Martyrs 75009, Paris, France. **Solaglas**, 23a Glasshill Street, London SE1 OQR, UK. **Antoni Solanas i Canovas**, C/Girona 113, 2. 1a, 08009 Barcelona, Spain. **Solo Metals**, 521 West 26th Street, New York, NY 10001, USA. **Spectrum**, 8 Thomas Street, Cirencester, Gloucester GL7 2AX, UK. **SPI Lighting**, 10400 North Enterprise Drive, Mequon, Wisconsin 53092, USA. **SS Fabrications**, Meadow Works, Great North Road, Barnet, Herts., UK. **Ernst Stair**, Beechwood and Second Street, New Rochelle, NY 10801, USA. **Philippe Starck**, 3 rue de la Roquette, 75011 Paris, France. **Konrad Steffen**, Muhlstrasse 14, 3504 Meisunger-Rohrenfurth, Germany. **Bíró Steinar**, Smidjvvegi 2, is 200 Kopavogur, Iceland. **James Stirling, Michael Wilford and Associates Ltd**, 8 Fitzroy Square, London W1P 5AH, UK. **Stoakes Systems Ltd**, Astralite House, 1 Banstead Road, Purley, Surrey CR2 4EB, UK. **Stone Age Ltd**, The Studio, 40 St John's Hill Grove, London SW11 2RG, UK. **Stone Cladding International**, Dakota House, Brunel Road, Newton Abbott TQ12 4PB, UK. **Stoneyford Design Ltd**, The Coach House, Matfen Hall, Matfen, Northumberland NE20 ORH, UK. **Stucco Lustro Veneziano**, 117 St John's Place, Brooklyn, New York, NY 11217, USA. **Studio Granda**, Fjolnisvigi 2, is 101 Reykjavik, Iceland. **STUDIOS Architecture**, 99 Green Street, San Francisco, CA 94111, USA. **Suminoe Co. Ltd**, 3-11-20 Minami-Senba, Chuo-ku, Osaka-City 542, Japan. **Sun-Ad Company Ltd**, Palace Bldg, 1-1-1 Chiyoda-ku, Tokyo, Japan.

Taborsky VertriebsgesmbH, Unterwaltersdorfer Strasse 32, 2440 Moosbrunn, Germany. **Taisei Co. Ltd**, 14-10 Nishinomaru-cho, Takamatsu-City, Kagawa, 760 Japan. **Taiyo Kanamono Co. Ltd**, 3-15-34 Kozu, Chuo-ku, Osaka 542, Japan. **Akiko and Hiroshi Takahashi**, Work Station, 5-131-605 Hanasaki-cho, Nishi-ku, Yokohama 220, Japan. **Takano Sasshu Kogyo Co. Ltd**, 3-30 Zaimoku, Niigata City, Niigata, Japan. **Takenaka Corporation**, 21-1, 8 chome Ginza, Tokyo, Japan. **Ste Taravella**, 108 rue du Regard des Luats, 94500 Champigny Sur Marne, France. **Tarkett**, 114 Mayfield Avenue, P.O. Box 3053, Edison, NJ 08818-9869, USA. **Taylor Maxwell & Co. Ltd**, 4 Newmarket Road, Cambridge CB5 8DT, UK. **Technical Blinds**, Old Town Lane, Wooburn Town, High Wycombe HP10 OPN, UK. **Tecnics**, Plaza Onze de Septembre 5, 17190 Salt-Girona, Spain. **Tecno (UK) Ltd**, 19 New Bond Street, London W1Y 9HF, UK. **Tema Collection**, Indecassa, Escuelas Pias, 250817 Barcelona, Spain. **Temmel Glass GesmbH**, Gradnerstrasse 66, A-8055 Graz, Austria. **Terra Design Woodworking Company**, 11711 Clark Street No. 101, Arcadia, CA 91006, USA. **Ticoflex**, Hipley Street, Old Woking, Surrey GU22 9LL, UK. **Tikino**, 57 rue de Chartres, 78610 Le Perray en Yvelines, France. **Times Square Lighting**, 318 West 47th Street, New York, NY 10036, USA. **Tokyo Glass Art Institute**, 333-1 Ichinotsubo, Nakahara-ku, Kawasaki City, Kanagawa, Japan. **Trésmidjan Borg**, Borgarmyri 1, is 551 Savdarkrokur, Iceland. **Trésmidján Grein**, Smidhvvegi 16, is 200 Kopavogvr, Iceland. **Trésmidjaverkstaedi Reykjavíkur**, Skulatun 2, is 105 Reykjavik, Iceland. **Steven Truslow**, 125 West 26th Street, 9th Floor, New York, NY 10001, USA. **August Truss**, Franzgraben 6, Postfach 10 37 20, 3500 Kassel, Germany. **Yannis Tsiomis Architecture**, 29 rue Miguel Hidalgo, 75019 Paris, France. **Tsuneishi Ship Building Co. Ltd**, 1083 Tsuneishi Numasumi-cho, Numasumi-gun, Hiroshima, Japan. **Tubeworkers Ltd**, Kingston Works, Claverdon, Warwick, UK.

Shigeru Uchida, Studio 80, 1-17-14 Minami-Aoyama, Minato-ku, Tokyo 107, Japan. **Unika Vaev USA**, 305 East 63rd Street, New York, NY 10021, USA. **Urbas**, Billroth-Strasse 7, A-9100 Volermarkt, Austria. **Ushio Spax Inc.**, 2-43-15 Tomigaya, Shibuya-ku, Tokyo 151, Japan.

Etablissement Van Mullem, 49 avenue du Maine, 75014 Paris, France. **Chantier Van Praet**, 62 quai Alfred Sisley, 92394 Villeneuve La Garenne, France. **Vignelli Associates**, 475 Tenth Avenue, New York, NY 10018, USA. **Vincon S.A.**, Paseo de Gracia 96, 08008 Barcelona, Spain. **Entreprise Vita Germain**, 339 avenue de Provence 83300, Draguignan, France. **Vitra**, 2 Charles Eames Strasse, 7858 Weil am Rhein, Germany. **V'soske Joyce (UK) Ltd**, Coda Centre, Munster Road, London SW6 6AW, UK.

Waiko Systembüro, Genferstrasse 10, 6000 Frankfurt/M 56, Germany. **Wakasa Tekko Ltd**, 31-22-4 Fukuhara Kohama City, Fukui, Japan. **Howard Waller**, 60 Neal Street, London WC2H 9PA, UK. **Weerschild B.V.**, Nijerheidstraat 8, 4143 HM Leerdam, The Netherlands. **Whitby & Bird**, 53-54 Newman Street, London W1P 3PQ, UK. **Paul White**, 24a Grafton Crescent, London NW1 8SL, UK. **Wickham & Associates Architects**, 4-5 Crawford Passage, London EC1R 3DP, UK. **Jean-Michel Wilmotte**, Governor Sarl, 68 rue du Faubourg Saint-Antoine, 75012 Paris, France. **Sarah Williams**, 65 Ashburn Place, Greenwich, London SE10 8UG, UK. **Shelby Williams**, A & D Building, 15 East 58th Street, Suite 300, New York, NY 10155, USA. **Metallkonstruktionen Wippel GmbH**, Industriegelande 1, 2491 Steinbrunn, Neue Siedlung, Austria. **Woodline**, 55 Mabledon Avenue, Ashford, Kent TN24 8BN, UK. **WORKSHOP Inc.**, 6-14-11 Roppongi, Minato-ku, Tokyo 106, Japan. **Workshop 119 (now The Woodwork Shop)**, 22 Gordon Street, London NW1, UK. **Wrulich**, Adi-Dassler-Gasse 7, A-9073 Klagenfurt, Austria.

Yamagiwa Labo, Kourakuen Bldg, 4-15-7 Nishi-Shinjuku, Shinjuku-ku, Tokyo, Japan. **YRM Anthony Hunt Associates**, 24 Britton Street, London EC1M 5NQ, UK.

Zanetti & Bailey, 110 Ashley Down Road, Bristol BS7 9JR, UK. **Zanotta S.p.A**, Via Vittorio Veneto 57, 20054 Nova Milanesa, Italy. **Marco Zanuso**, Corso di Porta Romana 111, Milan, Italy. **Zeidler & Himmel**, Konsul Metzingstrasse 7-9, 8701 Kirchheim, Germany. **Tischlerei Günter Zimmermann**, Magarethenstrasse 41a, 2000 Hamburg 6, Germany. **Ingenieurbüro alois Zitnik**, Liebigstrasse 43, 6000 Frankfurt/M 1, Germany.

Index of Architects, Designers & Projects

Académie Musicale de Villecroze, Villecroze, Salernes, Var, France 244
Agence Berbesson Racine et Associés, Asnières, France 26
Ahrends Burton and Koralek 146
Allies and Morrison Architects 100
Amadó, Roser 174
Anderson/Schwartz Architects 12
Arad, Ron, Associates 16
Architekturbüro Bolles-Wilson and Partner 178
Ark, The, London, UK 48
Australian Embassy, The, Tokyo, Japan 46

B Braun Melsungen AG, Melsungen, Germany 82
Badalona Sports Palace, Badalona, Barcelona, Spain 182
Bar Maddalena, Prato, Italy 118
Bar Rothko, Barcelona, Spain 128
BASF-France, Levallois-Perret, Paris, France 94
Bausman-Gill Associates 20
Beers, Jeffrey G., Architects 104
Behnisch & Partners 24
Ben Kelly Design 68
Berbesson Racine et Associés 26
Bergström, Lennart 48
Bonell, Esteve 182
Branson Coates Architecture 148
Brenac, Olivier 28
Bru, Eduard 184

Calvi, Luisa 30
Can Felipa Cultural Centre, Barcelona, Spain 226
Chiat/Day Advertising Inc., London, UK 42
Chiat/Day/Mojo, Venice, California, USA 56
Chipperfield, David, Architects 32
Circulo de Lectores, Madrid, Spain 234
Ciriani, Henri 186
Citterio, Antonio and Terry Dwan Architects 152
Coenen, Jo, & Co. 36
Cortés, Pepe 110
Cruz, Antonio 190

David Bentheim Interior Design 106
David Mellor, London, UK 154
Davis, Lynn, Architects 114
de Architekten Cie 40
de Bruijn, Pi 40
DEGW London Ltd 42
de Martino, Stefano 42
Denton Corker Marshall 46
Designers' Guild, London, UK 52
Domènech, Lluís 174

El Tragaluz, Barcelona, Spain 110
Erskine, Ralph 48

Fausto Santini, Paris, France 152
Fifth Floor, Harvey Nichols, London, UK 168
Fitzwilliam College Chapel, Cambridge, UK 224
Foster, Sir Norman, and Partners 198
Foster Associates 194
Fretton, Tony 202
Fundació Antoni Tàpies, Barcelona, Spain 174
Fung, Spencer, Architects 52

Galí, Beth 204
Gehry, Frank O., & Associates, Inc. 56
Giencke, Volker 58

Giovannoni, Stefano 118
Glynn-Smith, Peter, Associates 122
Gonzalez, Xavier 28
Guggenheim Museum, The, New York, USA 206
Gwathmey Siegel & Associates 206

Historial de la Grande Guerre, Peronne-Somme, France 186
Holl, Steven, Architects 60
Hollein, Hans 210
Hopkins, Michael, and Partners 154
Hôtel du Cheval Blanc, Nîmes, France 142
Hôtel Montalembert, Paris, France 124

Isaac Mizrahi & Company, New York, USA 12
Israel, Franklin D., Design Associates 64
Ito, Toyo, & Associates 214

J.C.J. Haans, Tilburg, The Netherlands 36
Jestico + Whiles 66
Jigsaw, Knightsbridge, London, UK 148
Jiménez, Carlos 218
Joan Miró Library, Barcelona, Spain 204
John Lewis, Kingston upon Thames, UK 146
Julia Binfield, Milan, Italy 30

King Kong Production 118
Kita Griesheim-Süd, Frankfurt am Main, Germany 178
Knoll International, Frankfurt am Main, Germany 90
Koolhaas, Rem 42
Kuramata, Shiro 156

Lapeña, José Antonio Martinez 220
La Ranarita/Guest Room, Tokyo, Japan 140
Liaigre, Christian 124
Lievore, Alberto, & Asociados 128
Limelight Productions, Los Angeles, California, USA 64
Lisson Gallery, London, UK 202
Lum, John 158
Lynn Goode Gallery, Houston, Texas, USA 218
Lynne Franks PR, London, UK 68

MacCormac Jamieson Prichard 224
Mateo, José Luis 226
Mather, Rick, Architects 132
Matsumoto Corporation, Okayama, Japan 32
Mazda Lietz, Waidhofen, Austria 164
Merlini, Marco 30
Miller, John, + Partners 230
Minema Café, London, UK 106
Ministry of Sound, The, London, UK 114
Miralles, Enric 234
Monastery of Sant Pere de Rodes, Port de la
Selva, Catalunya, Spain 220
Moss, Eric Owen 72
Moya, Carlos 30
Mozuna, Kiko, Architects & Associates 238
Museo del Juguete, Ibi, Alicante, Spain 184
Museum für Moderne Kunst, Frankfurt am Main, Germany 210

Nägeli, Walter 82
Neeland, Torsten 160
New Line Cinema East and West, New York and Los Angeles, USA 78
Nexus-III, Kyoto, Japan 134
Notojima Glass Art Museum, Noto Island, Ishikawa
Prefecture, Japan 238

Now & Zen, London, UK 132

Odörfer, Klagenfurt, Austria 58
One Off Ltd, London, UK 16
Ortiz, Antonio 190

Paramount Hotel, New York, USA 136
Plenary Complex of the German Federal
Parliament, Bonn, Germany 24
Podrecca, Boris 164

Quintana, Màrius 204

Reid & Tarics Associates 158
Reykjavik City Hall, Reykjavik, Iceland 86
Rius, Francesc 182
Roberto Verino, Barcelona, Spain 166
Rock Townsend 48

S-Lattice, Sendagaya, Tokyo, Japan 96
Sackler Galleries, The, Royal Academy of Arts, London, UK 198
Saishunkan Seiyaku Women's Dormitory, Kumamoto City,
Kumamoto Prefecture, Japan 74
Sakamoto Ryoma Memorial Hall, Urato, Kochi City, Japan 240
Salas, Fernando 166
Santa Justa Railway Station, Seville, Spain 190
Santini, Milan, Italy 122
Scarpa, Afra and Tobia 134
Scott Mednick Associates, Culver City, California, USA 72
Second Chamber of Parliament, The, The Hague, The Netherlands 40
Sejima, Kazuyo, Architect & Associates 74
Shaw, D.E. & Company, New York, USA 60
Smith-Miller + Hawkinson Architects 78
Solanas, Antoni 204
SPIRAL, AXIS Building, Tokyo, Japan 156
Stansted Airport Terminal, Stansted, UK 194
Starck, Philippe 136
Stephen Bull's Bistro and Bar, London, UK 100
Stevens Building, The, Royal College of Art, London, UK 230
Stirling, James, Michael Wilford and Associates 82
Studio 80 140
Studio Granda 86
STUDIOS Architecture 90

Takahashi, Akiko & Hiroshi 240
Torres Tur, Elías 220
Tour sans Fins, Arche de la Défense, Paris, France 28
Tsiomis, Yannis 244
20-22 Stukeley Street, London, UK 66

Uchida, Shigeru 140
Urban Eyes, San Francisco, California, USA 158
Uta Raasch, Hamburg, Germany 160

Venturini, Guido 118

Warner Bros. Records, New York, USA 20
Wickham & Associates 168
Wilmotte, Jean-Michel 94, 142
WORKSHOP 96
Work Station 240

Yatsushiro Municipal Museum, Kumamoto Prefecture, Japan 214

Zoë, New York, USA 104